ASSESSMENT
with Audio CD and Test Generating CD-ROM

2 FOCUS ON GRAMMAR
AN INTEGRATED SKILLS APPROACH

THIRD EDITION

JOAN JAMIESON
CAROL A. CHAPELLE

WITH
LESLIE GRANT
BETHANY GRAY
XIANGYING JIANG
HSIN-MIN LIU
KEVIN ZIMMERMAN

Focus on Grammar 2: An Integrated Skills Course
Assessment Pack

Copyright © 2006 by Pearson Education, Inc.

The pages in this publication are designed to be reproduced for classroom use. Longman grants permission to classroom teachers to reproduce these pages.

Pearson Education, 10 Bank Street, White Plains, NY 10606

Staff credits: The people who made up the *Focus on Grammar 2: An Integrated Skills Course, Assessment Pack* team, representing editorial, production, design, and manufacturing, are listed below:

Rhea Banker
Nancy Blodgett
Elisabeth Carlson
Christine Edmonds
Margot Gramer
Laura Le Dréan
Wendy Long
Michael Mone
Linda Moser
Julie Schmidt

ISBN: 0-13-193141-5

LONGMAN ON THE WEB

Longman.com offers online resources for teachers and students. Access our Companion Websites, our online catalog, and our local offices around the world.

Visit us at **longman.com**.

Printed in the United States of America
3 4 5 6 7 8 9 10—BAH—10 09 08 07

Contents

Introduction — v

Part Diagnostic Tests, Unit Achievement Tests, and Part Achievement Tests — 1

General Information — 1

- Part I Diagnostic Test — 5
- Units 1–3 Achievement Tests — 9
- Part I Achievement Test — 17
- Part II Diagnostic Test — 21
- Units 4–7 Achievement Tests — 25
- Part II Achievement Test — 35
- Part III Diagnostic Test — 38
- Units 8–10 Achievement Tests — 43
- Part III Achievement Test — 52
- Part IV Diagnostic Test — 57
- Units 11–14 Achievement Tests — 61
- Part IV Achievement Test — 70
- Part V Diagnostic Test — 75
- Units 15–19 Achievement Tests — 80
- Part V Achievement Test — 94
- Part VI Diagnostic Test — 100
- Units 20–22 Achievement Tests — 104
- Part VI Achievement Test — 113
- Part VII Diagnostic Test — 117
- Units 23–25 Achievement Tests — 121
- Part VII Achievement Test — 129
- Part VIII Diagnostic Test — 134
- Units 26–29 Achievement Tests — 138
- Part VIII Achievement Test — 150
- Part IX Diagnostic Test — 154
- Units 30–32 Achievement Tests — 159
- Part IX Achievement Test — 169
- Part X Diagnostic Test — 174
- Units 33–35 Achievement Tests — 179
- Part X Achievement Test — 189
- Part XI Diagnostic Test — 194
- Units 36–39 Achievement Tests — 200
- Part XI Achievement Test — 216
- Part XII Diagnostic Test — 222
- Units 40–43 Achievement Tests — 226
- Part XII Achievement Test — 241

Audioscript	**245**
Answer Key	**263**

Test Generating Software 299
General Information 299

Introduction

The *Focus on Grammar 2 Assessment Pack* includes the following assessment tools to help you determine students' grammar proficiency level and monitor their progress and achievement in the *Focus on Grammar* course.

In addition to the tools listed below, a separately packaged *Focus on Grammar Placement Test* (ISBN 0-13-199437-9) is also available. To obtain a copy of the *Placement Test,* contact your local Longman ELT specialist.

FOG Student Book Assessment Tools

- Part Diagnostic and Achievement Tests
- Unit Achievement Tests
- Audio CD with the listening portions of the Diagnostic and Achievement Tests

Supplementary Assessment Tools

- Two ETS Grammar Proficiency Tests (Levels 4 and 5)
- Test Generating Software

You can find detailed descriptions of each type of assessment tool, as well as instructions on administering and scoring the tests, in the "General Information" sections that precede the test forms.

About the Authors

Joan Jamieson, Project Director, is a Professor in the Applied Linguistics program in the English Department at Northern Arizona University. She received her Ph.D. from the University of Illinois at Urbana-Champaign. Dr. Jamieson is the author of several publications on English as a Second Language assessment and computer-assisted language learning. She has collaborated with Pearson Longman and Carol Chapelle in the past on several projects, including *Longman English Assessment* and the testing program for *Longman English Interactive*.

Carol A. Chapelle, Project Director, is a Professor of TESL/Applied Linguistics at Iowa State University. She received her Ph.D. from the University of Illinois at Urbana-Champaign. She is the author of *Computer applications in second language acquisition: Foundations for teaching, testing and research* (Cambridge University Press, 2001), *English language learning and technology: Lectures on teaching and research in the age of information and communication technology.* (John Benjamins Publishing, 2003), and *ESOL tests and testing: A resource for teachers and program administrators* (TESOL Publications, 2005). Dr. Chapelle was until recently the editor of *TESOL Quarterly*. She has collaborated with Joan Jamieson and Pearson Longman in the past on several projects, including *Longman English Assessment* and the testing program for *Longman English Interactive*.

Project Staff

The following people worked on the development of the tests under the guidance of Joan Jamieson and Carol Chapelle:

Leslie Grant, Ph.D., Northern Arizona University

Bethany Gray, MA-TESL student, Iowa State University

Xiangying Jiang, Ph.D. student, Northern Arizona University

Hsin-min Liu, MA-TESL, Iowa State University

Kevin Zimmerman, MA-TESL, Brigham Young University

and

Liza Armstrong, MA-TESL, Northern Arizona University

Maja Grgurovic, Ph.D. student, Iowa State University

James McCormick, Ph.D., Michigan State University

Erin Kate Murphy, MA-TESL, Northern Arizona University

Pamela Pearson, MA-TESL student, Iowa State University

Lia Plakans, Ph.D. student, University of Iowa

Kornwipa Poonpon, Ph.D. student, Northern Arizona University

Kerri Quinn, MA-TESL, Northern Arizona University

Betsy Tremmel, MA student, Iowa State University

Part Diagnostic Tests, Unit Achievement Tests, and Part Achievement Tests

General Information

Overview

The *Focus on Grammar* Part Diagnostic, Unit Achievement, and Part Achievement Tests have set a new standard in ELT grammar teaching and testing. Developed under the direction of applied linguists Joan Jamieson and Carol A. Chapelle, these tests:

- are manageable in length and easy to administer and score;
- accurately reflect the material presented in the Grammar in Context, Grammar Charts and Notes, and Focused Practice sections of the course;
- offer a sufficient number of items to assess students' knowledge of each grammar point;
- include a wide variety of item types;
- provide a powerful remediation tool.

About the Test Development

These tests have been carefully developed so that the weighting and distribution of test items mirror those of the Student Book content. For example, if 40 percent of the items in a unit practice the simple present and 60 percent of the items practice the present progressive, then the Unit Achievement Test maintains the same balance. The Part Diagnostic and Achievement Tests additionally reflect the distribution of items across the units in a part. For example, if one unit in a part has 110 practice items, and the second unit in the part has 53 practice items, then the Part Diagnostic and Achievement Tests maintain the same balance.

Using the Tests for Remediation Purposes

Codes provided in the Answer Key help you determine what grammar points students might be having difficulty with. In the Unit Achievement tests, each answer has a code that refers to one or more of the Grammar Notes or to the Grammar Chart. In the Part Diagnostic and Part Achievement tests, each answer has a code that refers to the unit where the item was presented. By referring to these codes, both you and the student can try to pinpoint grammar points that are causing confusion or proving to be difficult.

EXAMPLE:

Item 5 in Exercise 2 of the Unit 14 Achievement Test has the code **N3**. This means that the item is testing the grammar point associated with Grammar Note 3 in the student book: "Use *one* or *ones* after an adjective in place of a singular or plural count noun." If a student answered this item incorrectly, that student may need more help with this grammar point.

NOTE: If a test item has two codes separated by a comma (for example, `N1, N2` or `U1, U2`), that item is testing two grammar points or two units.

Test Purpose and Design

The **Part Diagnostic Tests** help you determine how well students know the material they are about to study in the next part of the Student Book. Since the material they are about to study is usually new, students often score low on these tests.

Each Part Diagnostic Test takes 50 minutes and includes 60 items. The test begins with a listening exercise, includes several contextualized grammar exercises, and ends with an editing exercise.

The **Unit Achievement Tests** help you assess students' knowledge of the specific grammatical topics presented in the unit. If students have mastered the material presented in the unit, they should answer most of the questions correctly. The codes provided in the Answer Key help you determine what grammar topics students may need to review.

Each Unit Achievement Test takes 30 minutes and includes 30 items. The test begins with a listening exercise, includes two to three contextualized grammar exercises, and ends with an editing exercise.

The **Part Achievement Tests** help you determine how well students have mastered the material they have studied in that part of the student book. If students have mastered the material presented in the part, they should answer most of the questions correctly. The codes provided in the Answer Key help you determine what units students may need to review.

Each Part Achievement Test is identical in structure to the Part Diagnostic Test for the part, including the same number of items and testing the same grammar points with equal balance and weighting. By comparing a student's results on the Part Diagnostic Test and on the Part Achievement Test, you can determine how much students have learned.

Administering the Tests

Before administering a test:

- Make photocopies of the test form.
- Set up your CD player in the testing room and check the volume.
- Check the track list on the inside back cover for which track you will need to play.

The listening section in the Part Diagnostic, Unit Achievement, and Part Achievement Tests is the first section of the test so that it may be administered to all students at the same time without interfering with the other parts of the test. When students are ready to begin the test, play the audio CD and have students listen and answer the questions. You should play each track two times.

After students have completed the listening section, stop the CD and ask students to work on the remaining sections of the test.

Scoring the Tests

To determine a student's score on the tests, add up the number of questions the student answered correctly, using the Answer Key on pages 263–298. You may also wish to subtract the number incorrect from the total number of items. The total number of items for each test is shown on the first page of the test.

To determine the percentage score, first divide the number correct by the total number of items; then, multiply that proportion by 100. (Use the total number of items on the test, not the number of items that a student answered.)

EXAMPLE:

The Part VI Achievement Test includes 60 items.
A student answered 47 items correctly.

$47 \div 60 = .78 \rightarrow .78 \times 100 = 78$

The student's percentage score is 78%.

A scoring box is provided on the first page of each test to record the student's score.

Name _____ Date _____

PART I Diagnostic Test

60 Items
Score: _____

1 | LISTENING: DINNER PLANS

🎧 **A.** *Dave and Tammy are friends. They want to eat at a restaurant. Listen to their conversation. Complete the conversation by writing the words that you hear. You will hear the recording two times.*

DAVE: ____I'm____ hungry. _____ hungry?
            0.   1.

TAMMY: _____. I'm very hungry. Let's go to Caruso's Restaurant.
          2.

DAVE: My friend Nancy was there _____. She wasn't happy with the food. It wasn't very good.
                              3.

TAMMY: _____ sure? I was there last week, too. The food _____ bad at all!
          4.   5.

DAVE: OK. Let's go to Caruso's.

B. *Complete these questions and answers based on the conversation above. Circle the correct words or phrases.*

0. **A:** (Is) / Am / Are Dave hungry?

   B: Yes, he is.

1. **A:** Is Tammy hungry?

   B: Yes, she is / No, she isn't / No, she wasn't hungry.

2. **A:** Nancy wasn't happy with the food at Caruso's.

   B: Was you / she / they there before?

3. **A:** Tammy is / was / were there before.

   B: Yes, and she was happy with the food.

4. **A:** Was the food bad at Caruso's?

   B: No, they aren't / they weren't / it wasn't.

5. **A:** Are Dave and Tammy at Caruso's now?

   B: No, she isn't. / Yes, he is. / No, they aren't.

Name _____ Date _____

2 | AT THE RESTAURANT

Dave and Tammy are at the restaurant. Complete their conversation. Use the words in the box.

am	I don't know	~~Is~~	No, he isn't	Was	were
are	I'm	Is	No, it isn't	was	Yes, it is
are	is	it's	was	wasn't	Yes, she is

TAMMY: _____Is_____ your spaghetti good?
                0.

DAVE: _____. It _____ delicious. _____ your pizza
           1.   2.   3.
good?

TAMMY: Yes, _____ wonderful. _____ your friend Nancy here or at
              4.   5.
a different restaurant last week?

DAVE: _____. _____ not sure. I think she _____
          6.   7.   8.
here, and the food _____ good. But maybe I _____ wrong.
                        9.   10.
Maybe she _____ at a different restaurant.
               11.

3 | TALKING WITH THE SERVER

Dave and Tammy finished eating. Now Dave is talking with the server. Use the present or past and the words in parentheses to complete their conversation.

SERVER: ___Was the food___ (be / the food) OK?
              0.

DAVE: Yes, _____ (the food / be / delicious). _____ (be / there)
              1.   2.
another restaurant in town named Caruso's?

SERVER: No, _____ (there / be / not). Why?
              3.

DAVE: I have a friend. I think she _____ (be / here) last week, and she said the
                                        4.
food _____ (be / not) good. But I don't think _____ (it /
         5.   6.
be / possible). The food here _____ (be / not / bad). It
                                    7.
_____ (be / wonderful)!
     8.

6 | PART I ■ DIAGNOSTIC TEST

Name _____ Date _____

SERVER: _____ (be / she) at Colucci's?
          9.

DAVE: _____ (be / there) a restaurant named Colucci's? Maybe she
        10.

_____ (be / there)!
    11.

4 | NEW ACQUAINTANCES

Dave and Tammy are walking home when Dave sees his friend Nancy. Complete the conversation with the correct forms of **be**.

DAVE: Oh! I see Nancy now! Come meet her. . . . Hi, Nancy! This ___is___ my
                                                                   0.
friend Tammy.

NANCY: Hi, I _____ pleased to meet you. _____ you from here?
              1.   2.

TAMMY: Yes, I _____ . _____ you from here, too?
              3.   4.

NANCY: No, I _____ from Toronto, in Canada.
             5.

TAMMY: Wow! Toronto _____ far from here!
                      6.

NANCY: Yes, it _____ . But it _____ a wonderful city.
               7.   8.

TAMMY: Yes, it _____ . I'm sure it _____ fun for you to grow up
               9.   10.
there.

NANCY: Yes, it _____ !
               11.

DAVE: Nancy and I _____ in high school together ten years ago. We
                   12.

_____ in the school band. Nancy _____ a drummer. I
    13.   14.
played the trumpet.

TAMMY: _____ you good musicians in high school?
        15.

NANCY: I _____ not very good, but Dave _____ great!
         16.   17.

Name _____ **Date** _____

TAMMY: Hey, Nancy . . . Dave and I _____ at Caruso's for lunch.
18.

_____ you there last week?
19.

NANCY: No, I _____ at Colucci's. The food _____ bad. How
20.   21.

was the food at Caruso's?

DAVE: It _____ great! Hey, let's all go there for lunch next week, OK?
22.

NANCY AND
TAMMY: OK!

5 | EDITING: GOOD FOOD

Nancy is at Caruso's for the first time. She is talking to Dave and Tammy. Correct their conversation. There are seven mistakes. The first mistake is already corrected.

                                    is
DAVE: My pizza ~~are~~ very good. Are your salad good?

NANCY: Yes, they are! They are delicious.

TAMMY: Are you happy we're not at Colucci's?

NANCY: Yes! The food at Colucci's were bad. Also, the restaurant were dirty and the prices was high.

Name _____ Date _____

Unit 1 Achievement Test

30 Items
Score: _____

1 | LISTENING: THE PRICE FAMILY, PART I

🎧 **A.** *Lydia is showing pictures to her friend Caroline. Listen to their conversation. Complete the conversation by writing the words that you hear. You will hear the recording two times.*

CAROLINE: Who's in this picture?

LYDIA: This is the Price family. ____*They're*____ my friends. _____ from
        0.   1.
California. Mr. Price is a professor there. His first name is Ralph.

_____ married to Pat. Ralph and Pat have three children. This is
   2.
Lynnette. _____ 27. This is Michelle. _____ 24. And
            3.   4.
this is Nate. _____ 19.
                 5.

CAROLINE: _____ all very good-looking! They look rich and famous!
            6.

LYDIA: They _____ rich or famous, but they are wonderful!
              7.

B. *Complete these sentences based on the conversation. Circle the correct words or phrases.*

0. My friends (are)/ is from California.

1. Ralph and Pat are / are not married.

2. Lynnette, Michelle, and Nate are / are not brothers and sisters.

3. The Price family is / is not rich or famous, but they are wonderful.

Name _____ Date _____

2 | THE PRICE FAMILY, PART II

Circle the contractions (short forms) in each sentence. Check (✓) the negative statements.

0. ____ (They're) Lydia's friends.

0. ✓ They are not from Washington.

1. ____ He's a professor.

2. ____ They are not rich.

3. ____ They are not famous.

4. ____ They're very good-looking.

5. ____ They're friends of Lydia's.

3 | THE PRICE FAMILY, PART III

*Complete the sentences with the correct forms of **be** or pronouns.*

Ralph Price ____is____ a professor at the University of California in San Diego.
       0.

____He____ is a professor of Spanish. His classes _____ popular because
   0.   1.

he _____ a good teacher.
      2.

Pat plays the piano. She's a good piano player but she _____ a very good cook.
                                                            3. (not)

Lynnette and Lydia _____ best friends. _____ talk on the phone
                         4.   5.

a lot. Lydia _____ from Mexico. _____ is the same age as Lynnette.
                  6.   7.

Michelle is an artist. She _____ famous yet, but her art _____
                              8. (not)   9.

good.

Nate is a student at the University of California. _____ is a film student.
                                                         10.

4 | EDITING: LYDIA'S FAMILY

Correct this paragraph about Lydia's family. There are six mistakes. The first mistake is already corrected. (Note: Use the full forms of the verbs.)

                          is
My family ^ in Mexico. My mother a teacher, and my father an engineer. They in Mexico

City. They sad because I am far away from them. I am here because I a student of English.

Name _____   Date _____

Unit 2 Achievement Test

30 Items
Score: _____

PART 1

1 | LISTENING: FIRST DAY OF CLASS

🎧 *It is Tim's first day of acting class. Listen to the conversation between Tim and Dale. Complete the conversation by writing the words that you hear. You will hear the recording two times.*

TIM: Excuse me. ____Is this____ Acting 101?
                     0.

DALE: _____ . _____ in the class?
           1.   2.

TIM: _____ . Are you?
          3.

DALE: _____ .
          4.

TIM: You look familiar. . . . I know! Are you Molly's friend?

DALE: Molly? I _____ .
                    5.

TIM: Well. . . . _____ from Washington?
                       6.

DALE: _____ . I'm from Michigan.
          7.

TIM: Michigan? That's pretty far away from here!

DALE: You're right. _____ close at all.
                           8.

TIM: _____ this a good class?
         9.

DALE: _____ . I'm the teacher!
          10.

TIM: Oh! You're Dale Shumway, the actor! I'm Tim.

UNIT 2 ■ ACHIEVEMENT TEST | 11

Name _____   Date _____

2 | ASKING QUESTIONS

Match the questions and the answers.

Questions

__d__ 0. Excuse me. Are you in this class?

____ 1. Are we on time?

____ 2. Is Mr. Shumway a good teacher?

____ 3. Is he famous?

____ 4. Is the class good?

____ 5. Are we in the right room?

____ 6. Is she in this class?

Answers

a. Yes, it is a good class.

b. Yes, he's very famous.

c. Yes, we are. Room 208.

~~d.~~ Yes, I am.

e. No, she isn't.

f. Yes, he's a very good teacher.

g. Yes, we are. It is 10:00.

h. No, she is.

i. Yes, I don't think so.

3 | WAITING FOR CLASS

Complete the conversations between Tim and Gina before class. Rewrite the sentences in parentheses as questions. Some items may have more than one right answer.

0. GINA: (It is 10:00.) _____ Is it 10:00 _____ ?
   TIM: No, it isn't.

1. GINA: (I am early.) _____ ?
   TIM: Yes, you are. It's before 10:00.

2. GINA: (This is the right room.) _____ ?
   TIM: I think so.

3. GINA: (You are a new student.) _____ ?
   TIM: No, I'm not. I was here last year.

4. GINA: (You are from Ireland.) _____ ?
   TIM: No, I'm not.

5. GINA: (This is your bag.) _____ ?
   TIM: Yes, it is.

Name _____ **Date** _____

6. GINA: (This is my pen.) _____?
   TIM: Yes, I think so.

7. GINA: (This is your first class.) _____?
   TIM: No, it isn't. I had a class at 9:00.

8. GINA: (They are in this class.) _____?
   TIM: I don't know.

9. GINA: (She is the teacher.) _____?
   TIM: No, she isn't.

10. GINA: (The teacher is late.) _____?
    TIM: No, he isn't. He is here now.

11. GINA: (Dale Shumway is our teacher.) _____?
    TIM: Yes, he is! We're lucky!

4 | EDITING: LUNCHTIME

Tim and Gina are looking for the cafeteria. Correct their conversation. There are four mistakes. The first mistake is already corrected.

TIM: I'm hungry. ~~Hungry you are~~? *Are you hungry?*

GINA: Yes, am I.

TIM: The cafeteria is close?

GINA: I think.

Name _____ Date _____

Unit 3 Achievement Test

29 Items
Score: _____

1 | LISTENING: LAST NIGHT'S PLAY

🎧 **A.** Linda is visiting Nancy. Listen to their conversation. Complete the conversation by writing the words that you hear. You will hear the recording two times.

LINDA: __Were you__ at your sister's play _____?
             0.   1.

NANCY: Yes! It _____ great! All of her friends _____ there. They
                   2.   3.

_____ in the play. It was really funny!
    4.

LINDA: Were your parents there to watch it?

NANCY: _____. They were out of town _____.
           5.   6.

LINDA: _____ in the play?
           7.

NANCY: No. Julie wrote the play, but she's not an actor.

B. Complete these sentences based on the conversation. Circle the correct words.

0. (Was)/ Were / Is Nancy at her sister's play?

1. Was / Were / Is Nancy's parents at the play?

2. Nancy's parents was / were / is out of town.

3. The play were / is / was really funny.

Name _____   Date _____

2 | SENTENCE ORDER

Put the sentences in the correct order to make a conversation.

Example:
- Yes, it was fun.
- Did you go to the concert?
- Was it fun?
- No, I didn't. I was at a party.

A: *Did you go to the concert?*

B: *No, I didn't. I was at a party.*

A: *Was it fun?*

B: *Yes, it was fun.*

- Yes, they were. Why?
- Were Tim and Gina in class on Monday?
- I was in the cafeteria. They weren't there.
- They were at a restaurant during lunch.

A: _____
1.
B: _____
2.
A: _____
3.
B: _____
4.

Unit 3 ■ Achievement Test

Name _____   Date _____

3 | AFTER A TRIP

*Julie returned from a trip. Read her phone conversation with her friend Roger. Complete the conversation with the correct forms of be. Add **not** if needed.*

JULIE: Hello?

ROGER: Hi, Julie. This is Roger. How ____was____ your trip?
                                         0.

JULIE: It _____ great! I _____ at the beach. It _____
          1.   2.   3.
beautiful.

ROGER: _____ you with Susan?
         4.

JULIE: Yes, I _____. We _____ sad to come home.
              5.   6.

ROGER: You _____ in class today. _____ you sick?
            7.   8.

JULIE: Yes, we _____. We _____ in the sun too long. Today we
                9.   10.
_____ very tired. We _____ in bed all day.
    11.   12.

4 | EDITING: JULIE'S PLAY

Correct this conversation between Nancy and Julie. There are four mistakes. The first mistake is already corrected.

                         was
NANCY: Julie, your play ^ great. Your friends were happy with the play?

JULIE: Yes, they was. But I was no. It was bad!

NANCY: No, it wasn't!

Name _____ Date _____

Part I Achievement Test

60 Items
Score: _____

1 | LISTENING: THIRSTY

🎧 **A.** Ryan and Denise are thirsty. Listen to their conversation. Complete the conversation by writing the words that you hear. You will hear the recording two times.

RYAN: It's hot, and ____I'm____ thirsty. _____ thirsty?
           0.   1.

DENISE: _____. I'm very thirsty. Let's go to Tom's Diner.
           2.

RYAN: My friend Shinji was there _____. He wasn't happy. It was very dirty.
                                    3.

DENISE: _____ sure? I was there on Monday. The restaurant _____
          4.   5.
dirty!

RYAN: OK. Let's go.

B. Complete these questions and answers based on the conversation above. Circle the correct words or phrases.

0. A: (Is)/ Am / Are Ryan thirsty?

   B: Yes, he is.

1. A: Is Denise very thirsty?

   B: Yes, she is / No, she isn't / No, she wasn't thirsty.

2. A: Shinji didn't like Tom's Diner.

   B: Was he / we / they there before?

3. A: Shinji said the place are / was / were very dirty.

   B: Oh, really?

4. A: Denise was / were / are there on Monday.

   B: Yes, and the restaurant was fine.

5. A: Are Ryan and Denise at Tom's Diner now?

   B: No, he isn't. / Yes, he is. / No, they aren't.

Name _____ Date _____

2 | AT TOM'S DINER

Ryan and Denise are at the restaurant. Complete their conversation. Use the words in the box.

am	I'm	~~is~~	No, it isn't	was	weren't
are	is	it's	was	wasn't	Yes, it is
I don't know	Is	No, he isn't	Was	were	Yes, she is

DENISE: ____Is____ your lemonade good?
          0.

RYAN: _____. It _____ great. _____ your soda good?
        1.   2.   3.

DENISE: Yes, it is. And _____ good to be inside. I think the restaurant is very
                         4.
clean. _____ Shinji really here last week?
        5.

RYAN: _____. _____ not sure. I think he _____ here
        6.   7.   8.
last week, and he said the tables _____ not clean. But maybe I
                                    9.
_____ wrong. Maybe he _____ at a different restaurant.
   10.   11.

3 | TALKING WITH THE SERVER

Ryan and Denise finished their drinks. Now Ryan is talking with the server. Use the present or past and the words in parentheses to complete their conversation.

SERVER: __Were the drinks__ (be / the drinks) OK?
           0.

RYAN: Yes, _____ (the drinks / be / fine). _____ (be / there)
             1.   2.
another restaurant in town named Tom's Diner?

SERVER: No, _____ (there / be / not). Why?
              3.

RYAN: I have a friend, and I think he _____ (be / here) last week. He said the
                                         4.
restaurant _____ (be / not / clean). But I don't think _____
              5.   6.
(it / be / possible). Everything _____ (be / very / clean) today! The floor
                                    7.
and tables _____ (be / not / dirty) at all.
              8.

18 | PART I ■ ACHIEVEMENT TEST

Name _____ Date _____

SERVER: I don't think he _____ (be / here). _____ (be / he) at Joe's
                                              9.   10.

            Diner?

RYAN: _____ (be / there) a restaurant called Joe's Diner? Maybe that's it!
          11.

4 | AN OLD FRIEND

Ryan and Denise are walking home when Ryan sees his friend Shinji. Complete the conversation with the correct forms of **be**.

RYAN: I see my friend Shinji. Come meet him. . . . Hi, Shinji! This __is__ my
                                                                                      0.

        friend Denise.

SHINJI: Hello, Denise. I _____ Shinji. _____ you from here?
                                   1.   2.

DENISE: Yes, I _____ . _____ you from here, too?
                          3.   4.

SHINJI: No, I _____ from Kyoto, in Japan.
                   5.

DENISE: Kyoto! Wow! Japan _____ far from here!
                              6.

SHINJI: Yes, it _____ . But it _____ a fantastic place.
                      7.   8.

DENISE: Yes, it _____ ! I'm sure it _____ great for you to grow
                     9.   10.

        up there.

SHINJI: Yes, it _____ !
                 11.

RYAN: Shinji and I _____ in college together three years ago. Shinji
                      12.

    _____ in my history class. He _____ very smart in that
      13.   14.

    class!

DENISE: And you, Ryan? _____ you good at history in college, too?
                                    15.

RYAN: No, I _____ not very good. History _____ hard for me.
                 16.   17.

DENISE: Hey, Shinji . . . Ryan and I _____ at Tom's Diner for a cold drink.
                                             18.

    _____ you there last week?
      19.

SHINJI: No, I _____ at Joe's Diner. It _____ very dirty. How
                  20.   21.

    was Tom's Diner?

RYAN: It _____ great! Hey, let's all go there for lunch next week, OK?
              22.

DENISE AND
   SHINJI: OK!

5 | EDITING: GOOD FOOD

Shinji is at Tom's Diner for the first time. Correct his conversation with Ryan and Denise. There are seven mistakes. The first mistake is already corrected.

RYAN: These fries ~~is~~ *are* very good. Are your hamburger good?

SHINJI: Yes, they are! They are delicious.

DENISE: I'm happy we're here and not at the other diner.

SHINJI: Yes. The food at Joe's Diner weren't good. The diner were dirty and the prices was high.

Name _____ Date _____

PART II Diagnostic Test

57 Items
Score: _____

1 | LISTENING: DIRECTIONS TO THE MUSEUM

🎧 **A.** *Paul and Judy are meeting at the museum. Listen to their conversation. Complete the conversation by writing the words that you hear. You will hear the recording two times.*

PAUL: _____*Where*_____ is the museum?
              0.

JUDY: Downtown. It's near the train station. There is a _____ sign in front of it.
                                                                    1.

      It's next to the park with the tall _____ .
                                                    2.

PAUL: Oh. Where's the park?

JUDY: It's on First Avenue. It's called Jefferson _____ .
                                                                   3.

PAUL: OK. It looks like rain. Bring _____ umbrella.
                                                                    4.

B. *Reread the conversation. Find one contraction of a* wh- *question, one short answer to a* wh- *question, and three prepositions of place. Write them in the table below. An example is given.*

1. One contraction of a *wh-* question: _____

2. One short answer to a *wh-* question: _____

3. Three prepositions of place: _____ , _____ ,

_____

PART II ■ DIAGNOSTIC TEST | 21

Name _____ Date _____

2 | E-MAIL FROM LONDON

Complete the e-mail from Jaime to his friend Eugene. Use the words in the box. Some items may have more than one right answer.

a	between	~~in~~	people	where
an	Birmingham Prep	in front of	picture	Who
at	England	near	school	why

Dear Eugene,

Are you ____*in*____ school? I am. I'm at _____ school
          0.   1.

_____ London, _____. The name is _____. It's a small
   2.   3.   4.

_____.
  5.

Pictures of famous _____ are in the room. A _____ of Thomas
                                  6.   7.

Gainsborough is _____ my desk. _____ is he, and
                           8.   9.

_____ is he famous?
  10.

Jaime

3 | EUGENE'S ANSWER

Read Eugene's e-mail back to Jaime. Look at the underlined words. Write each word in the correct category. An example is given.

Dear Jaime,

    <u>Gainsborough</u> is <u>an artist</u>. He is from <u>Sudbury</u>, <u>England</u>. His art is <u>in</u> the British Museum.

    My classes are finished. Now I'm <u>lonely</u>. I want to visit my <u>friends</u>. They live <u>near</u> Chicago.

    <u>What</u> is your phone number there? Have a <u>good</u> time <u>in</u> London!

Eugene

1. Prepositions of place: _____, _____, _____

2. Singular noun: _____

3. Plural noun: _____

4. Proper nouns: __*Gainsborough*__, _____, _____

5. Adjectives: _____, _____

6. *Wh-* word: _____

4 | EUGENE'S PICTURES

Eugene is showing pictures to his friend David. Complete their conversation. Circle the correct words or phrases.

EUGENE: I have a pictures / picture / (pictures) to show you. This is
0.
a picture / an picture / pictures of my family. These are
1.
my grandparent / my grandparents / a grandparent, and these are
2.
my brothers / my brother / a brother. This brother is still on / in / near school. And
3. 4.
this is my sister, between / on / at my grandfather and me.
5.

DAVID: Who / When / Where is your sister now?
6.

EUGENE: She's at / on / in Tokyo, japan / Japan / Japans. She works at
7. 8.
a international bank / internationals banks / an international bank there. She's
9.
smart / a smart / a girl smart and friendly.
10.

5 | DAVID'S PICTURES

Now David is showing his pictures to Eugene. Use the words in parentheses to complete their conversation. Put the words in the correct order.

EUGENE: So, those are my pictures. __Where are your pictures?__ (your / are / pictures? /
0.
Where)

DAVID: Here they are. Here is a picture of my family. _____
1.
(were / We / at / home.) That is my dad. My brother is behind my dad. And my sister is

next to my brother.

EUGENE: _____ (the / picture. / like / I) This picture is good,
2.
too. _____ (it? / Who / is)
3.

DAVID: Oh, that's my mother. _____ (in / She / Frankfurt,
4.
Germany. / was) Here's another picture. _____
5.
(a / It's / in / hotel / famous / Frankfurt.) _____
6.
(hotel / was / The / beautiful.) _____
7.
(on / were / We / floor. / the 20th) The view was incredible!

Name _____ Date _____

6 | EDITING: THINGS TO SEE IN LONDON

Eugene is going to London. Correct his conversation with David. There are 12 mistakes. The first mistake is already corrected. (Note: There can be more than one way to correct a mistake.)

EUGENE: ~~Who~~ *What* are your favorite place in London?

DAVID: There are some wonderfuls museums. The British Museum is interest. And the Tower of London is famous building. Also, the Royal botanic Gardens are beautifuls now. Where is your hotel?

EUGENE: My hotel is the corner of Knightsbridge and Wilshire. The name is king george Hotel. I have room on fourth floor.

Name _____ Date _____

Unit 4 Achievement Test

30 Items
Score: _____

1 | LISTENING: PICTURES OF PARIS

🎧 **A.** Holly is visiting Jen. Listen to their conversation. Complete the conversation by writing the words that you hear. You will hear the recording two times.

JEN: Hi, ____*Holly*____! Wow! I like your earrings!
　　　　　　0.

HOLLY: Thanks. And I really like your _____.
　　　　　　　　　　　　　　　　　　　　　　1.

JEN: Thank you! My pants and shirt are from _____. I was in Europe last
　　　　　　　　　　　　　　　　　　　　　　　　2.
summer.

HOLLY: Really? Do you have _____?
　　　　　　　　　　　　　　　　3.

JEN: Yes! In fact, I have an album. . . . Here it is. OK, here I am at the Eiffel Tower.

HOLLY: Very nice! Who's the woman with you?

JEN: Oh, she's _____ from class. Her name is Cheryl. She's
　　　　　　　　　　　4.
_____.
　　　5.

B. Reread the conversation. Write each noun from the box below in the correct category. An example is given.

| an album | Europe | shirt | the woman |
| ~~earrings~~ | pants | the Eiffel Tower | |

PROPER NOUNS	SINGULAR NOUNS	PLURAL NOUNS
1. _____	1. _____	0. ____*earrings*____
2. _____	2. _____	1. _____
	3. _____	

UNIT 4 ■ ACHIEVEMENT TEST 25

Name _____ Date _____

2 | FRIENDS IN ITALY

*Jen is showing Holly her photographs of Europe. Complete their conversation. Use the correct forms of the nouns in parentheses. Add **a** or **an** if necessary.*

HOLLY: These are good ___pictures___. Tell me about them.
             0. (picture)

JEN: This is _____ of a friend. His name is _____. He is
          1. (picture)   2. (antonio)
_____. He lives in _____. He lives in _____
    3. (actor)   4. (rome)   5. (apartment)
with three _____.
            6. (friend)

HOLLY: You were in _____, too! I love Italian ice cream!
                     7. (italy)

JEN: Me, too! I know _____ with really good ice cream! Look at this picture of
                      8. (restaurant)
us there. These two _____ are my _____. He's an architect,
                       9. (man)   10. (friend)
and he's _____.
           11. (teacher)

3 | EDITING: POSTCARD

Correct this postcard from Jen. There are nine mistakes. The first mistake is already corrected. (Note: There can be more than one way to correct a mistake.)

       Erin
Hello, ~~erin~~!

I am in rome, italy. The peoples are very nice. This postcard is picture of downtown. The

building are beautiful. Last week, I was in paris, france.

I will show you picture when I return.

Love,

Jen

26 | UNIT 4 ■ ACHIEVEMENT TEST

Name _____ Date _____

Unit 5 Achievement Test

30 Items
Score: _____

1 | LISTENING: THE PAINTED DESERT

A. Listen to the description of the Painted Desert. Complete the description by writing the words that you hear. You will hear the recording two times.

The Painted Desert is an ____unusual____ place in Arizona. It is very colorful. You can
                              0.
drive through it, or you can walk on _____ trails. There are helpful signs with
                                          1.
interesting information. It is _____ in the summer but nice in the winter. It is
                                    2.
almost always sunny and dry. If you walk, take a _____ bottle of water and a good
                                                       3.
hat. It is a beautiful place to visit.

B. Reread the description of the Painted Desert. Find seven adjectives. Write them below. (Note: Only use words that are given in the description. Do not use any words that you wrote.) An example is given.

0. ____colorful____

1. _____

2. _____

3. _____

4. _____

5. _____

6. _____

7. _____

2 | A SPECIAL PLACE

Read Jody's description of a special place. Circle 10 adjectives. An example is given.

I'm in a motel in Oregon. The motel is in a (little) town by the ocean. The motel is old, but it is comfortable. The rates are not expensive. The ocean is blue, and the air is fresh and salty. The beach is clean. This place is fun, and I am relaxed. It's easy to forget about time here.

UNIT 5 ■ ACHIEVEMENT TEST | 27

Name _____ Date _____

3 | SYDNEY, AUSTRALIA

Use the words to write sentences. Put the words in the correct order.

0. cool / in / is / It / a / night / Sydney.

   It is a cool night in Sydney.

1. lights / bright. / The / are

   _____

2. seafood / fresh. / is / The

   _____

3. The / friendly. / are / people

   _____

4. is / The / Sydney Opera House / big.

   _____

5. are / to be here. / We / happy

   _____

4 | EDITING: PICTURES

Petra is showing Tim some pictures. Correct their conversation. There are six mistakes. The first mistake is already corrected.

TIM: This is a ^good picture ~~good~~ of you. The colors are beautifuls.

PETRA: Thank you. The picture is from the Painted Desert. It was a few years ago. The weather perfect.

TIM: I was there last year, but the weather unusual was. There were very strongs winds, and it was cold.

PETRA: That interesting.

Name _____ Date _____

Unit 6 Achievement Test

30 Items
Score: _____

1 | LISTENING: DIRECTIONS TO MOLLY'S PARTY

🎧 **A.** *Jay needs directions to Molly's party. Listen to their conversation. Complete the conversation by writing the words that you hear. You will hear the recording two times.*

JAY: I need directions to your party. Do you live ____in____ the city?
　　　　　　　　　　　　　　　　　　　　　　　　　　　　　　0.

MOLLY: Well, I live _____ the city. I'm at 301 Cherry Avenue. It's an apartment
　　　　　　　　　　　　　1.

　　　building _____ the train station. It's _____ Cherry Avenue
　　　　　　　　　　　2.　　　　　　　　　　　　　　　　　　　3.

　　　and Main Street.

JAY: So is the entrance on Cherry or Main?

MOLLY: It's on Cherry. There's a big sign _____ the building that says Mountain
　　　　　　　　　　　　　　　　　　　　　　　　4.

　　　Plaza Apartments. The parking lot is in back of the building.

JAY: What's your apartment number?

MOLLY: My apartment number is 217, but the party is in the clubhouse. The clubhouse is

　　　_____ the pool. It's easy to find.
　　　　　　5.

JAY: Great! I'll see you tonight.

B. *Reread the conversation. Complete these sentences. Circle the correct words or phrases.*

0. Molly lives (in) / in front of / near an apartment.

1. The train station is in front of / behind / near Molly's apartment building.

2. Molly's apartment building is next to / between / on Cherry Avenue.

3. The building is in front of / in back of / at the parking lot.

4. Molly's apartment is on the / at the / in the second floor.

5. Molly's party isn't at / on / in work.

Name _____ Date _____

2 | NUMBERS GAME

Look at the numbers. Complete the sentences. Use **under**, **next to**, **between**, and **near**. The first answer is already given. Some items may have more than one right answer.

$$0\ 1\ 2\ 3\ 4$$
$$5\ 6\ 7\ 8\ 9$$

0. The 0 is ____next to____ the 1.

1. The 6 is _____ the 1.

2. The 8 is _____ the 7 and the 9.

3. The 2 is _____ the 6.

4. The 7 is _____ the 8.

5. The 3 is _____ the 2 and the 4.

6. The 9 is _____ the 4.

3 | DIRECTIONS

Carrie is e-mailing her friend Collin directions to her apartment. Complete the sentences. Use the words in the box and the map. Some items may have more than one right answer.

| next to | near | of | in | in front of | on the | at | ~~on~~ |

Name _____ Date _____

Hi Collin,

Here are directions from your apartment to my apartment. Near your apartment building there is a big bank. It's ____*on*____ the corner _____ Washington and
                                     0.   **1.**
Willow. Walk there and turn right on Willow. My apartment building isn't on the corner, but it's

_____ there. I live _____ 1743 Willow Road. There's a newsstand
     2.   **3.**

_____ my building. My building is _____ a doctor's office. My
     4.   **5.**

apartment is number 313, and it's _____ third floor. I'll be _____
                                        6.   **7.**
school until 3:00, so come at 4:00.

See you then!

Carrie

4 | EDITING: PEOPLE AND PLACES

Put a ✓ next to the correct sentences. Put an X next to the incorrect sentences. Correct the incorrect sentences. (Note: There can be more than one way to correct a mistake.)

            of
__X__ 0. The car is in front ʌ the house.

__✓__ 0. I'm at the store.

____ 1. He lives Main Street.

____ 2. We live near a river.

____ 3. They live on first floor.

____ 4. He's Canada now.

____ 5. She's at home.

____ 6. We are in back the house.

____ 7. They are on the corner of Broadway and Main Street.

Name _____   Date _____

Unit 7 Achievement Test

30 Items
Score: _____

1 | LISTENING: NEW ROOMMATES

🎧 *Tony and Allan are new roommates. Listen to their conversation. You will only see Allan's part of the conversation. Complete Allan's questions by writing the words that you hear. You will hear the recording two times.*

0. ALLAN: OK. _____Where_____ are you?

1. ALLAN: I'm here. _____ is it?

2. ALLAN: Oh, interesting. _____ that next to you?

3. ALLAN: It's a beautiful photo. _____ were you?

4. ALLAN: Segovia? _____ that?

5. ALLAN: I like Spain. _____ were you there?

6. ALLAN: So, your family is Spanish. _____ your last name?

2 | THE PHOTOGRAPH

Read the conversation. Find two contractions of wh- *questions and two short answers to questions. Write them below.*

NICK: What's this?
SIMON: It's a photograph of water.
NICK: Why's it orange?
SIMON: The photographer made it orange on the computer. And look at this picture.
NICK: Who is it?
SIMON: Me.
NICK: Who's the photographer?
SIMON: My sister, Jana.

1. Contraction 1 of a *wh-* question: _____

2. Contraction 2 of a *wh-* question: _____

3. Short answer 1: _____

4. Short answer 2: _____

Name _____   Date _____

3 | QUESTIONS FOR A NEW ROOMMATE

Megan and Rachel are new roommates. Complete their conversation. Use **who**, **why**, **what**, **what's**, *and* **where**.

0. MEGAN: _____*What*_____ is this?

   RACHEL: It's the book for my art class.

1. MEGAN: _____ is the name of the class?

   RACHEL: Art History 103.

2. MEGAN: _____ is it interesting for you?

   RACHEL: Because I like art and art history.

3. MEGAN: _____ is the teacher for the class?

   RACHEL: The teacher's name is Professor Budai. She's a painter.

4. MEGAN: _____ is your favorite artist?

   RACHEL: Claude Monet. He's famous for impressionism in his art.

5. MEGAN: _____ is impressionism?

   RACHEL: It's a painting style.

6. MEGAN: Oh. _____ is he from?

   RACHEL: France.

7. MEGAN: _____ the name of the city?

   RACHEL: Paris.

8. MEGAN: _____ are Monet's paintings?

   RACHEL: They're in museums.

4 | GEOGRAPHY QUIZ

Allan is in a geography class. These are questions from a quiz. Complete each question with the correct wh- *word.*

0. Q: _____*Where*_____ is the Amazon River?

   A: In Brazil.

1. Q: _____ is the Taj Mahal?

   A: A beautiful building in India.

Name _____ **Date** _____

2. Q: _____ was George Washington?

   A: He was the first president of the United States.

3. Q: _____ is Sri Lanka?

   A: In Southern Asia.

4. Q: _____ is the name of a big city in Turkey?

   A: Ankara.

5. Q: _____ is the Thames River?

   A: In England.

6. Q: _____ was Simón Bolívar?

   A: He was an important leader in South America.

7. Q: _____ is Rhode Island called an island?

   A: I don't know the reason. That's just its name.

8. Q: _____ is the name of that mountain?

   A: Mount Everest.

5 | EDITING: MORE GEOGRAPHY QUESTIONS

Correct five more questions from the quiz. There are five mistakes. The first mistake is already corrected.

0. Q: Where ~~is~~ *are* the Andes Mountains?

   A: In South America.

1. Q: Where is the name of a big city in Hungary?

   A: Budapest.

2. Q: What is the names of the Great Lakes?

   A: Huron, Ontario, Michigan, Erie, and Superior.

3. Q: What is the country of Namibia?

   A: Namibia is in Southern Africa.

4. Q: Who Winston Churchill was?

   A: He was a very famous prime minister of England.

Name _____ Date _____

Part II Achievement Test

57 Items
Score: _____

1 | LISTENING: DIRECTIONS TO THE RESTAURANT

A. *Paula and James are meeting at a restaurant. Listen to their conversation. Complete the conversation by writing the words that you hear. You will hear the recording two times.*

PAULA: ____Where____ is the restaurant?
         0.

JAMES: On the corner of First Avenue and Main Street. It's near the art museum. There are

  _____ in front of it. The building is very _____.
         1.   2.

PAULA: Oh, yes. It's behind the mall. What's the name of the mall?

JAMES: Mall of the _____.
                     3.

PAULA: That's right. OK. See you there in _____ hour.
                                            4.

B. *Reread the conversation. Find one contraction of a* wh- *question, one short answer to a* wh- *question, and three prepositions of place. Write them below.*

1. One contraction of a *wh-* question: _____

2. One short answer to a *wh-* question: _____

3. Three prepositions of place: _____ , _____ , _____

2 | E-MAIL FROM MELBOURNE

Complete the e-mail from Nancy to her friend Lori. Use the words in the box.

a	~~at~~	in	paintings	where
Albert Namatjira	Australia	in	photograph	Who
an	Australian Art	on	store	why

Dear Lori,

   Are you ____at____ work? I'm not! I'm _____ Melbourne,
            0.   1.

_____. I was at _____ art store yesterday. The name of the store is
    2.   3.

_____. There were many paintings _____ the _____.
    4.   5.   6.

PART II ■ ACHIEVEMENT TEST | 35

Name _____ **Date** _____

There was also a _____ of a man. The man was _____.
                      7.   **8.**

_____ is Albert Namatjira, and _____ is he famous?
   9.   **10.**

Nancy

3 | LORI'S ANSWER

Read Lori's e-mail back to Nancy. Look at the underlined words. Write each word in the correct category. An example is given.

Dear Nancy,

   Namatjira is an artist. He is from Canberra, Australia. His art is in the Melbourne Museum.

   I'm on vacation, too, but I'm at home. I'm bored. I want to visit my parents. They live near Denver.

   What is the name of your hotel?

   Have a great time in Melbourne!

Lori

1. Prepositions of place: _____, _____, _____

2. Singular noun: _____

3. Plural noun: _____

4. Proper nouns: *Namatjira*, _____, _____

5. Adjectives: _____, _____

6. *Wh-* word: _____

4 | NANCY'S PICTURES

Nancy is showing pictures to her friend Amy. Complete their conversation. Circle the correct words or phrases.

NANCY: I have a photos / photo /(photos) to show you. This is a photo / an photo / photos of
              0.   **1.**
   my daughter. These are my parent / my parents / a parent, and these are
                              2.
   my sisters / my sister / a sister. This sister is still on / in / near school. This is my
         3.   **4.**
   brother, between / on / at my dad and me.
              5.

AMY: Who / When / Where is your daughter now?
         6.

36 | PART II ■ ACHIEVEMENT TEST

Name _____ Date _____

NANCY: She's <u>at / on / in</u> Seoul, <u>korea / Korea / Koreas</u>. She works at
        7.   8.

<u>a computer company / computers companies / an computer company</u> there. She's
                                 9.

beautiful and <u>intelligent / an intelligent / a girl intelligent</u>.
                          10.

5 | AMY'S PICTURES

Amy is showing her pictures to Nancy. Use the words in parentheses to complete their conversation. Put the words in the correct order.

NANCY: Amy, <u>where are your pictures?</u> (your / Where / pictures? / are)
              0.

AMY: Oh, _____ (have / photos. I)
           1.

 _____ (an / in / album. They're)
           2.

NANCY: Let's look at them. Oh, this picture is great! _____
                                                3.

 (you? / Where / were)

AMY: _____ (was / Puerto Rico. / in / I) I was there with
          4.

 my friends Laura and Jenny. _____ (good / They're /
                                         5.

 friends.)

NANCY: Oh, look at this picture!

AMY: _____ (in front of / I / was / building. / famous / a)
          6.

 _____ (in / It's / San Juan.) The name is El Morro. It
          7.

 was an old fort.

6 | EDITING: THINGS TO SEE IN MELBOURNE

Nancy is going to Melbourne. Correct her conversation with Amy. There are 12 mistakes. The first mistake is already corrected. (Note: There can be more than one way to correct a mistake.)

                 What
NANCY: ~~Who~~ are your favorite thing in Melbourne?

AMY: The National gallery of Victoria is interest. It is museum. Most person like to see the beach. There are some greats restaurants. Also, the melbourne Aquarium is funs. Where is your hotel?

NANCY: My hotel is on the corner Queen and Lonsdale. I have room on seventh floor.

Name _____   Date _____

PART III Diagnostic Test

60 Items
Score: _____

1 | LISTENING: DINNER PLANS

🎧 *A. Pam is having a party. Frank and Susan meet there and start to talk. Listen to their conversation. Complete the conversation by writing the words that you hear. You will hear the recording two times.*

SUSAN: Hi, I'm Pam's friend Susan. Are you a friend of Pam's, too?

FRANK: Yes, I am. I'm Frank. It's nice to meet you.

SUSAN: You, too. So, how do you know Pam?

FRANK: _She and I take_ a Japanese cooking class together.
       0.

SUSAN: Oh, that's interesting. I love sushi. _____ how to make it?
                                                    1.

FRANK: Yeah, it's pretty easy.

SUSAN: Really? That's great. _____ the class?
                                    2.

FRANK: A Japanese professor from the community college. He's really good. Come to class with Pam sometime—it's a lot of fun!

SUSAN: Do I sign up somewhere?

FRANK: _____. Just come by and visit. Actually, there is a little party in class next
        3.
       week. That's a good day to go.

SUSAN: That _____ great! When does the party start?
                4.

FRANK: Well, the class is at 7:45 on Tuesday.

SUSAN: Oh no. I _____.
                    5.

FRANK: Are you busy on Tuesday?

SUSAN: Yes, _____. I have dinner plans.
              6.

FRANK: Well, maybe another time.

SUSAN: Yes, I hope so. . . .

B. Reread the conversation. Find two wh- questions and two yes / no questions. Write them on the lines provided on the next page. (Note: Only use words that are given in the conversation. Do not use any words that you wrote.)

Name _____ Date _____

1. Wh- question 1: _____

2. Wh- question 2: _____

3. Yes / no question 1: _____

4. Yes / no question 2: _____

2 | DINNER CONVERSATION

Pam, Susan, and Frank are at a Japanese restaurant. Complete their conversation. Use the words in the box.

am	cook	does	eat	is	sounds	Who
aren't	Do	doesn't	has	isn't	what	Who
buy	do	don't	how	~~like~~	Where	

FRANK: Do you ____like____ the sushi?
                      0.

SUSAN: Yes, I _____. It _____ delicious! Do you make sushi like
                 1.   2.
this in your cooking class?

FRANK: Well, yes, our teacher _____. But my sushi _____ taste like
                                   3.   4.
this. I _____ still a new student.
          5.

SUSAN: So, _____ do you make the rice?
              6.

PAM: It's pretty easy. First you _____ it in water on the stove.
                                     7.

SUSAN: _____ you wash the rice before you cook it?
          8.

FRANK: Well, it's a good idea to wash the rice, but I _____ wash it all the time.
                                                          9.

PAM: And after you cook it, you put in some sushi vinegar.

SUSAN: Oh, a special ingredient? _____ sells that?
                                     10.

FRANK: The Asian food store downtown has it.

SUSAN: And _____ does the vinegar do?
              11.

FRANK: It _____ sugar and salt in it. So it helps you form the rice, and it also
            12.
tastes good.

SUSAN: Well, your class sounds great. _____ eats all the food you make?
                                          13.

FRANK: We do!

Name _____ Date _____

3 | AN ARTIST

*Complete the conversation between George and Tina. Use the correct forms of the words in parentheses to make questions and statements. Add **do / does** and wh- words if necessary.*

GEORGE: What ___do you do___ for a living?
0. (you / do)

TINA: I'm an artist.

GEORGE: Really? _____?
1. (you / paint)

TINA: Yes, and I also draw, and I _____ sculptures.
2. (make)

GEORGE: Wow, that's really interesting. So how _____ ideas for your work?
3. (you / get)

TINA: Many things _____ me ideas. Sometimes I look at paintings by other
4. (give)
artists.

GEORGE: Oh, really? _____ your favorite artist?
5. (be)

TINA: Probably Picasso. He's amazing.

GEORGE: That's great. I'm interested in art, but I _____ a lot about it.
6. (not know)

TINA: That's OK. You _____ to know a lot about art to like it.
7. (not need)

GEORGE: _____ your art?
8. (you / sell)

TINA: Yes, _____.
9. (I / do)

GEORGE: And _____ it?
10. (buy)

TINA: Many people and stores buy it. And sometimes I have shows. People

_____ and see my work, and they buy things. Hey, _____
11. (come)   12. (you / want)

to see my art?

GEORGE: Sure. _____ your next show?
13. (be)

TINA: Saturday night. It's at the Art Center downtown.

GEORGE: Great. I'll be there.

Name _____ Date _____

4 | COMPUTER BUSINESS

*Tina and George are talking about George's business. Use the words in parentheses to complete their conversation. Put the words in the correct order. Add **do / does** if necessary.*

TINA: So, __what do you do__ (you / do / what), George?
0.

GEORGE: I _____ (computer / have / a / business). I
1.
_____ (new / sell / computers). I also
2.
_____ (repair / computers / old).
3.

TINA: _____ (you / your work / like)?
4.

GEORGE: _____ (yes / love / I / it).
5.

TINA: _____ (you / sell / to / your services / who)?
6.

GEORGE: I work with a lot of owners of small businesses. But I also sell computers for personal use. _____ (you / a / have / computer)?
7.

TINA: _____ (no / not / I). I want to buy one.
8.
_____ (your / computers / are / inexpensive)?
9.

GEORGE: _____ (yes / are / they).
10.

TINA: And _____ (how / know / I) what I need?
11.

GEORGE: Well, I'm happy to help you. Here's my card. It has all my information.

TINA: Oh, _____ (you / have) your business in your home?
12.

GEORGE: _____ (yes / do / I).
13.

TINA: But if you don't have a store or office, _____ (people / how / find) you?
14.

GEORGE: It's easy: on the Internet! I have a website.

TINA: Oh, I need to learn so much. I want to make my own website, too. _____ (learn / I / who) that from?
15.

GEORGE: Well, I sometimes teach the basics. _____ (have / you) time
16.
this week? I'm free in the evenings.

PART III ■ DIAGNOSTIC TEST | 41

Name _____ Date _____

5 | EDITING: WORKING FROM HOME

Correct George and Tina's conversation. There are nine mistakes. The first mistake is already corrected.

TINA: Your business ~~seem~~ *seems* great. Do is it easy to have a business in your home?

GEORGE: It's not always easy, but I like it. I don't drive or don't sit in traffic to get to work, and that's nice. Some of my neighbors thinks that I not work because they don't see me leave the house every day. But I'm very busy at home.

TINA: Who does helps you?

GEORGE: What do you mean?

TINA: Well, for example, who does brings you the computers?

GEORGE: The mail carrier.

TINA: Oh, that makes sense. And whom helps you do the repairs?

GEORGE: A friend works with me two days a week. On the other days, it's just me.

TINA: Wow, it sounds like a lot of work.

GEORGE: It is, but I love it.

TINA: Well, I need to go now. But do are you busy tomorrow? I want to look at your computers.

Name _____ Date _____

Unit 8 Achievement Test

30 Items
Score: _____

1 | LISTENING: SHOPPING

🎧 **A.** *Listen to Megan and Kevin's conversation. Complete the conversation by writing the words that you hear. You will hear the recording two times.*

MEGAN: I don't have a car, but I ____need____ to go to the store.
         　　　　　　　　　　　　　　　　　0.

KEVIN: You don't need a car. I _____ to the store. I _____ twice a
                               　　　　1.　　　　　　　　　　　　　　2.
week because I don't buy a lot. I _____ my backpack with me, and I
                                 　　　　3.
_____ my food home in it.
　　4.

MEGAN: That _____ a good idea. I _____ you're right. I don't need
              　　5.　　　　　　　　　　　　　　6.
a car.

B. *Reread the conversation. Find three negative statements. Write them below. An example is given.*

0. *I don't have a car.*

1. _____

2. _____

3. _____

2 | MY FAMILY

Complete the sentences. Circle the correct words.

0. I (want)/ wants to tell you about my family.

1. My brother study / studies hard.

2. He doesn't / don't work.

3. My sister work / works at a store.

4. You doesn't / don't know them.

5. They come / comes home for dinner.

6. We eat / eats at 7:00.

7. I drink / drinks milk with dinner.

Name _____ Date _____

3 | AFFIRMATIVE AND NEGATIVE STATEMENTS

Complete each pair of sentences with the verb in parentheses. Make affirmative statements for a and negative statements for b.

0. (like)　　a. My brother has a lot of books. He _____likes_____ to read.

　　　　　　b. My sister prefers to watch TV. She ____doesn't like____ to read.

1. (drive)　　a. My sister lives far from work. She _____ a long time to get there.

　　　　　　b. My mother lives near work. She _____ a long time to get there.

2. (go)　　　a. Bob and Donna love concerts and plays. They _____ to concerts and plays often.

　　　　　　b. Dan and Jill like to stay home. They _____ to concerts and plays often.

3. (want)　　a. I'm hot. I _____ to go swimming.

　　　　　　b. Danny is cold. He _____ to go swimming.

4. (wear)　　a. Businesspeople _____ business clothes.

　　　　　　b. Farmers _____ business clothes.

5. (practice)　a. I want to learn how to play the saxophone. I _____ it every day.

　　　　　　b. My sister already plays perfectly. She _____ at all.

4 | EDITING: WITHOUT A CAR

Correct the paragraph. There are five mistakes. The first mistake is already corrected.

　　　　　　shops
　　Megan ~~shop~~ at the store twice a week. She usually walk with her friend Kevin. They doesn't have cars, but that be fine with them. They don't work or don't study far from home.

44 | UNIT 8 ■ ACHIEVEMENT TEST

Name _____ Date _____

Unit 9 Achievement Test

30 Items
Score: _____

1 | LISTENING: LOOKING FOR A JOB

🎧 **A.** Listen to Andrés's conversation with Harvey, a worker at The Music Shop. Complete the conversation by writing the words that you hear. You will hear the recording two times.

ANDRÉS: Excuse me, ___*do you work*___ here?
                        0.

HARVEY: _____. Do you need some help?
              1.

ANDRÉS: Actually, I need a job.

HARVEY: Well, the owner isn't here right now. But you can leave your name and number for her.

_____ experience with music?
      2.

ANDRÉS: Yeah, I'm in a band.

HARVEY: That's cool. Is it popular?

ANDRÉS: Well, we play at Jake's Steaks every Tuesday, Wednesday, and Thursday night, so

_____.
     3.

HARVEY: Does your band play on weekends?

ANDRÉS: _____. In fact, I want to work on weekends. Hey, let me ask you
              4.

something about the owner. _____ good care of the employees?
                                         5.

HARVEY: _____. She's great.
              6.

ANDRÉS: Excellent. Here's my name and phone number. She can call me anytime.

B. Reread the conversation. Find three yes / no questions. Write them below. (Note: Only use words that are given in the conversation. Do not use any words that you wrote.)

1. _____

2. _____

3. _____

UNIT 9 ■ ACHIEVEMENT TEST | 45

Name _____ Date _____

2 | TALKING ABOUT FRIENDS

Complete the short conversations. Circle the correct words or phrases.

A: (Do) / Does / Are you have many friends?
     0.

B: Yes, I am / have / (do).
        0.

A: Do your friends visit / visits / are visit you often?
                  1.

B: No, they aren't / do visit / don't.
             2.

A: Do you has / have / does one best friend?
          3.

B: Yes, I have / do / does.
        4.

A: Does she lives / live / is in town?
           5.

B: No, she doesn't live / doesn't / isn't.
           6.

A: Do / Does / Are we need our friends?
    7.

B: Yes, we do / need / are.
        8.

3 | QUESTIONS AND ANSWERS

Complete the short conversations. Use **do** *or* **does** *and the verbs in parentheses.*

0. A: (know) _____*Do*_____ you _____*know*_____ her?

   B: Yes, _____*I do*_____ .

1. A: (have) _____ you _____ a brother?

   B: Yes, _____ .

2. A: (live) _____ he _____ at home?

   B: No, _____ .

3. A: (visit) _____ your parents _____ you?

   B: No, _____ .

4. A: (walk) _____ they _____ to school?

   B: Yes, _____ .

5. A: (go) _____ she _____ to school, too?

   B: No, _____ .

4 | EDITING: WHERE ARE YOU FROM?

Correct the conversation between Shannon and Gabriel. There are four mistakes. The first mistake is already corrected.

SHANNON: You have an accent. ~~Is~~ Are you from Mexico?

GABRIEL: No, I'm not. Guess again.

SHANNON: Do are you from Spain?

GABRIEL: No. Try again.

SHANNON: Do live you in Brazil?

GABRIEL: No.

SHANNON: I give up. Does you come from Argentina?

GABRIEL: Yes! I'm from Argentina.

Name _____ Date _____

Unit 10 Achievement Test

30 Items
Score: _____

1 | LISTENING: HELP FROM MOTHER

🎧 **A.** *Listen to Gretchen's phone conversation with her mother, Mrs. Tomkins. Complete the conversation by writing the words that you hear. You will hear the recording two times.*

GRETCHEN: Hello?

MRS. TOMKINS: Hi, Gretchen. It's your mother. How are you?

GRETCHEN: Terrible!

MRS. TOMKINS: Oh no! ___What do you___ need? Tell me everything.
                         0.

GRETCHEN: Thanks. I'm fine, I'm just so tired. The kids are noisy, the house is messy, I have so much work. . . . _____ people have kids *and* a life?!
                                                1.

MRS. TOMKINS: What do you mean?

GRETCHEN: I never finish my work. I'm always busy!

MRS. TOMKINS: Oh, that's simple! Let me ask you a question: How do you relax?

GRETCHEN: Relax?! _____ have time to relax?
                      2.

MRS. TOMKINS: Well, if you don't have time, you need to make time to relax. Listen, _____ when you're tired and stressed?
                3.

GRETCHEN: I feel terrible. I get angry easily.

MRS. TOMKINS: Right. And _____ to feel like that? You need to take 15 minutes
                            4.
each day to rest, relax, or do something that you enjoy.

GRETCHEN: _____ the children go while I'm relaxing? What do they do?
            5.

MRS. TOMKINS: They can read or draw or relax in their rooms. Explain that it is a special time just for you. They can understand.

GRETCHEN: Thanks, Mom. _____ told you all this?
                            6.

MRS. TOMKINS: My mother, of course!

48 | UNIT 10 ■ ACHIEVEMENT TEST

Name _____ Date _____

B. *Reread the conversation. Find three questions. Write them below. (Note: Only use words that are given in the conversation. Do not use any words that you wrote.) An example is given.*

0. <u>How are you?</u>

1. _____

2. _____

3. _____

2 | MUSIC QUESTIONS AND ANSWERS

Match the questions with the answers.

Questions

___g___ 0. What kind of music do you like?

_____ 1. Who do you like to listen to?

_____ 2. Who has a lot of CDs, you or your roommate?

_____ 3. When does your roommate listen to music?

_____ 4. Where do you listen to music?

_____ 5. Whom do you borrow music from?

_____ 6. How many CDs do you have?

_____ 7. Who listens to music at night?

Answers

a. In the car.

b. My roommate has a lot.

c. It is very good.

d. My sister. She lets me listen to her CDs.

e. I do.

f. My favorite group is the Beatles.

g. I like rock.

h. At night.

i. Very often.

j. About 100.

Name _____ Date _____

3 | QUESTIONS

Read each sentence. Write questions about the underlined words. Use the answers to help you.

He goes to work after school.

    Q: *Who goes to work after school* ?
                                0.

    A: He does.

    Q: *Where does he go after school* ?
                                0.

    A: To work.

The student calls his friend every week.

    Q: _____ ?
                                1.

    A: The student.

    Q: _____ ?
                                2.

    A: His friend.

The computer stays on the desk.

    Q: _____ ?
                                3.

    A: The computer.

    Q: _____ ?
                                4.

    A: On the desk.

Jack has a cell phone.

    Q: _____ ?
                                5.

    A: Jack.

    Q: _____ ?
                                6.

    A: A cell phone.

Tom and Linda see their dad every day.

Q: _____ 7. ?

A: Tom and Linda do.

Q: _____ 8. ?

A: Their dad.

The apartment feels hot because the air conditioner doesn't work.

Q: _____ 9. ?

A: The apartment.

Q: _____ 10. ?

A: Because the air conditioner doesn't work.

4 | EDITING: A NEW DOG

Correct the conversation between Sherry and Barbara. There are five mistakes. The first mistake is already corrected.

SHERRY: Hey, Barbara. I hear you have a new dog. How ~~it feels~~ *does it feel* to have an addition to your family?

BARBARA: Great! The dog is wonderful. Hey, I have a question. Where does your dog sleeps?

SHERRY: In my bed, with me. Why you do ask?

BARBARA: Well, I don't want my dog to sleep in the bed. How I teach him to sleep on the floor?

SHERRY: I don't know the answer to that. Let me think. . . . Who know a lot about dogs? Oh, Mike knows a lot about dogs. Ask him.

BARBARA: OK, thanks. I will.

Name _____ Date _____

Part III Achievement Test

60 Items
Score: _____

1 | LISTENING: LISA AND ALEX

🎧 **A.** Lisa and Alex are classmates. Listen to their conversation during lunch. Complete the conversation by writing the words that you hear. You will hear the recording two times.

ALEX: Hey, Lisa, you ____carry____ that camera with you everywhere. Why do you do
             0.
that? _____ a photographer?
          1.

LISA: _____. Not professionally, anyway. But I _____ pictures all
          2.   3.
the time.

ALEX: What do you take pictures of?

LISA: Oh, anything. People, nature . . . I _____ photography.
                                                       4.

ALEX: Are you a good photographer?

LISA: I guess so. Yeah, I'm pretty good.

ALEX: I _____ pictures, but I love to look at them.
          5.

LISA: Oh. Do you want to see my photos?

ALEX: I'd love to. _____ some with you?
                             6.

LISA: _____. But I'll bring some tomorrow. When do you have some time?
          7.

ALEX: Umm . . . let's have lunch again tomorrow. You can show them to me then.

LISA: OK, great.

B. Reread the conversation. Find two wh- questions and two yes / no questions. Write them below. (Note: Only use words that are given in the conversation. Do not use any words that you wrote.)

1. Wh- question 1: _____

2. Wh- question 2: _____

3. Yes / no question 1: _____

4. Yes / no question 2: _____

52 | PART III ■ ACHIEVEMENT TEST

Name _____ Date _____

2 | LOOKING AT PICTURES

Complete Lisa and Alex's conversation at lunch the next day. Use the words in the box.
Some items may have more than one right answer.

are	does	give	know	teaches	~~what~~	Who
Do	doesn't	How	like	use	When	who
do	don't	is	need	What	Where	why

LISA: So, ___what___ do you think about my pictures? Do you _____
                0.   1.
them?

ALEX: Yes, I _____. They _____ wonderful! _____
             2.   3.   4.
do you find things to photograph?

LISA: Lots of places. I always look for interesting things.

ALEX: And what about people? _____ do you take pictures of?
                                    5.

LISA: Anyone—old people, young children, my friends, my family.

ALEX: What _____ a photographer need to take a really good picture?
            6.

LISA: A good photographer doesn't _____ much—just a camera and someone or
                                       7.
something to photograph.

ALEX: _____ do you feel about digital cameras?
        8.

LISA: Well, they're convenient, but I don't _____ them much. Hey,
                                                9.
_____ do you have so many questions?
   10.

ALEX: I'm very interested. I _____ about some other kinds of art, but I
                                 11.
_____ know much about photography.
   12.

LISA: Do you want to learn? There is a class on Saturday.

ALEX: Oh, who _____ it?
                13.

LISA: My friend Jack does.

ALEX: And _____ goes to the class? Is everyone there really good at photography?
            14.

LISA: No, beginners go. Don't worry! It's a lot of fun.

3 | CLASSICAL MUSIC

*Complete the rest of Lisa and Alex's conversation. Use the correct forms of the verbs in parentheses to make questions and statements. Add **do / does** and **wh-** words if necessary.*

LISA: So, what about you? What ____do you do____ in your free time?
0. (you / do)

ALEX: Well, I really _____.
1. (like / music)

LISA: Yeah? _____ an instrument?
2. (you / play)

ALEX: Yes, _____ the piano. I also _____ music.
3. (I / play) 4. (write)

LISA: Wow! That's so interesting. _____ a favorite kind of music?
5. (you / have)

ALEX: Actually, classical music _____ my favorite.
6. (be)

LISA: Oh, I love classical, too. _____ most?
7. (who / you / listen to)

ALEX: Well, I have many favorite musicians, but I love Rachmaninov. _____ his music?
8. (you / know)

LISA: No, _____.
9. (I / not)

ALEX: It's really wonderful. _____?
10. (who / you / like)

LISA: I like Beethoven.

ALEX: Oh, there's a Beethoven concert this weekend. It's at the park.

LISA: That's great! I want to go.

ALEX: Cool! It's on Saturday night. It _____ at 7:30.
11. (start)

LISA: Sounds good. _____ from?
12. (who / I / buy / tickets)

ALEX: You don't need a ticket. Just meet me at the park around 7:00.

54 | PART III ■ ACHIEVEMENT TEST

Name _____ Date _____

4 | A SMALL BUSINESS

*Megan and Neil are talking about Megan's small business. Complete their conversation. Use the words in parentheses. Put the words in the correct order. Add **do / does** if necessary*

NEIL: So _____*what do you do*_____?
　　　　　　　0. (you / do / what)

MEGAN: I _____. I give classes.
　　　　　　1. (a / school / have / small)

NEIL: _____?
　　　　　2. (you / what / teach)

MEGAN: I _____, and I also
　　　　　　3. (teach / English)
_____ sometimes.
4. (give / Spanish and French / classes)

NEIL: _____?
　　　　　5. (you / your work / like)

MEGAN: _____. _____?
　　　　　6. (yes / I / it / love)　　　　　7. (you / want / language classes)

NEIL: _____. But my friend wants to take Spanish.
　　　　　8. (no / not / I)
_____?
9. (studies / with you / who)

MEGAN: _____?
　　　　　10. (you / mean / what)

NEIL: Well, _____, or are some of your students adults?
　　　　　　11. (work / you / with children)

MEGAN: Oh, I understand. I only teach adults.

NEIL: Great. _____ to sign up?
　　　　　　12. (who / my friend / call)

MEGAN: He can call me. Here's my card. It has the phone number of the school. Even if I'm not there, _____.
13. (answer / someone / the phone)

NEIL: And do you offer advanced level classes?

MEGAN: _____.
　　　　　14. (yes / do / I)

NEIL: That's great. His Spanish is pretty good.

Name _____ **Date** _____

5 | EDITING: OWNING A BUSINESS

Correct the rest of Megan and Neil's conversation. There are ten mistakes. The first mistake is already corrected.

                        sounds
NEIL: Your job ~~sound~~ fun. Do is it nice to have your own business?

MEGAN: I like it. I doesn't want to work for someone else. Some people think teachers not work much, but we do!

NEIL: Does the work is hard?

MEGAN: Yes, it is, but I enjoy it. And I have help.

NEIL: Oh, who does helps you?

MEGAN: I have a secretary, and there are two other teachers.

NEIL: Do the teachers work every day?

MEGAN: Yes, they do work.

NEIL: Who find the students?

MEGAN: We advertise online. Students come to us.

NEIL: You have a lot of students?

MEGAN: Yes, business is very good right now. In fact, we doesn't have enough classes for all our students. We plan to offer more classes soon.

Name _____ Date _____

PART IV Diagnostic Test

60 Items
Score: _____

1 | LISTENING: GOING TO THE CONCERT

🎧 **A.** *Chris and Stacie are going to a concert. Listen to their conversation. Complete the conversation by writing the words that you hear. You will hear the recording two times.*

CHRIS: Hi! Sorry I'm late. I took the car to the shop. ____*It*____ will be ready
                                                          0.

tomorrow. _____ does the concert start tonight?
              1.

STACIE: _____ 7:30. We need to get ready! They say _____ is going
          2.   **3.**

to be the best concert of the year. The orchestra and its conductor are from Italy.

CHRIS: Great! So, whose car can we take?

STACIE: I called our neighbors. . . . We can take Kim's car. It's in the driveway.

CHRIS: Do you have the key?

STACIE: Yes, I have her extra key. It's right here.

CHRIS: Great! By the way, _____ are nice earrings. Your dress is nice too.
                              4.

STACIE: Thank you!

B. *Reread the conversation. Find six possessive nouns or possessive adjectives. Write them below. (Note: Only use words that are given in the conversation. Do not use any words that you wrote.)*

1. _____

2. _____

3. _____

4. _____

5. _____

6. _____

PART IV ■ DIAGNOSTIC TEST | 57

Name _____ **Date** _____

2 | AN EVENING WITH FRIENDS

Chris and Stacie are playing a game with friends. Complete their conversation. Circle the correct words.

CHRIS: Thanks for coming over to play their / his /(our)/ these new game with us.
　　　　　　　　　　　　　　　　　　　　　　　　　　0.

KIM: Thanks for inviting us. We always have fun at my / your / our / their house! And
　　　　　　　　　　　　　　　　　　　　　　　　　　　　　　1.

these / this / those / your is a great game. It / One / Ones / These is so fun! I want to
　　2.　　　　　　　　　　　　　　　　　　　　　3.

buy those / one / ones / that.
　　　　　　4.

STACIE: You can find it at any store. . . . So, where / what / when / whose turn is it? Is it my
　　　　　　　　　　　　　　　　　　　　　　　　　5.

turn is / and / or / one your turn, Chris?
　　　　　　6.

CHRIS: I started, and Jamie is two / second / secondth / one. Kim is third, so it's
　　　　　　　　　　　　　　　　　　　　　7.

she's / her / she / hers turn.
　　　8.

KIM: I don't think so. I think it's Jamie's / Jamie / Jamies / hers turn.
　　　　　　　　　　　　　　　　　　　9.

JAMIE: It's not my / myself / mine / me turn, but it's time for us to go anyway. It's already
　　　　　　　　10.

10:00.

STACIE: Oh, really? That's too bad.

KIM: Yeah, I have an early meeting tomorrow. And I have to stop at the grocery store first.
But let's play again in / at / on / for Friday.
　　　　　　　　　　　　11.

CHRIS: OK! See you Friday!

3 | AT THE STORE

Kim and Jamie are at the grocery store the next morning. Complete their conversation. Use the words in the box. Some items may have more than one right answer.

at	her	it	my	ones	these	When
boss's	his	~~my~~	on	or	this	whose
boss's	in	my	one	These	those	your

KIM: Thanks for coming with me to get food for _____my_____ meeting.
　　　　　　　　　　　　　　　　　　　　　　　　　　0.

JAMIE: You're welcome. _____ is your meeting?
　　　　　　　　　　　　　　1.

KIM: It's at 9:00 _____ the morning.
　　　　　　　　　　2.

58 | PART IV ■ DIAGNOSTIC TEST

JAMIE: Did you prepare _____3._____ report?

KIM: Yes, I prepared it yesterday. I hope _____4._____ boss likes it. Sometimes he doesn't like _____5._____ reports.

JAMIE: Good luck! . . . So, what's your _____6._____ favorite food? Get something he likes.

KIM: I don't know what his favorite food is! Do you know your _____7._____ favorite food?!

JAMIE: No, but _____8._____ doughnuts here look good. Do you want _____9._____ box of doughnuts?

KIM: No, people eat too much sugar _____10._____ days. I want to buy fruit.

JAMIE: Grapes and oranges are on sale. What sounds better, grapes _____11._____ oranges?

KIM: I want to get pineapples. Here are some nice _____12._____.

4 | AT THE MEETING

Kim is at her meeting. Read the conversation. Write each underlined word in the correct category. An example is given.

TOM: Thank you for <u>your</u> report, Kim. Now, I want to talk about <u>our</u> computers. The IT department says that some of them are in bad shape. We have <u>ten</u> new computers and <u>four</u> old computers. The new <u>ones</u> are fast, but there's an old <u>one</u> that takes 20 minutes to start up. It's an IMP, I think. <u>Whose</u> computer is the IMP?

KIM: That's <u>my</u> computer. <u>It</u> is very slow.

TOM: OK, so <u>Kim's</u> computer is slow. I want to replace <u>her</u> computer. Does anyone else need a new <u>one</u>, too?

1. Pronouns: _____, _____, _____, _____, _____

2. Possessive adjectives: ___your___, _____, _____, _____, _____, _____

3. Cardinal numbers: _____, _____

Name _____ Date _____

5 | SLEEP WELL

*Chris is visiting his friend Jamie. Complete their conversation. Use prepositions, pronouns, possessive adjectives, possessive nouns, ordinal numbers or **one** or **ones**. Some items may have more than one right answer.*

CHRIS: I'm so tired. But I have a problem. I can't sleep ____at____ night. Do you have
0.
any ideas about how to sleep better?

JAMIE: Well, I talked to my doctor about sleep. This is _____ advice: First, don't
1.
watch TV _____ the evening. TV can excite _____ mind.
2. **3.**
_____, take a warm bath. This helps _____ muscles relax.
4. **5.**
Finally, use a comfortable pillow.

CHRIS: I don't have _____. Maybe that's the problem.
6.

JAMIE: Here, use this _____. I don't use _____.
7. **8.**

6 | EDITING: THE NEW PILLOW

Correct the conversation between Stacie and Chris. There are eight mistakes. The first mistake is already corrected.

　　　　　　 Whose
STACIE: ~~Who's~~ pillow is this?

CHRIS: It's Jamies pillow.

STACIE: Which Jamie? Ours neighbor Jamie, and our friend Jamie?

CHRIS: The two Jamie, our friend. I don't sleep well in night, so he thinks I should try pillow his. I like.

60 | PART IV ■ DIAGNOSTIC TEST

Name _____ Date _____

Unit 11 Achievement Test

30 Items
Score: _____

1 | LISTENING: NEW YEAR'S DAY

🎧 *Listen to this information about New Year's Day. Complete the information by writing the words that you hear. Use the words in the box. You will hear the recording two times.*

at	eleven	fifteen	1st	in	✗	one	13th
at	11th	15th	in	in	on	thirteen	20th

Most people celebrate New Year's Day ____on____ January _____. In
                                                 0.   1.
some countries, New Year's Day is _____ the winter. In other countries, it is
                                                    2.
_____ the summer. On New Year's Eve, or December 31st, people stay up late
      3.
_____ night. They watch fireworks that begin _____ 12:00
      4.   5.
midnight. They go to bed early _____ the morning. Most people do not work
                                          6.
_____ January 1st. People in Ethiopia celebrate the new year on September
    7.
_____. People in Thailand celebrate the new year from April _____
    8.   9.
to April _____.
         10.

2 | GRANDPARENTS DAY

Complete the paragraph about Grandparents Day in the United States. Circle the correct words.

Grandparents Day in the United States is always (on)/ in / at the Sunday after Labor Day.
                                                                           0.
Labor Day is on / in / at the one / first / firsth Monday on / in / at September. Grandparents
                    1.   2.   3.
Day is usually on / in / at the two / second / secondth Sunday on / in / at September, but it is
                       4.   5.   6.
on / in / at the one / first / firsth Sunday every seven / seventh / sevenst years. Grandparents Day
   7.   8.   9.
is on / in / at September 7th on / in / at 2008, which is the one / first / firsth Sunday.
   10.   11.   12.

Name _____ Date _____

3 | GRADUATION

Complete the conversation between Louis and Sara. Use wh- words or prepositions.

LOUIS: _____When_____ is your last day of class?
           0.

SARA: Wednesday.

LOUIS: _____ is your graduation?
           1.

SARA: It's _____ May 30th.
              2.

LOUIS: _____ time does it start?
           3.

SARA: It's _____ 5:30.
              4.

LOUIS: Great. I'll be there.

4 | EDITING: AFTER GRADUATION PLANS

Correct the conversation about Sara's plans after she graduates. There are five mistakes. The first mistake is already corrected.

        What
LOUIS: ~~When~~ are your plans after you graduate?

SARA: My one plan is to visit my parents in Ohio. My two plan is to visit my third brothers. They live in California.

LOUIS: When day do you start work?

SARA: Work? Umm . . .

Name _____ Date _____

Unit 12 Achievement Test

29 Items
Score: _____

1 | LISTENING: BEFORE CLASS

🎧 **A.** *Greg and Kathy are talking before class. Listen to their conversation. Complete the conversation by writing the words that you hear. You will hear the recording two times.*

KATHY: Hi. __*My name*__ is Kathy. What's your name?
               0.

GREG: _____ is Greg. Nice to meet you.
         1.

KATHY: Nice to meet you, too. Do you like our professor?

GREG: Yes, I do. I like his way of teaching. . . . Hey, _____ is this?
                                                                    2.

KATHY: It's not my book. Maybe it's Asami's book.

GREG: Whose book?

KATHY: _____. Asami is the girl from Japan. Maybe it's her book.
           3.

GREG: Oh. I'll ask her.

B. *Reread the conversation. Find six possessive nouns or possessive adjectives. Write them below. (Note: Only use words that are given in the conversation. Do not use any words that you wrote.) An example is given.*

0. *your*

1. _____

2. _____

3. _____

4. _____

5. _____

6. _____

PART IV

UNIT 12 ■ ACHIEVEMENT TEST | 63

Name _____ Date _____

2 | ASAMI'S FAMILY

Asami is in English class. The class is talking about their families. Complete the conversation. Use the words in the box.

Asami	Her	His	our	Whose	your
brother's	her	its	sister	~~your~~	your
Her	Hiroshi	My	their	Your	Yuka

TEACHER: Thank you, Felipe, for telling us about ____your____ family.
0.
_____ turn is it now? Asami! Tell us about _____ family.
1.   2.

ASAMI: _____ name is Asami. I have a brother named Hiroshi and a sister
3.
named Yuka. Hiroshi owns a restaurant. My _____ work is difficult.
4.
_____ wife is a doctor. _____ work is also difficult. My
5.   6.
_____, Yuka, and _____ husband are in Africa. It's
7.   8.
_____ first time there. _____ husband doesn't like the
9.   10.
food, but she does.

TEACHER: _____ family sounds very interesting. Thank you, Asami. Paulo, now
11.
you talk about _____ family.
12.

3 | BOOKS

Asami is visiting Kathy's house. Use the correct possessive forms of the words in parentheses to complete their conversation.

ASAMI: Wow, you have a lot of books. Are they all ____your____ books?
0. (you)
KATHY: No, they're not all _____ books. These are _____
1. (I)   2. (I)
_____ books, and those are _____ books.
3. (mother)   4. (my brother Jack)

ASAMI: _____ poetry book is this?
5. (who)
KATHY: It's _____ poetry book. I love poetry.
6. (I)

4 | EDITING: THE ART BOOK

Correct the rest of the conversation between Asami and Kathy. There are three mistakes. The first mistake is already corrected.

                                            Whose
ASAMI: This is a beautiful art book. ~~Who~~ is it? Is it you're book?

KATHY: No, it's my dads book.

64 | UNIT 12 ■ ACHIEVEMENT TEST

Name _____ Date _____

Unit 13 Achievement Test

30 Items
Score: _____

1 | LISTENING: AT THE MUSEUM

🎧 **A.** *Josh and his sister Megan are at a museum. Listen to their conversation. Complete the conversation by writing the words that you hear. You will hear the recording two times.*

MEGAN: _____*This*_____ is a big museum. Let's start on this side. Oh, look at that! Are
            0.

      those dinosaur bones _____ elephant bones?
                                     1.

JOSH: These are bones of an old animal that was like an elephant. It's called a mammoth.

      Mammoths lived during the last Ice Age. In _____ days, early man ate
                                                     2.

      them. But the mammoths all died about 10,000 years ago.

MEGAN: Did they all die because of humans or because of another reason?

JOSH: _____ a good question. No one knows.
         3.

MEGAN: Interesting. Where do you want to go next, this way or that way?

B. *Read each sentence based on the conversation. Write **P** if the underlined word is a pronoun and **A** if it is an adjective.*

0. ___P___ <u>This</u> is a big museum.

1. _____ Let's start on <u>this</u> side.

2. _____ Oh, look at <u>that</u>!

3. _____ <u>Those</u> bones are big.

4. _____ <u>These</u> are bones of an old elephant.

5. _____ Do you want to go <u>this</u> way?

C. *Reread the conversation. Find two questions that ask for a choice. Write them below. An example is given.*

0. Are those dinosaur bones or elephant bones? _____

1. _____

2. _____

UNIT 13 ■ ACHIEVEMENT TEST | 65

Name _____ Date _____

2 | THE BLUE WHALE

Josh and Megan visit the ocean room at the museum. Complete their conversation. Use **this, that, these, those,** *and* **or**. *Some items may have more than one right answer.*

JOSH: Do you want to go ___this___ way to the insect room _____
0.   1.

_____ way to the ocean room?
2.

MEGAN: Let's go _____ way to the ocean room. Wow, look at
3.

_____ big whale! Are whales really that big, _____ are
4.   5.

they smaller in real life?

JOSH: _____'s a model of a blue whale, the largest animal in the world. And
6.

yes, they're really that big. There are not as many blue whales _____
7.

days. _____'s the reason they are protected.
8.

MEGAN: And look here. What are _____? Are they shrimp _____
9.   10.

fish?

JOSH: _____ are called "krill." They're like shrimp, and blue whales eat them.
11.

3 | BUTTERFLIES

Josh and Megan visit the insect room at the museum. Complete their conversation. Use **this, that, these, those,** *and* **or**. *Some items may have more than one right answer.*

MEGAN: ___That___ was really interesting. Do you want to see the insects now,
0.

_____ do you want to watch the movie about birds?
1.

JOSH: The movie starts in 15 minutes. Let's go _____ way to see the insects.
2.

MEGAN: Oh, look at all _____ butterflies! They're beautiful! Are their colors real
3.

_____ painted?
4.

JOSH: They're all real. _____ part of the museum with the butterflies is new.
5.

_____ butterflies come from all over the world.
6.

Name _____ Date _____

4 | EDITING: AFTER THE MUSEUM

Josh and Megan get ready to leave the museum. Correct their conversation. There are four mistakes. The first mistake is already corrected.

JOSH: I think ~~these~~ *this* is the exit.

MEGAN: That movie was really good. And that butterflies were beautiful. Thank you for bringing me to those museum.

JOSH: You're welcome. Now, do you want to see the gift shop, and do you want to eat lunch?

Name _____ Date _____

Unit 14 Achievement Test

30 Items
Score: _____

1 | LISTENING: BUYING PET FISH

🎧 *Dan and Mara want to buy some pet fish. Listen to their conversation. Complete the conversation by writing the words that you hear. You will hear the recording two times.*

DAN: Look at these orange fish. Those are nice ___ones___.
    0.

MARA: They're OK. Do you like this black fish?

DAN: That's a strange _____. Here are some blue fish.
    1.

MARA: Those are interesting _____. But I like these red fish. They're better than
    2.
    the blue _____.
    3.

DAN: Here are some frogs. They're cute!

MARA: I don't think so. I don't want _____. But look at that suckerfish.
    4.
    _____ helps keep the tank clean.
    5.

DAN: Let's get one. And we need a big fish tank. Here's _____.
    6.

MARA: Let's put it in the shopping cart. Where is _____?
    7.

DAN: _____'s right here.
    8.

MARA: Did you bring your wallet?

DAN: Yes, _____'s in my pocket.
    9.

2 | LUNCH

Dan and Mara are having lunch. Complete their conversation. Circle the correct words or phrases.

MARA: I made some sandwiches. Do you want (one) / it / ones ?
    0.

DAN: Sure, I want one / it / ones .
    1.

MARA: Do you want this one or that one / it / that ones ?
    2.

DAN: I want the one / it / ones with tuna.
    3.

MARA: We also have red grapes and green one / it / ones .
    4.

DAN: I want the red one / it / ones . Thank you!
    5.

68 | UNIT 14 ■ ACHIEVEMENT TEST

Name _____ Date _____

MARA: How's the sandwich?

DAN: <u>One / It / Ones</u>'s great.
         6.

MARA: Good. I'm glad you like <u>one / it / ones</u>.
                                       7.

DAN: How's your sandwich?

MARA: <u>One / It / Ones</u>'s delicious.
         8.

3 | LOOKING AT CARS

*Dan wants to buy a car. He's looking at cars with his friend Mike. Complete their conversation. Use **one**, **ones**, and **it**.*

DAN: Is this the right place?

MIKE: Yes, this is the _____one_____.
                          0.

DAN: It looks like they have new cars and used _____. I want a used
                                                    1.

_____.
   2.

MIKE: Here are some nice cars. Do you like this _____?
                                                    3.

DAN: It's OK. But it's an American car, and I want a Japanese _____.
                                                                  4.

MIKE: Here's _____. Do you like _____?
               5.   **6.**

DAN: _____'s too expensive. But look at this little car. I really like this
       7.

_____.
   8.

MIKE: That _____ is yellow! It looks like a taxi!
              9.

4 | EDITING: NO NEW CAR

Dan is telling Mara about the cars. Correct their conversation. There are five mistakes. The first mistake is already corrected.

DAN: Mike and I looked at cars, but I didn't buy ~~it~~.
                                                  one

MARA: Really? Why not?

DAN: Well, I liked one a lot, but one was yellow. Mike thinks it looks like a taxi. I like the

model of the car. Sometimes they have white one and silver one, but not right now.

MARA: That's OK. Our car is old, but we don't need a new ones right now.

Name _____   Date _____

Part IV Achievement Test

60 Items
Score: _____

1 | LISTENING: GOING TO THE MOVIES

🎧 **A.** Rich and Wendy are going to a movie. Listen to their conversation. Complete the conversation by writing the words that you hear. You will hear the recording two times.

RICH: I'm home! I took ____*your*____ dress to the cleaners. It will be ready tomorrow.
                                     0.
 _____ does the movie start tonight?
     1.

WENDY: _____ 6:45. Hey, did you read _____ review of the movie
        2.   **3.**
 in the newspaper last night? They say it's wonderful! And its director is famous.

RICH: Good! Hey, whose pants are those?

WENDY: They're my sister's pants. All my pants are dirty.

RICH: _____ are nice. Your sister has nice clothes.
     4.

WENDY: I know. I like them, too. So, do you have the key to the house?

RICH: Yes, I do. Do you have your purse?

WENDY: Yes. Let's go.

B. Reread the conversation. Find six possessive nouns or possessive adjectives. Write them below. (Note: Only use words that are given in the conversation. Do not use any words that you wrote.) An example is given.

0. *its*

1. _____

2. _____

3. _____

4. _____

5. _____

6. _____

Name _____ Date _____

2 | THE NEW APARTMENT

Helen and Will are at Rich and Wendy's new apartment. Complete their conversation. Circle the correct words.

RICH: I'm glad you like (our)/ their / those / that apartment.
                                                 0.

HELEN: We love it! These / This / Those / That is a great apartment. Is that
                                     1.

       my / your / our / their stove, or was it already in the apartment?
            2.

       It / One / Ones / These's so nice—I love gas stoves. I want it / one / ones / that just
            3.   4.

       like it.

RICH: Yeah, it is our stove, and you're right—gas stoves are great! Oh, this is one of the bedrooms.

WILL: So, where / what / when / whose bedroom is this? Is it your bedroom is / and / or / one
             5.   6.
       the guest bedroom?

RICH: It's our bedroom. The guest bedroom is the two / second / secondth / one door on
                                                              7.

       the right, and this is your / our / their / that office. Actually, it's
                                       8.

       Wendy / Wendys / Wendy's / hers office. This is all her / hers / she's / her's stuff.
                      9.   10.

WILL: It's a beautiful apartment.

RICH: Thanks. Hey, we're having a party in / at / on / for Saturday. Can you come?
                                                                    11.

WILL: OK! Thanks!

Name _____   **Date** _____

3 | AT THE MALL

Helen and Will are at the mall. Complete their conversation. Use the words in the box.

at	In	mom's	my	ones	These	When
her	in	My	on	or	this	whose
his	mom's	~~my~~	one	that	those	your

HELEN: I need to get a birthday present for ____my____ mom.
                                             0.

WILL: _____ is her birthday?
         1.

HELEN: It's _____ Tuesday.
              2.

WILL: Did you send _____ mom a card yet?
                       3.

HELEN: Yes. _____ mom loves cards. But I actually sent it to _____
             4.   5.
dad. He's giving it to her on her birthday.

WILL: So what's your _____ idea of a good gift? What kinds of things does she
                         6.
like?

HELEN: Useful things. My _____ favorite gift last year was a microwave oven. It
                             7.
was from my dad.

WILL: _____ dishes are nice. Do you want to get her _____ box
         8.   9.
of dishes?

HELEN: No, I don't want _____. There were nice dishes on sale last week, but she
                            10.
didn't want them. I want to buy her a cookbook.

WILL: These cookbooks are on sale. What sounds better, Mexican food _____
                                                                         11.
Italian food?

HELEN: She likes French food, so maybe a French cookbook. Here are some nice
_____.
    12.

72 | PART IV ■ ACHIEVEMENT TEST

Name _____ Date _____

4 | AT THE BIRTHDAY PARTY

Helen and Will are at Helen's mother's birthday party. Read the conversation. Write each underlined word in the correct category below.

HELEN'S MOM: Thank you for <u>your</u> gift, Helen. I always love <u>your</u> gifts.

HELEN: Thanks, Mom. There were <u>two</u> big French cookbooks at the store and <u>one</u> small French cookbook, but the big <u>ones</u> were in French, and the smaller <u>one</u> didn't have any pictures. So I got the Chinese cookbook.

HELEN'S MOM: Well, it's great!

WILL: <u>Whose</u> piece of cake is <u>this</u>?

HELEN'S MOM: <u>That</u>'s <u>my</u> piece. <u>It</u>'s delicious!

WILL: I know. Helen is a great cook. <u>Her</u> cakes are always delicious.

HELEN: Thanks. The recipe for this cake is an old one from <u>our</u> family.

1. Pronouns: _____, _____, _____, _____, _____

2. Possessive adjectives: ___*your*___, _____, _____, _____, _____, _____

3. Cardinal numbers: _____, _____

Name _____ Date _____

5 | HELEN'S SECRET

Rich is visiting Will. Complete their conversation. Use prepositions, pronouns, possessive adjectives, possessive nouns, or ordinal numbers. Some items may have more than one right answer.

RICH: I liked ____Helen's____ cake at the party _____ Saturday. How does
            0.   1.

she make _____ wonderful chocolate cake?
              2.

WILL: Well, she uses an old family recipe, and she buys very expensive chocolate. That's

_____ secret: really good chocolate.
      3.

RICH: I didn't know that! Next time I make a chocolate cake, the _____ thing I'll
                                                                          4.

buy will be good chocolate. Maybe then _____ cake will be as delicious as
                                                 5.

_____ cake.
      6.

WILL: Hey, we have more pieces of cake. Do you want _____?
                                                                7.

RICH: Sure!

WILL: Choose any _____ you want.
                          8.

6 | EDITING: THE JACKET

Correct the conversation between Helen and Will. There are eight mistakes. The first mistake is already corrected.

                Whose
HELEN: ~~Who's~~ jacket is this? I like.

WILL: It's Richs jacket.

HELEN: Ours friend Rich and our neighbor Rich?

WILL: Our friend Rich. He was here this morning, but he forgot his jacket.

HELEN: This is the two time that he forgot jacket his at our house!

WILL: I'll give it to him in Monday.

Name _____ Date _____

PART V Diagnostic Test

| 60 Items |
| Score: _____ |

1 | LISTENING: AT THE COLD CUT CAFÉ

🎧 **A.** *Alice and Joanne are at a café. Listen to their conversation. Complete the conversation by writing the words that you hear. You will hear the recording two times.*

ALICE: Is this the only café around here? It seems so unfriendly. Where are the employees?

__Who is working__ ? Let's go somewhere else.
       0.

JOANNE: Wait. I think that guy over there is a waiter. Is he coming this way?

ALICE: Yeah, he sees us.

WAITER: Welcome to the Cold Cut Café. _____ me. . . . Here are your menus.
                                            1.

_____ me know when you're ready.
      2.

JOANNE: OK. These chairs are so uncomfortable. And it's so cold in here. Look, you're shaking.

Excuse me! _____ up the heat, please? We're really cold.
              3.

WAITER: Sorry, our heater _____ .
                        4.

ALICE: You know, this part of Vancouver needs a good café. Let's start our own café, where

people can be comfortable! We _____ it the Comfort Café!
                                        5.

JOANNE: That's a great idea!

B. *Reread the conversation. Find two present continuous verbs, one suggestion, and one response to a suggestion. Write them in the table below. (Note: Only use words that are given in the conversation. Do not use any words that you wrote.) An example is given.*

PRESENT CONTINUOUS VERBS	SUGGESTION	RESPONSE TO SUGGESTION
1. _____	0. *Let's go*	1. _____
2. _____	1. _____	

PART V ■ DIAGNOSTIC TEST | 75

Name _____ Date _____

2 | PLANNING THE COMFORT CAFÉ

Joanne and Alice are making plans for their new café. Complete their conversation. Write the letter of the best answer on each line.

JOANNE: Hi! __a__ (a. Can I sit b. Can sitting c. Can be sitting d. I'm sit) here with you?
         0.

ALICE: Sure.

JOANNE: So, _____ (a. what's happening b. what happen c. what happens d. what can happen)?
        1.

ALICE: Well, _____ (a. why don't working on b. am I working on c. I'm working on d. can working on) a
        2.
business plan for our café.

JOANNE: Really? _____ (a. What do you look at b. Why don't you look at c. Why are you looking at
        3.
d. What are you looking at) right now?

ALICE: I _____ (a. 'm review b. 'm reviewing c. reviewing d. can review) our finances, and I have
       4.
good news. I think _____ (a. we can doing b. we do can c. can we do d. we can do) it!
                    5.

JOANNE: Oh, I'm so excited! _____ (a. Let's buying b. Let us buy c. Let's buy d. Let buy us) some
                            6.
furniture and things right away. _____ (a. Why not we b. Why not us c. Why don't us
                                 7.
d. Why don't we) get big sofas for people to sit on? And we _____ (a. can have
                                                             8.
b. can having c. have d. 're having) wooden tables and soft chairs, too.

ALICE: _____ (a. Don't forgetting b. Don't forget c. Not forget d. Not forgetting) the soft, yellow
       9.
lighting. What kind of food do you want to serve?

JOANNE: Well, we _____ (a. can't serving b. can't serve c. not serve d. let's not serve) anything too
                 10.
greasy. People _____ (a. are trying b. please try c. can trying d. try) to eat more healthily
                11.
these days.

Name _____ Date _____

3 | A COOK FOR THE COMFORT CAFÉ

Alice and Joanne are looking for a cook for the Comfort Café. Complete their conversation. Use the words and phrases in the box.

can	Don't	Is he making	is thinking	~~let's~~
can't	is buying	Is he working	is visiting	Let's
can't	is he looking	is taking	is working	Why don't we

ALICE: OK, ____let's____ think about a cook now. How _____ we find a
                    0.   1.
cook?

JOANNE: _____ ask me! I have no idea!
             2.

ALICE: Well, I have one idea. My friend Steve is a cook. He _____ at the
                                                                    3.
Carlton Hotel right now. But he doesn't like his job there because it's not very

interesting. He _____ create new dishes there. He always makes the same
                       4.

thing. _____ call him?
            5.

JOANNE: Good idea. But _____ for another job?
                                6.

ALICE: Yes. He _____ about a job at another hotel downtown.
                     7.

JOANNE: _____ give him a call. Maybe he can work for us! _____
              8.   9.
today? Maybe we can call him at the hotel right now.

ALICE: No. This is his day off. He _____ his parents in Cloverdale. I
                                            10.
_____ talk to him today, but I can call him tomorrow.
      11.

4 | CLOSING TIME

Alice's friend Pete is visiting her at the Comfort Café at the end of the day. Complete their conversation. Use the imperative, present progressive, **could**, or suggestions and the words in parentheses.

PETE: Did you hear that the Cold Cut Café ____is closing____ (close)?
                                                    0.

ALICE: No! I can't believe it! _____ (why / they / close)?
                                       1.

PETE: They _____ (could / not get) any business after the Comfort Café opened.
                  2.
_____ (business / go) well here nowadays?
      3.

PART V ■ DIAGNOSTIC TEST | 77

Name _____ Date _____

ALICE: Yeah, at the moment we _____ (do) really well. People
4.
_____ (come in / and / buy) lunch *and* dinner these days. We
5.
_____ (finish) our first year now, so we're very happy. But, we
6.
_____ (not stop) there! We're working to make the café even better!
7.

PETE: I knew you _____ (could / do) it! _____ (let's / go) eat.
8. 9.

ALICE: OK. _____ (please / help) me push in the chairs; then we can go.
10.

5 | OLD FRIENDS

*Joanne sees her friend Kate. Complete their conversation. Use the imperative, present progressive, **can / could**, or suggestions and the words in the box.*

can	come	enjoy	go	help	not say	sit	want
can't	do	go	have	not	not worry	~~tell~~	work

KATE: Joanne? Is that you? I never see you anymore! ___Tell___ me all about your
0.
life. What _____ you _____ these days?
1.

JOANNE: Oh, I'm working a lot.

KATE: Really? Where _____ you _____ right now?
2.

JOANNE: Well, Alice and I have a café. It's about a year old. It's a lot of work, but we
_____ it! It's fun! Actually, I _____ there right now. Hey,
3. 4.
are you hungry? _____ with me for lunch there!
5.

KATE: Thanks, Joanne, but I _____ eat there today. I don't have any money.
6.

JOANNE: _____ about it. You don't need to pay. It's my café, remember? Please
7.
_____ no.
8.

KATE: OK, but _____ you wait five minutes? I want to finish this first.
9.
_____ down, please.
10.

78 | PART V ■ DIAGNOSTIC TEST

Name _____ Date _____

6 | EDITING: ANOTHER COMFORT CAFÉ

Alice and Joanne are planning to open another Comfort Café. Correct their conversation. There are 10 mistakes. The first mistake is already corrected. (Note: There can be more than one way to correct a mistake.)

ALICE: We ^are having a busy week! Business not slowing down at all! You can check how much money we have in the bank?

JOANNE: Sure. I can check it online. OK, here is our bank information.

ALICE: Are we do well this week?

JOANNE: We are make a lot of money right now. People are coming and are bringing their friends.

ALICE: Print please our bank statement. . . . This is great. Why we don't open another Comfort Café?

JOANNE: That a good idea.

ALICE: You call tomorrow and see if there are any good places for a second café.

JOANNE: OK!

Name _____ Date _____

Unit 15 Achievement Test

30 Items
Score: _____

1 | LISTENING: AFTER THE EARTHQUAKE

🎧 *Listen to this radio report after an earthquake. Complete the report by writing the words that you hear. You will hear the recording two times.*

ANNOUNCER: You're listening to NRI, Network Radio International.

ERIC ENSLEY: Early this morning, there was a sudden, violent shaking across the city of Kobe, Japan. People soon realized that it was an earthquake. NRI's Yoko Arisaka ____is reporting____ live from Kobe. Yoko, tell us what you _____ there at the moment.
                                     0.   1.

YOKO ARISAKA: Well, right now, Eric, I _____ in downtown Kobe. Many homes are badly damaged, so there are many people on the streets. Thousands of
                                     2.
people _____ on the sidewalks. Many people want to leave the
         3.
city. But taxis are full, and the subway _____. Buses and trains
                                                            4.
are not on schedule. So people _____ for other ways to get
                                     5.
around. Far away, smoke from a fire _____ in the sky. It is a
                                           6.
difficult day for many people in Kobe.

ERIC ENSLEY: And I understand that people from all over the country _____ to
                                                                              7.
help. Everyone wants to cooperate.

YOKO ARISAKA: That's true, Eric. The government _____ people to give food,
                                                       8.
water, and clothes, and people are giving as much as they can.

ERIC ENSLEY: Thank you, Yoko. That was NRI's Yoko Arisaka in Kobe, Japan.

Name _____ Date _____

2 | SATURDAY MORNING

It is Saturday morning. Complete these sentences about what the Aragons are doing. Circle the correct words or phrases.

0. Denise Aragon (is listening) / listens / listening to news about the earthquake on the radio.

1. She stands / standing / is standing in the kitchen right now.

2. She making / makes / is making breakfast at the moment.

3. She is frying / frying / fry eggs.

4. She does not working / is not working / is not work as much these days, so she is home more.

5. The cat sits / sitting / is sitting on the chair right now.

6. At the moment, her husband runs / is running / running in the park.

7. He is exercising / exercise / exercising more nowadays.

3 | SCENES FROM A STORE

Complete the sentences about people at a store. Use the present progressive forms of the verbs in the box.

| ask | do | give | leave | play | ~~shop~~ | talk |
| become | eat | help | look | read | sit | walk |

0. People ____are shopping____ for shoes.

1. They _____ at the prices of things.

2. A young man _____ in a chair because he is tired.

3. A man _____ money to the salesperson to pay for his new coat.

4. A woman _____ the store with her children. They are finished shopping.

5. The store _____ good music these days.

6. An old woman _____ a question about prices.

7. Two college students _____ on their phones.

8. A child _____ an apple.

9. A salesperson _____ a boy find a shirt.

Name _____ **Date** _____

4 | EDITING: AT THE PARTY

Correct this conversation among three friends at a party. There are seven mistakes. The first mistake is already corrected.

SHELLY: Great party, Dean. Everything is ~~being~~ wonderful!

RHONDA: Yeah, everything is very good. People are eating and are drinking a lot.

DEAN: Well, I'm glad they are enjoy everything.

SHELLY: Everyone is has a great time, too. This party was a great idea. A lot of us don't going out much nowadays. . . . Hey, where are Kevin and Heather?

RHONDA: They're walking around and are talking outside.

DEAN: They are not spend enough time together these days.

RHONDA: I know. I think that's why they want to be alone now.

Name _____   Date _____

Unit 16 Achievement Test

30 Items
Score: _____

1 LISTENING: GOOD NEIGHBORS

🎧 **A.** Amy is at her neighbor Gina's house. Listen to their conversation. Complete the conversation by writing the words that you hear. You will hear the recording two times.

AMY: Hi, Gina. I need to borrow your cake pan, please. ____Are you using____ it?
                                                                   0.

GINA: No, I'm not. _____?
                              1.

AMY: A cake—a chocolate one with vanilla frosting. Oh! Is your refrigerator working?

GINA: _____! What's going on? Are you feeling OK?
              2.

AMY: Yes, I'm fine. I'm just busy. I'm cooking, and I need more room for the food.

GINA: Why are you making so much food? _____ a party?
                                                      3.

AMY: Yes! The birthday party!

GINA: _____ a birthday?
              4.

AMY: David! Don't you know about the party?

GINA: No, I don't. Is David working today?

AMY: Yes. It's a surprise party. It's at 6:30. Can you come?

GINA: Of course! Do you need help? Where are the kids? Are they playing outside?

AMY: Yes, thank goodness! I have to run and get some eggs.

GINA: Wait! Where _____? Use my eggs! And I'll get the cake pan.
                              5.

AMY: Perfect! Thanks so much!

B. Reread the conversation. Find three present progressive yes / no questions. Write them on the lines below. (Note: Only use questions that are given in the conversation. Do not use any questions with words that you wrote.) An example is given.

0. _Is your refrigerator working?_____

1. _____

2. _____

3. _____

UNIT 16 ■ ACHIEVEMENT TEST | 83

Name _____ Date _____

2 | QUESTIONS

Everyone is at David's birthday party. Complete these questions from people's conversations. Circle the correct phrases.

0. (Are you having) / Do you have / Are you have a good birthday?

1. You sitting / Are you sitting / Do you sitting here?

2. What you are talking / you talk / are you talking about?

3. Why they laughing / are they laughing / they are laughing?

4. What are you eating / you eating / you are eating? It looks delicious!

5. Who you are talking / are you talking / do you talk about?

6. Your wife feeling / Are your wife feeling / Is your wife feeling OK? I don't see her here.

7. Where are the children? Are they playing / They are playing / They playing a game?

8. Where you working / you are working / are you working now?

9. Are you look / Are you looking / You looking for the plates?

10. Is your friend travel / traveling / travels?

3 | BUSINESS TRIP

David is out of town on a business trip. He is talking to Amy on the phone. Use the present progressive and the words in parentheses to complete their conversation.

AMY: Hello?

DAVID: Hi, Honey. _____How are you doing_____ (How / you / do)?
                              0.

AMY: I'm OK, but I'm feeling a little sick. How's your trip going?

DAVID: _____ (It / go / OK), but I'm a little tired. I'm sorry
                  1.
you're not feeling well.

AMY: Thanks. _____ (Where / you / call) from?
                          2.

DAVID: I'm in the hotel. It's a nice one! And I'm in a huge, fancy room—a suite!

AMY: _____ (Why / you / stay) in a suite?
              3.

DAVID: It was the only room left. The hotel is full, so the manager gave me a nice room at a

good price.

84 | UNIT 16 ■ ACHIEVEMENT TEST

Name _____ Date _____

AMY: That's great! _____ (you / get) a lot of work done?
                              4.

DAVID: Yes, I am. I'm reading a lot.

AMY: _____ (What / you / read)?
              5.

DAVID: Just reports. They're pretty boring. _____ (What /
                                                      6.
happen) at home?

AMY: Not much. I'm doing a little laundry, and the kids are doing their homework.

DAVID: _____ (What / they / work) on?
                7.

AMY: Jacob is doing some math homework, and Sarah is writing a paper for English.

DAVID: _____ (they / behave) well?
                8.

AMY: Yeah, they are. Well, we miss you.

DAVID: I miss you too. I hope you feel better. See you tomorrow night.

AMY: OK, bye.

4 | EDITING: AT THE DOCTOR'S OFFICE

Amy is at the doctor's office. Correct her conversation with the doctor. There are five mistakes. The first mistake is already corrected.

DR. MONTOYA: How are you ~~feel~~ feeling?

AMY: I am not cough. But I'm sneezing all the time.

DR. MONTOYA: Are you taking any medication?

AMY: Yes, I am.

DR. MONTOYA: Is it working?

AMY: Yes, it does, but only for a few hours. I'm also taking some vitamins now.

DR. MONTOYA: What kind of vitamins you use?

AMY: Vitamin C and a multivitamin.

DR. MONTOYA: How is you sleeping?

AMY: Just fine.

DR. MONTOYA: Good. Let me check your throat. Say "Ah!"

Name _____ Date _____

Unit 17 Achievement Test

30 Items
Score: _____

1 | LISTENING: CAR SALE

🎧 **A.** *Listen to this radio advertisement. Complete the advertisement by writing the words that you hear. You will hear the recording two times.*

OK, everyone . . . listen to this! ____Come____ to Gary's Downtown Auto Mall today.
0.
Bring your family and friends! _____ the biggest car sale of the year! Find the car
1.
of your dreams at a low, low price. Choose from our huge selection, and _____
2.
away in a new car or truck the same day! Get $1,000 cash back. Don't wait because these deals
won't be around for long! _____ us today!
3.

B. *Reread the radio advertisement. Find five imperatives. Write them below. (Note: Only use words that are given in the advertisement. Do not use any words that you wrote.) An example is given.*

0. _listen_____

1. _____

2. _____

3. _____

4. _____

5. _____

2 | CLASS RULES

Complete the rules for an English class. Circle the correct words or phrases.

0. (Show)/ Shows / Showing respect to others.

1. Arriving / Arrive / You arrive at class before the bell rings.

2. Not / Doesn't / Don't leave class early. I give assignments at the end of class.

3. Being / Be / You be prepared for class every day.

4. Don't / Doesn't / Not forget to bring your books to class.

5. Don't / Doesn't / Not eat in class.

6. Clean / Cleaning / You clean up after yourself.

7. Putting / Put / You put all trash in the garbage can by the door.

8. Turn / Turning / You turn in your homework on time.

9. You may not turn in work late. Don't please / Please don't / Please not ask.

10. Pay / Paying / You pay attention in class.

11. Please speaking / Speak please / Please speak only English in the classroom.

12. Please don't / Please not / Don't please be shy. If you have a question, ask!

13. Please not / Please don't / Don't please speak when others are talking.

14. Please don't / Don't please / Please not worry. Try your best.

15. Stay / Staying / You stay positive!

3 | EDITING: WIN A TRIP!

Correct these instructions on a form for a contest at Gary's Downtown Auto Mall. There are eight mistakes. The first mistake is already corrected.

    Win
~~Winning~~ a trip for two to Hawaii!

    Thank you for buying your car or truck from Gary's Downtown Auto Mall. Now try to win a trip to Hawaii! Completes this form. Write please your name and address. Use blue please or black ink. Send not money. Mailing your entry before December 31. You visit our website for more contest information at www.garyauto.com. You enjoy your new car or truck!

Name _____ Date _____

Unit 18 Achievement Test

30 Items
Score: _____

1 | LISTENING: PRESTO PESTO'S

🎧 **A.** Listen to this radio advertisement for Presto Pesto's Italian Restaurant. Complete the advertisement by writing the words that you hear. You will hear the recording two times.

Are you hungry, but you __can't decide__ what to eat? Presto Pesto's
                              0.

_____. We offer a variety of traditional Italian dishes. And you can dine in, you
     1.

_____ out, or we can deliver. Also, you can enjoy your meal on our garden patio.
     2.

And now, for a short time only, you _____ two pizzas for the price of one! That's
                                           3.

right: two for one! You can look, but you _____ better prices or better food
                                                  4.

anywhere in town! Next time you're hungry, remember Presto Pesto's. Presto Pesto's—when you

just _____ to eat!
        5.

B. Reread the radio advertisement. Find three verb phrases with can. Write them below. (Note: Only use phrases that are given in the advertisement. Do not use any phrases that you wrote.) An example is given.

0. _can dine_

1. _____

2. _____

3. _____

88 | UNIT 18 ■ ACHIEVEMENT TEST

Name _____ Date _____

2 | TANYA IS HUNGRY!

Match the statements with the reasons.

	Statements		Reasons
_c_	0. Tanya couldn't call Presto Pesto's.	a.	She was at the library yesterday.
____	1. She can't drive to a restaurant.	b.	She was busy at lunch time.
____	2. She can't find anything to eat at home.	~~c.~~	Her cell phone was broken.
____	3. She couldn't go to the store yesterday.	d.	Her television was broken.
____	4. She couldn't go to the store this morning.	e.	She can't find her car keys.
____	5. She couldn't eat lunch at work.	f.	Presto Pesto's is across the street.
____	6. She can walk to Presto Pesto's.	g.	She doesn't have food.
		h.	She was at work this morning.
		i.	She couldn't go to class today.

3 | JOB HUNTING

Stacie wants to play in a rock band. Mark wants to be a maintenance man. Complete the questions and answers about their abilities. Use **can** *or* **could** *and the words in parentheses. Some items may have more than one right answer.*

Q: <u>Can Stacie play the piano</u> (Stacie / play the piano) now?

A: She <u>   couldn't play the piano   </u> (not / play the piano) last year, but she can now.
           0.

Q: _____ (she / sing) now?
      1.

A: Yes. She _____.
           2.

Q: _____ (she / dance) now?
      3.

A: She _____ (not / dance) last year, but she can now.
        4.

Q: _____ (she / play the drums) now?
      5.

A: No. She _____ last year, but now she can't.
         6.

UNIT 18 ■ ACHIEVEMENT TEST

Name _____ Date _____

Q: _____ (Mark / drive) last year?
     7.

A: He _____ (not / drive) last year, but now he can.
        8.

Q: _____ (he / cut grass) now?
     9.

A: Yes. He _____.
              10.

Q: _____ (he / lift heavy boxes)?
     11.

A: No, he can't. He has a bad back.

Q: _____ (he / paint) now?
     12.

A: He _____ (not / paint) last month because he broke his arm, but he
        13.

can now.

4 | EDITING: A RIDE TO THE STORE

Correct this conversation between Tanya and her neighbor Ron. There are four mistakes.
The first mistake is already corrected.

           Can you
TANYA: ~~You can~~ take me to the grocery store? I could find not anything to eat today.

RON: No problem. When do you want to go? I can to take you now or later.

TANYA: Can you to be ready in 15 minutes?

RON: Sure.

Name _____ Date _____

Unit 19 Achievement Test

30 Items
Score: _____

1 | LISTENING: PLANS FOR THE DAY

🎧 **A.** *Four friends are on vacation in Hong Kong. Listen to their conversation. Complete the conversation by writing the words that you hear. You will hear the recording two times.*

GREG: It's a beautiful day. _____*Why don't we*_____ go to the beach today?
                                      0.

JEFF: Great idea. But let's not go to the same one we went to the other day.

_____ to Lantau Island and see the Giant Buddha statue
              1.

near the beach.

SHARON: I don't know. I want to see the Dragon Boat Festival. Why don't we see that today?

STEPHANIE: That _____ to me. I'm really interested in the festival. And I
                            2.

want to see the Dragon Boat races. _____ out when they are.
                                                3.

SHARON: I'm sure there's information about them on the Internet.

_____ check online?
            4.

JEFF: OK.

SHARON: Tonight I want to watch the Symphony of Lights. Let's go to the Tsim Sha Tsui

waterfront. I hear that's the best place to see the lights.

GREG: _____ on the waterfront. Let's take a harbor cruise tour.
              5.

The view is even better from the water!

STEPHANIE: _____. Why don't you call and reserve our tickets?
                    6.

GREG: OK.

Name _____ **Date** _____

B. *Reread the conversation. Find four examples of suggestions. Write them below. (Note: Only use suggestions that are given in the conversation. Do not use any suggestions with words that you wrote.) An example is given.*

0. let's not go

1. _____

2. _____

3. _____

4. _____

2 | LUNCHTIME

The four friends are talking about restaurants for lunch. Complete their conversations. Circle the correct phrases.

SHARON: (Let's have) / Let us have / Let's having lunch. I'm hungry!
  0.

GREG: Me too. Let's getting / Let us get / Let's get pizza.
  1.

JEFF: I don't want to eat pizza in Hong Kong. Why

  not we have / we don't have / don't we have some Chinese food?
  2.

STEPHANIE: This restaurant looks good. Why don't we try / not we try / we don't try it?
  3.

GREG: It's sounding good / They sound good / That sounds good.
  4.

[After lunch . . .]

SHARON: That food wasn't very good. Let's don't go / Let's not go / Let's not going there
  5.
  again.

GREG: Let's looking for / Let's look for / Let's will look for pizza next time.
  6.

JEFF: No, let's not eat / let's not eating / let's eat not pizza.
  7.

  Let's trying / Let's will try / Let's try another Chinese restaurant next time.
  8.

Name _____ Date _____

3 | PLANS FOR THE EVENING

The four friends are talking about what to do next. Complete their conversation. Use the words and phrases in the box. Some items may have more than one right answer.

let's	let's	That sounds like a plan	Why don't you
~~Let's~~	let's not	That's a good idea	why don't you
Let's	No, I don't have time	why don't we	

SHARON: _____Let's_____ go downtown for some live music.
　　　　　　　　　0.

JEFF: No, _____ do that. I'm tired. _____
　　　　　　　　1.　　　　　　　　　　　　　　　　　　　2.
go to the hotel.

STEPHANIE: I can go with you. But _____ walk on Jaffe Road to get
　　　　　　　　　　　　　　　　　　　　　3.
there? On the way, _____ stop and see if there are any good
　　　　　　　　　　　　4.
bands. If there aren't, _____ go straight to the hotel.
　　　　　　　　　　　　　　5.

GREG: Well, I want to stay out for a little while. Jeff and Stephanie, _____ go
　　　　　　　　　　　　　　　　　　　　　　　　　　　　　　　　　　　　　　6.
back to the hotel? Sharon and I will go back when we're ready.

JEFF: _____.
　　　　　7.

SHARON: _____ take the camera to the hotel? I don't think we'll need
　　　　　　　8.
it.

STEPHANIE: _____. We'll see you later.
　　　　　　　　9.

4 | EDITING: THE NEXT TRIP

Greg and Jeff are talking about their next trip. Correct their conversation. There are four mistakes. The first mistake is already corrected.

JEFF: This trip was so great, ~~let us~~ let's plan another one for next year.

GREG: Sounds good to me. Where do you want to go?

JEFF: Let's go to Tahiti.

GREG: That's good idea. Why you don't talk to your friend the travel agent?

JEFF: OK. Let's to plan to go in June next year.

GREG: Perfect!

Name _____   Date _____

Part V Achievement Test

60 Items
Score: _____

1 | LISTENING: AT THE FIESTA TACO RESTAURANT

🎧 **A.** *Alfred, Jamie, and Luis are at a Mexican restaurant. Listen to their conversation. Complete the conversation by writing the words that you hear. You will hear the recording two times.*

ALFRED: I hope we can sit down and eat soon. I'm really hungry.

LUIS: Me, too. Where <u>is the waitress going</u> ?
                              0.

JAMIE: I don't think she sees us. Let's try to get her attention.

LUIS: Is she coming over here yet? . . . Finally! The service here is *so* slow!

WAITRESS: Welcome to Fiesta Taco. _____ this way. . . . Our special today is the
                                                  1.

taco salad. _____ at the menu, and I can come back to take your order.
                    2.

JAMIE: Uh . . . It's so hot in here. Look, I'm sweating. Excuse me, _____ on
                                                                                         3.

the air conditioning? We're really hot.

WAITRESS: I'm sorry, I know it's hot. But our air conditioning _____ .
                                                                                 4.

ALFRED: Hey, I have an idea. Let's open our own Mexican restaurant. I think we can make a

lot of money. We _____ it the Tres Amigos.
                              5.

LUIS: That's a good idea!

JAMIE: Yeah, I like it.

ALFRED: I can start to check out how to do it.

B. *Reread the conversation. Find two present continuous verbs, one suggestion, and one response to a suggestion. Write them in the table below. (Note: Only use words that are given in the conversation. Do not use any words that you wrote.) An example is given.*

PRESENT CONTINUOUS VERBS	SUGGESTION	RESPONSE TO SUGGESTION
1. _____ 2. _____	0. <u>Let's try</u> 1. _____	1. _____

94 | PART V ■ ACHIEVEMENT TEST

Name _____ Date _____

2 | PLANNING THE TRES AMIGOS RESTAURANT

Alfred, Jamie, and Luis are talking about their new restaurant. Complete their conversation. Write the letter of the best answer on each line.

JAMIE: Hey, Alfred. We got your phone message. You were so excited.

What __a__ (a. 's happening b. can happen c. be happening d. 's happens)?
         0.

LUIS: Yeah, _____ (a. what's going b. what going c. what goes d. what can go) on?
              1.

ALFRED: Well, at the moment I _____ (a. work b. can work c. 'm working d. can be working) on
                                  2.

some ideas for the restaurant.

JAMIE: Yeah? _____ (a. What do you look at b. What are you looking at c. What can you look at
              3.

d. What are you look at) right now?

ALFRED: This is just a list of some general ideas. I _____ (a. 'm think b. think c. 'm thinking
                                                          4.

d. can think) about many possibilities these days. I'm not finished, but I _____
                                                                         5.

(a. can telling b. can to tell c. can be telling d. can tell) you what I know so far.

LUIS: Great! _____ (a. Let's hearing b. Let us hear c. Let's hear d. Let hear us) it.
              6.

ALFRED: All right. Well, first, we need a place for the restaurant. _____ (a. Why not we
                                                                         7.

b. Why not us c. Why don't us d. Why don't we) look at some buildings next week?

JAMIE: Sounds good.

LUIS: We need a nice building. People like attractive restaurants. Oh, and we _____
                                                                              8.

(a. can have b. can having c. have d. 're having) live music too.

JAMIE: _____ (a. Don't forgetting b. Don't forget c. Not forget d. No forgetting) the food!
         9.

ALFRED: Right! We need a chef. But we _____ (a. can't paying b. can't pay c. couldn't pay d. aren't
                                          10.

pay) a lot at the beginning.

LUIS: Yeah, we _____ (a. are trying b. could trying c. can trying d. try) to make some money!
                  11.

ALFRED: OK, I can call today about places.

JAMIE: Great.

LUIS: Yeah, thanks.

Name _____ Date _____

3 | A CHEF FOR THE TRES AMIGOS

Alfred, Jamie, and Luis are looking for a chef for their new restaurant. Complete their conversation. Use the words and phrases in the box.

can tell	Don't	is thinking	tell
Can we find	is she doing	is working	That sounds good
could	Is she working	~~let's~~	Why don't you
couldn't	is staying	Let's	Why is she doing

ALFRED: OK, ____let's____ look at our list. We still need a chef. _____
                    0.   1.
a chef if we put an ad in the newspaper?

JAMIE: _____ ask me! I don't know if chefs look for jobs in the newspaper!
             2.

ALFRED: Luis, your friend Elena is a professional chef, right? What _____ these
                                                                                                              3.
days?

LUIS: She _____ at a beauty salon at the moment. But she doesn't like her job
                  4.
because there are a lot of rules. She _____ about cooking again.
                                                                    5.

ALFRED: Here's a suggestion: _____ give her a call. Maybe she can work for us!
                                                      6.

JAMIE: _____ at the beauty salon today? Maybe we can call her there right
             7.
now.

LUIS: No. She's on vacation. She _____ with a friend in California.
                                                              8.

JAMIE: _____ call her when she gets back?
             9.

LUIS: OK.

ALFRED: Yeah, that sounds good. You _____ her that she's our first choice for
                                                                  10.
chef!

JAMIE: Yeah! Make her a good job offer. And _____ her that she can make her
                                                                              11.
own rules!

Name _____ Date _____

4 | AFTER WORK

*Jamie's friend Adriana is visiting the Tres Amigos restaurant at the end of the night. Complete their conversation. Use the imperative, present progressive, **could**, or suggestions and the words in parentheses.*

ADRIANA: The Fiesta Taco ____is going____ (go) out of business!
0.

JAMIE: Really! _____ (why / they / close)?
1.

ADRIANA: They _____ (could / not / make) any money after the Tres
2.

Amigos opened. _____ (a lot of customers / come) in here
3.

these days?

JAMIE: Yeah, business _____ (grow) a lot right now. People
4.

_____ (come in / and / eat) a lot nowadays. Tres Amigos
5.

_____ (finish) its first year now, and we already have ideas
6.

for ways to improve the restaurant. But we _____
7.

(not / make) any big changes right now.

ADRIANA: You know, Jamie, I didn't think you _____ (could / do) it!
8.

Congratulations on your successful restaurant! _____
9.

(let's / go) have some ice cream and celebrate!

JAMIE: All right. _____ (help) me take out this garbage, please.
10.

Then we can go.

Name _____   Date _____

5 | DINNER

Alfred is visiting his friend Katya. Complete their conversation. Use the imperative, present progressive, **can / could***, or suggestions and the words in the box.*

buy	do	have	not forget	~~tell~~
can	give	make	not worry	wait
can	go	not	put	work

KATYA: . . . So, I'm only talking about me. _____Tell_____ me everything about you. How
                                                      0.
_____ you _____ these days?
                          1.

ALFRED: I'm fine. My friends and I have a restaurant. I _____ there now. It's a lot
                                                                 2.
of work, but I _____ a lot of fun!
                      3.

KATYA: How is the restaurant doing?

ALFRED: Great. It _____ a lot of money these days. I can't believe it! Hey! We can
                        4.
go there for dinner. _____ your shoes on, and we can leave.
                              5.

KATYA: _____ we go next week? I don't have much money.
              6.

ALFRED: Please _____ about it. I'm an owner, remember?
                      7.

KATYA: Thanks! _____ you get my purse? It's on the chair. _____
                      8.   9.
it to me, please. . . . Thank you.

ALFRED: Oh! _____ your keys!
                  10.

KATYA: No problem. They're in my purse.

98 | PART V ■ ACHIEVEMENT TEST

6 | EDITING: ANOTHER TRES AMIGOS RESTAURANT

Alfred, Jamie, and Luis are talking about opening another Tres Amigos restaurant. Correct their conversation. There are 10 mistakes. The first mistake is already corrected.

ALFRED: I ^am^ thinking about our bank account. You can look at it to see how much money we have? Check it on the Internet.

LUIS: OK.

ALFRED: How business going this month? Are we make more than last month?

JAMIE: Yes, Tres Amigos is make more these days! We do very well right now.

ALFRED: You let me see our bank statement. . . . This is excellent. Why we don't open another Tres Amigos?

LUIS: That a good idea.

ALFRED: Jamie, make please some calls. Let's find out if there are any good places for a second restaurant.

JAMIE: OK!

Name _____   Date _____

PART VI Diagnostic Test

60 Items
Score: _____

1 | LISTENING: HOME FOR THE WEEKEND

🎧 **A.** Pam is home from college for the weekend. Listen to her conversation with her mother. Complete the conversation by writing the words that you hear. You will hear the recording two times.

PAM: It feels so good to be home. I ____*missed*____ you.
                                          0.

MRS. UNVER: We missed you too! _____ your flight?
                                     1.

PAM: Perfect. I slept the whole way. I only woke up when we _____. I
                                                                2.
think I needed the rest! Maybe I'm trying to do too much.

MRS. UNVER: You *are* busy with work and school. _____ well on your English
                                                      3.
paper?

PAM: I don't know yet. We get them back next week.

MRS. UNVER: What _____ about?
                    4.

PAM: It was about my trip to South Africa _____. The professor wanted
                                                5.
us to write about a personal experience. At first, I _____ what to
                                                          6.
write, but I wrote about the trip. I realized it was really important to me.

MRS. UNVER: Great! I hope you do well.

PAM: Me, too!

B. Reread the conversation. Find three regular verbs and three irregular verbs in the simple past (not **be**). Write them in the table below. (Note: Only use words that are given in the conversation. Do not use any words that you wrote.) An example is given.

1. Simple past regular verbs: ____*missed*____, _____,

   _____, _____

2. Simple past irregular verbs: _____, _____, _____

100 | PART VI ■ DIAGNOSTIC TEST

Name _____   Date _____

2 | A BABY

Pam is telling her mother about her friend Sheryl's baby. Complete their conversation. Circle the correct words or phrases.

PAM: Oh, I have good news!

MRS. UNVER: What is it?

PAM: My friend Sheryl (had)/ have / did have her baby! He <u>is / was / did</u> born last night.
　　　　　　　　　　　　　　　0.　　　　　　　　　　　　　　　　1.

MRS. UNVER: That's wonderful! <u>Did you saw / Did you see / Were you see</u> the baby?
　　　　　　　　　　　　　　　　　　　　　　　2.

PAM: No, I <u>don't / wasn't / didn't</u>. Sheryl's husband <u>call / was called / called</u> me this
　　　　　　　3.　　　　　　　　　　　　　　　　　　　　　　4.

morning, but I <u>didn't had / not had / didn't have</u> time to go to the hospital before
　　　　　　　　　　　　　　5.

my flight.

3 | THE SPACE MUSEUM

Pam is talking with her mother and her little brother Jason. Use the simple past forms of the verbs in parentheses to complete their conversation.

MRS. UNVER: Jason ____had____ a fun week. Tell Pam where you _____
　　　　　　　　　　　　0. (have)　　　　　　　　　　　　　　　　　　　　　　1. (go)

this week.

PAM: Where _____ you _____, Jason?
　　　　　　　　　　　　　　　　2. (go)

JASON: We _____ the space museum.
　　　　　　　　3. (visit)

PAM: _____ they _____ a lot of cool things there?
　　　　　　　　　　　　　　4. (have)

JASON: Yeah. I _____ it was fun. The only bad part was that we
　　　　　　　　5. (think)

_____ for an astronaut to talk with us, but the astronaut
6. (wait)

_____. So we _____ around the museum and went
7. (not come)　　　　　8. (walk)

inside an old spaceship. That _____ cool.
　　　　　　　　　　　　　　　9. (be)

Name _____ Date _____

4 | AT AUNT HELEN'S

Jason is visiting his Aunt Helen. Complete their conversation. Use the correct forms of the words in parentheses to make simple past statements and questions.

JASON: Dinner __was delicious__ (be / delicious), Aunt Helen! I think I
0.
_____ (eat / too much)!
1.

AUNT HELEN: I know you love fried chicken. I _____ (prepare / it) especially for
2.
you! I _____ (not / have / any food) in the house, so I
3.
_____ (go / to the store) and _____ (buy / some
4. 5.
chicken).

JASON: _____ (you / know) that I _____ (go / to / the space
6. 7.
museum) yesterday?

AUNT HELEN: No, I _____ (not / know) that! Did you like it?
8.

JASON: Yeah, it _____ (be / great). Oh look! *Star Wars* is on TV!
9.

AUNT HELEN: Great! Why don't you stay and watch it with me?

5 | LAST NIGHT

Jason wrote in his journal about visiting his aunt. Complete the sentences. Use the simple past forms of the verbs in the box. Then circle the sound of each -ed ending (/t/, /d/, or /ɪd/).

| arrive | hug | ~~miss~~ | walk |
| cook | joke | visit | watch |

0. I __missed__ my bus this morning. (/t/) /d/ /ɪd/

1. I was out late last night because I _____ my aunt. /t/ /d/ /ɪd/

2. She _____ a delicious meal for me. /t/ /d/ /ɪd/

3. Then we _____ *Star Wars* on TV. /t/ /d/ /ɪd/

4. We had fun. She _____ me when I left. /t/ /d/ /ɪd/

5. I was really tired this morning. I _____ to the /t/ /d/ /ɪd/
   bus stop late.

6 | EDITING: AUNT HARRIETT

Pam and Jason are looking at family pictures with their dad. Correct their conversation. There are 16 mistakes. The first mistake is already corrected.

JASON: Who's in this picture, Dad?

MR. UNVER: You never ~~did knew~~ *knew* her, but this is your Great Aunt Harriett.

PAM: She was your dad's sister?

MR. UNVER: No, she not. She was my Uncle Hubert's wife. She born in Chicago in 1935.

JASON: Why she wear that funny uniform?

MR. UNVER: She work as a nurse.

PAM: It's a great picture of her. Who did take it?

MR. UNVER: Your Great Uncle Hubert taked it. He did had a very nice camera, and he know how to use it.

PAM: Do you still have the camera?

MR. UNVER: No. Your Aunt Helen borrow it two years but she never return it. I did asked her about it last month, but she not know where it was.

PAM: Oh no! I hope she didn't lost it.

Name _____   Date _____

Unit 20 Achievement Test

30 Items
Score: _____

1 | LISTENING: CARACAS

🎧 **A.** Stan is visiting Caracas, Venezuela. Listen to his conversation with his friend Raúl. Complete the conversation by writing the words that you hear. You will hear the recording two times.

RAÚL: How is your trip so far?

STAN: Good. I arrived two days ago. At the airport, a hotel shuttle ____picked____ me up.
0.
The driver _____ my suitcase. Now my suitcase is broken, and some of my
1.
clothes got dirty because it _____. But he was nice, and he was very sorry.
2.
He told me all about Caracas. At the hotel, I _____ to give him a tip, but
3.
he didn't take it.

RAÚL: Do you need to wash any of your clothes? You can wash them at my place.

STAN: That's OK. I _____ them last night at the hotel.
4.

RAÚL: So, how do you like Caracas?

STAN: I _____ around the city yesterday. The people are really nice. Yesterday
5.
afternoon it _____ to rain, so I returned to the hotel.
6.

RAÚL: Well, I'm glad you're here!

B. Reread the conversation. Find three simple past time markers. Write them below. (Note: Only use words that are given in the conversation. Do not use any words that you wrote.) An example is given.

0. _two days ago_

1. _____

2. _____

3. _____

104 | UNIT 20 ■ ACHIEVEMENT TEST

Name _____ Date _____

2 ROOMMATES

Annie and Julie are roommates. Complete the sentences about them. Circle the correct words or phrases.

Annie (cooked) / could cook / cooking spaghetti, but Julie (didn't like) / not liked / isn't liking the food.
       0.   0.

Julie talking / talked / could talk, but Annie not listen / isn't listening / didn't listen.
               1.   2.

Annie joked / joking / could joke, but Julie not laughed / didn't laughed / didn't laugh.
           3.   4.

Annie and Julie could bake / baked / baking cookies, but they didn't liked / didn't like / not liked the taste of them.
                  5.   6.

Annie could rent / renting / rented a movie, but they didn't watch / didn't watched / not watched it.
            7.   8.

Julie borrowing / could borrow / borrowed Annie's cell phone, but she didn't returned / didn't return / not returned it.
           9.   10.

3 NEGATIVES IN THE PAST

Complete the sentences. Make negative statements in the simple past. Use the verb in the sentence that comes before or after.

0. It snowed in the afternoon. It ____*didn't snow*____ in the morning.

1. I _____ outside in the afternoon. I walked outside in the morning.

2. Paco and Tim shopped at the grocery store. They _____ at the mall.

3. Christina _____ in the office for lunch. She stayed in the office for the meeting.

4. Maggie and I worked at the office. We _____ at home.

5. I _____ baseball after work. I played basketball instead.

4 | EDITING: E-MAIL FROM STAN

Correct this e-mail message from Stan to his friend Jen. There are seven mistakes. The first mistake is already corrected.

Hi, Jen,

~~I three days ago~~ *Three days ago I* arrived in Caracas, Venezuela. The plane lands, and I was happy to be here. I walked Monday around the city. Then it rains a little bit, so I returned to my hotel. My friend Raúl invites me to dinner yesterday evening. The food tastes delicious. Today morning I toured downtown.

I just want you to know that I am here and OK.

Take care,

Stan

Name _____ Date _____

Unit 21 Achievement Test

30 Items
Score: _____

1 | LISTENING: OVER THE VACATION

🎧 *Mr. Cooper's English class is starting again after vacation. Listen to the conversation. Complete the conversation by writing the words that you hear. You will hear the recording two times.*

MR. COOPER: Welcome back, everyone. How was your vacation?

YOLANDA: I ____had____ a great time. I _____ to see my friend in
                    0.   1.

Los Angeles. The weather was beautiful. My friend has a pool, so we

_____ every day.
      2.

MR. COOPER: That sounds wonderful. What about you, Maria? Did you have a nice vacation?

MARIA: Not really. I _____ anywhere. I was sick, so I just stayed home. I
                              3.

_____ two good books.
      4.

MR. COOPER: In English?

MARIA: No, in Spanish. What did *you* do, Mr. Cooper?

MR. COOPER: I _____ my sister. We talked a lot, and we went to the movies. It
                   5.

was fun!

2. | MARIA'S SICKNESS

After class, Mr. Cooper asks Maria about her sickness. Complete their conversation. Circle the correct words or phrases.

MR. COOPER: Are you feeling better?

MARIA: I'm fine now, but I (felt) / feeled / feeling terrible last week.
                                    0.

MR. COOPER: What was wrong with you?

MARIA: I don't know. I didn't went / didn't go / not went to the doctor, but I
                              1.

call / called / calling the doctor's office. The nurse there telled / told / tells me to
         2.   3.

rest. It was nice to stay home. I cook / cooking / cooked a lot, and I
                                              4.

listen / listening / listened to music. I feel much better now.
              5.

MR. COOPER: Good!

UNIT 21 ■ ACHIEVEMENT TEST

Name _____ **Date** _____

3 | YOLANDA'S TRIP

Yolanda visited her friend in Los Angeles. Complete her e-mail to her parents about her visit. Use the simple past forms of the verbs in parentheses.

Hi, Mom and Dad,

How are you? I'm fine. I ____visited____ my friends, Miriam and Paul, in Los Angeles
　　　　　　　　　　　　　　　　0. (visit)
this week. I _____. I _____ a car and _____. I left last
　　　　　　　1. (not fly)　　　2. (rent)　　　　　　　　　3. (drive)
week, and I _____ home yesterday. I _____ to see Miriam because
　　　　　　　4. (come)　　　　　　　　　　　　5. (want)
she just _____ a baby. The baby _____ born two months ago. I
　　　　　　6. (have)　　　　　　　　　　7. (be)
_____ lots of pictures of her. I _____ Miriam a nice baby gift, and it
8. (take)　　　　　　　　　　　　9. (buy)
_____ very expensive. Last Wednesday, I _____ some old friends and
10. (be not)　　　　　　　　　　　　　　11. (meet)
we _____ out for dinner. It was a nice vacation.
　　12. (go)

Love,

Yolanda

4 | EDITING: MR. COOPER'S VACATION

Mr. Cooper wrote about his vacation in his letter to a friend. Correct a paragraph from his letter. There are nine mistakes. The first mistake is already corrected.

　　　visited
I ~~visit~~ my sister in Idaho during the vacation. We go shopping, but I didn't spent a lot of money. I finded a nice pair of pants. They are on sale. They costed only $5. We also cook a lot together, and we make ice cream. Oh, my sister has a new little cat. She is born last month. The cat loved the ice cream!

Name _____ Date _____

Unit 22 Achievement Test

30 Items
Score: _____

1 | LISTENING: NORMA'S RING

🎧 **A.** Norma lost her ring. Listen to the conversation. Complete the conversation by writing the words that you hear. You will hear the recording two times.

ALICE: <u>What happened</u>, Norma? You look upset.
0.

NORMA: I lost my ring.

ALICE: Oh, that's terrible. Where _____ it?
1.

NORMA: I think I left it at school in the cafeteria. I reported it to the school office, but they didn't have it.

ALICE: Did it cost a lot?

NORMA: _____, but it was valuable to me. It belonged to my grandmother.
2.
My mother gave it to me a few days ago.

ALICE: When _____ the ring last?
3.

NORMA: Well, I know I had it at lunch this afternoon.

[Norma's cell phone rings.]

NORMA: Hello?

MR. JACKSON: Hi. Is this Norma Damron?

NORMA: Yes.

MR. JACKSON: This is Principal Jackson from the high school. I heard that you lost a ring. I found one in the cafeteria. Did you lose your ring there?

NORMA: Oh, yes, I think I did! Was it on the floor?

MR. JACKSON: _____.
4.

NORMA: Thank you very much for calling!

MR. JACKSON: You're welcome. You can pick it up at the front office.

NORMA: Thank you!

[Norma goes to the front office and picks up her ring the next day.]

Name _____   Date _____

B. Reread the conversation. Find three simple past yes / no questions. Write them below. (Note: Only use questions that are given in the conversation. Do not use any questions with words that you wrote.)

1. _____

2. _____

3. _____

C. Reread the conversation. Answer the questions. Write the letter of the best answer on each line.

_a_ 0. Did Norma lose her ring?
   a. Yes, she did.
   b. No, she didn't.
   c. It doesn't say.

____ 1. When did she get it?
   a. Many years ago.
   b. A few years ago.
   c. A few days ago.

____ 2. Where did she lose it?
   a. In the parking lot.
   b. In the cafeteria.
   c. In her car.

____ 3. Who called Norma?
   a. The principal.
   b. The math teacher.
   c. Her grandmother.

____ 4. Did Norma get her ring back?
   a. Yes, she did.
   b. No, she didn't.
   c. It doesn't say.

Name _____ Date _____

2 | BEKIR'S GRANDPARENTS

A. *Ali asked his friend Bekir some questions about his grandparents. Complete Ali's questions. Use the simple past and the words in parentheses.*

ALI: As a child, ___*did you live with your grandparents*___ ?
   0. (you / live / with your grandparents)

BEKIR: No. They lived far away.

ALI: _____ ?
   1. (where / your grandparents / live)

BEKIR: In the south of Turkey.

ALI: _____ ?
   2. (what / your grandfather / do)

BEKIR: He had a farm.

ALI: _____ ?
   3. (he / work / long hours)

BEKIR: Oh yes. He worked more than 12 hours a day.

ALI: _____ ?
   4. (he / have / a large farm)

BEKIR: Yes. It was really big.

ALI: _____ ?
   5. (your grandmother / work / too)

BEKIR: Yes. She helped my grandfather with the farm. She also raised my father and his brothers and sisters.

ALI: _____ ?
   6. (she / have / many children)

BEKIR: Yes, she had six children.

ALI: _____ ?
   7. (your grandparents / meet / a long time ago)

BEKIR: Yes, they met almost 70 years ago.

3 | THE REST OF THE CONVERSATION

B. *Ali and Bekir continue their conversation. Complete Bekir's answers. Use the simple past and the words in parentheses.*

ALI: Did they have a happy marriage?

BEKIR: _____
       1. (yes / they / have / a very happy marriage)

ALI: Did they have any animals?

BEKIR: _____. They raised wheat.
       2. (no / they / not)

ALI: Did they have a car?

BEKIR: _____.
       3. (no / they / have / not / a car)

ALI: Did your grandparents make a lot of money from the farm?

BEKIR: _____. But they were never hungry.
       4. (no / they / not)

ALI: Did you ever see their farm?

BEKIR: _____.
       5. (yes / I / visit / many times)

4 | EDITING: NORMA'S GRANDMOTHER

Correct the conversation between Alice and Norma. There are eight mistakes. The first mistake is already corrected.

ALICE: ~~You did~~ *Did you* get your ring?

NORMA: Yes, I did. I'm so glad I didn't lose it forever.

ALICE: Your grandmother wear it a lot?

NORMA: Yes, she was.

ALICE: What she was like? You were close to her?

NORMA: Yes. She was a very sweet woman. I loved her very much.

ALICE: Did she ever lived with you?

NORMA: No, she not, but she came to visit often.

ALICE: When she died?

NORMA: She died when I was 13.

Name _____ Date _____

Part VI Achievement Test

60 Items
Score: _____

1 | LISTENING: BROKEN LEG

🎧 **A.** Julie went home from college for the weekend. It's Tuesday, but she's not back at school yet. Her friend Linda calls. Listen to their conversation. Complete the conversation by writing the words that you hear. You will hear the recording two times.

JULIE: Hello?

LINDA: Hi, Julie! Finally, you're home! I ____tried____ to call you all day yesterday, but
                                                                         0.

no one answered. Where were you?

JULIE: I just _____. I was in the hospital.
                  1.

LINDA: Oh no! _____ in the hospital?
                 2.

JULIE: I fell and broke my leg on Sunday. I guess I picked the wrong day to go ice skating.

LINDA: Oh, wow, _____ anything else?
                     3.

JULIE: No, but my leg is bad enough. I have to stay home this week. You know, I

_____ my math test yesterday morning. I'm really worried about it. I
      4.

wanted to call my professor, but I _____ his phone number with me.
                                            5.

I hope I don't fail the class. He even told me _____ that I need to do
                                                     6.

better in his class.

LINDA: Oh, I'm sure you can take the test later. Just tell him what happened. I'm glad you're

OK. I was really worried!

B. Reread the conversation. Find three regular verbs and three irregular verbs in the simple past (not be). Write them in the table below. (Note: Only use words that are given in the conversation. Do not use any words that you wrote.)

1. Simple past regular verbs: _answered_, _____,

    _____ , _____

2. Simple past irregular verbs: _____, _____, _____

PART VI ■ ACHIEVEMENT TEST | 113

Name _____ Date _____

2 | HOME FOR THE WEEKEND

Patty and Linda are classmates. Complete their conversation. Circle the correct words or phrases.

LINDA: How was your weekend?

PATTY: OK. I (went)/ did went / go home.
　　　　　　　　0.

LINDA: Where is home?

PATTY: Albuquerque. I 'm born / was born / born there and am living / lived / did lived there
　　　　　　　　　　　　　　1.　　　　　　　　　　　　　　　　2.

most of my life. I got back last night.

LINDA: Did you had / Did you have / Were you had a good time?
　　　　　　　　　　　　3.

PATTY: No, I don't / wasn't / didn't. I was sick and in bed. I
　　　　　　　　　4.

didn't even saw / not even see / didn't even see my friends.
　　　　　　　　　　　　5.

LINDA: Too bad!

3 | THE WEEKEND

Travis and Martin are talking about their weekend. Complete their conversation. Use the simple past forms of the verbs in parentheses.

TRAVIS: <u>Did</u> you <u>have</u> a good weekend?
　　　　　　　　0. (have)

MARTIN: Yeah. I _____ a great movie yesterday.
　　　　　　　　1. (see)

TRAVIS: Oh yeah? What _____ you _____?
　　　　　　　　　　　　　　　　　2. (see)

MARTIN: It's called *The Cook*. It was about a guy who _____ how to cook, so he
　　　　　　　　　　　　　　　　　　　　　　　　　　　　3. (not know)

_____ a cooking class and _____ famous for his unusual
4. (take)　　　　　　　　　　　　5. (become)

food. It _____ really funny. What did you do?
　　　　6. (be)

TRAVIS: I _____ basketball on Saturday, but I _____ home after
　　　　7. (play)　　　　　　　　　　　　　　　　　8. (stay)

that and _____ a lot of homework.
　　　　　9. (do)

Name _____   Date _____

4 | THE LOST BASKETBALL

Travis is still talking to Martin. Complete their conversation. Use the correct forms of the words in parentheses to make simple past statements and questions.

TRAVIS: Listen, Martin, I have to tell you something. Do you remember that basketball I borrowed from you? Well, I ____lost it____ yesterday.
0. (lose / it)

MARTIN: What? You're kidding, right? _____ at the gym?
1. (you / lose / it)

TRAVIS: No, I _____ at the gym, because I _____ with me. I
2. (not / leave / it)   3. (take / it / to the car)
_____ in the parking lot. But when I _____, I
4. (have / it / with me)   5. (get / home)
_____ anywhere. I don't know _____.
6. (not / see / it)   7. (what / happen)

MARTIN: _____ in the parking lot?
8. (you / look for / it)

TRAVIS: No, I _____, but I will. I'll buy you a new one if I can't find it.
9. (not)

5 | WEEKEND BARBECUE

Linda wrote about her weekend in her journal. Complete the sentences. Use the simple past forms of the verbs in the box. Then circle the sound of each -ed ending (/t/, /d/, or /ɪd/).

| cook | land | rain | want |
| ~~invite~~ | play | talk | watch |

0. I ____invited____ some friends over on Saturday.   /t/   /d/   (/ɪd/)

1. I _____ to have a barbecue and cook outside.   /t/   /d/   /ɪd/

2. Unfortunately, it _____ all day.   /t/   /d/   /ɪd/

3. So I _____ dinner inside instead.   /t/   /d/   /ɪd/

4. We _____ games.   /t/   /d/   /ɪd/

5. We _____ about many interesting things.   /t/   /d/   /ɪd/

Name _____ **Date** _____

6 | EDITING: SUMMER BREAK

Martin and Linda are talking about their summers. Correct their conversation. There are 16 mistakes. The first mistake is already corrected.

LINDA: Did you ~~went~~ *go* anywhere over the summer?

MARTIN: No, I not. I work all summer.

LINDA: Where you worked?

MARTIN: I selled cell phones for Whitting Wireless. I leaved the company a week to come back to school. I maked pretty good money. You worked during the summer?

LINDA: No, I not. I did took summer classes. I also visit my parents in Kansas City for a week. I just got back from there yesterday.

MARTIN: Are you from there?

LINDA: I did born in Chicago, but I grow up in Kansas City.

MARTIN: Who watch your cat when you were away?

LINDA: My roommate. She not go anywhere.

Name _____ Date _____

PART VII Diagnostic Test

60 Items
Score: _____

1 | LISTENING: CAMERON LAKE

🎧 **A.** *Sandra and Heather are good friends and neighbors. Heather misses her home in Canada. Listen to their conversation. Complete the conversation by writing the words that you hear. You will hear the recording two times.*

SANDRA: You aren't eating very much of your lunch. Don't you like your chicken?

HEATHER: Yes, _____it's_____ delicious.
　　　　　　　　　　　0.

SANDRA: Then why do you look so sad? Do you still miss your home in Canada?

HEATHER: Yeah. This town is very different from my home. _____ a lake near the
　　　　　　　　　　　　　　　　　　　　　　　　　　　　　　　　　　　1.

　　　　　town I'm from in Alberta. It's called Cameron Lake.

SANDRA: Oh, I've been _____. It's gorgeous!
　　　　　　　　　　　　　　　2.

HEATHER: When did you go to Alberta?

SANDRA: Chad and _____ went there last year. He took _____ for
　　　　　　　　　　　　3.　　　　　　　　　　　　　　　　　　　　　　　　　　4.

　　　　　our anniversary. We had a picnic at the lake. In fact, Chad gave _____
　　　　　　　　　　　　　　　　　　　　　　　　　　　　　　　　　　　　　　　5.

　　　　　this watch there. The lake was beautiful. I liked _____ a lot.
　　　　　　　　　　　　　　　　　　　　　　　　　　　　　6.

HEATHER: Yeah, it's wonderful. There aren't _____ places like it in the world. I
　　　　　　　　　　　　　　　　　　　　　　　　　7.

　　　　　miss swimming there. The water is so beautiful. Are there _____ places
　　　　　　　　　　　　　　　　　　　　　　　　　　　　　　　　　　　　　　8.

　　　　　like that around here?

SANDRA: No, not like that.

B. *Complete these sentences based on the conversation. Circle the correct words.*

0. Chad and Sandra had **(a)** / an / the picnic at Cameron Lake for their anniversary.

1. There is a / an / the lake near the town where Heather is from.

2. Heather likes Cameron Lake. A / An / The lake is wonderful.

3. A / An / The water in Cameron Lake is very beautiful.

2 | HEATHER'S COOKIES

Complete the conversation between Sandra's husband, Chad, and Heather's husband, Bill. Chad and Bill are co-workers, and they are discussing the cookies Bill brought to the office. Write the letter of the best answer on each line.

BILL: _____b_____ (a. Any b. The c. Much d. Some) cookies are delicious! I just need
           0.

_____ (a. a b. some c. the d. a few) glass of milk now. I love cookies with milk.
     1.

CHAD: Did you say cookies?

BILL: Yeah. Didn't you get _____ (a. an b. two c. a d. the) cookie from the break
                                    2.

room? There _____ (a. is b. are c. aren't d. isn't) oatmeal cookies and chocolate
                  3.

chip cookies. Heather made them last night.

CHAD: Are there _____ (a. much b. any c. a little d. a) oatmeal cookies left?
                       4.

BILL: I don't know.

[later . . .]

CHAD: There _____ (a. are b. aren't c. is d. isn't) any more cookies.
                 5.

_____ (a. There are b. They is c. They're d. There is) all gone.
     6.

BILL: _____ (a. I'm b. Me am c. He's d. Him is) sorry. There were _____
            7.   8.

(a. any b. much c. a lot of d. a little) cookies. I don't know what happened to them.

CHAD: I guess _____ (a. one b. some c. much d. a little) people took too many. I see
                     9.

you have _____ (a. much b. a little c. any d. a few) cookies on your desk.
                10.

BILL: Oh, um, would you like _____ (a. a b. an c. the d. some) cookie? I'll sell one
                                          11.

to _____ (a. them b. her c. us d. you). I'm just kidding. Here, let me give
       12.

_____ (a. them b. her c. us d. you) one.
      13.

CHAD: No, that's OK. I brought _____ (a. any b. much c. some d. many) chocolate
                                             14.

cake with me from home, and I can eat that.

Name _____ Date _____

3 | A NEW TABLE

Complete this conversation between Bill and Heather. Use the words in the box.

a	are	he	is	money	the
an	chicken	him	it	much	them
any	furniture	I	me	some	They

BILL: Hi honey. How was your day?

HEATHER: Fine. Sandra and ____I____ went out to lunch. We ate some
0.

_____ 1. _____, and we talked about Cameron Lake. But enough about me! Did your co-workers like the cookies I baked?

BILL: Yeah, they were a hit! People liked them so much that Sandra's husband, Chad, wasn't able to get one in time.

HEATHER: That's too bad about Chad, but I'm glad everyone else liked _____ 2. _____.
Hey, I finally had time to look at _____ 3. _____ in that shop downtown. I saw a table that I liked, but they sold _____ 4. _____ to someone else. Anyway, their prices are very high. Maybe we can afford things like that when we get _____ 5. _____ money.

BILL: Yeah, maybe. So, are there _____ 6. _____ messages for _____ 7. _____?

HEATHER: There _____ 8. _____ two phone messages for you. _____ 9. _____ are both pretty short. One is from _____ 10. _____ guy named Barry. Who's he?

BILL: He's a guy at work. He makes furniture. In fact, he is probably _____ 11. _____ best furniture maker in town. He doesn't charge very _____ 12. _____ money, but his work is good quality, so I gave _____ 13. _____ our number.

Name _____ Date _____

4 | FOOD AT SCHOOL

Sandra and Chad are discussing an article about their son Joshua's school. Complete their conversation. Circle the correct words. Ø means that no word is necessary.

CHAD: Where's the newpaper? I didn't read them /(it)/ him yet.
                  0.

SANDRA: On the table. Oh, there are / they are / there's an article in a / an / the paper about
                               1.   **2.**

Joshua's school. It / They / There has a lot of overweight children. Much / A / Some
               3.   **4.**

parents are complaining that any / much / many children are gaining weight. All
                         5.

the / a / an food machines have a / the / ø junk food. There aren't much / any / some
  6.   **7.**   **8.**

machines with healthy food.

CHAD: Uh-huh.

SANDRA: So me / her / I called ø / an / the school principal. I asked her / she / them why the
         9.   **10.**   **11.**

school doesn't have much / a little / any machines with healthy food. She gave
                        12.

I / me / us a good explanation. There isn't / aren't / are any food machine companies
13.   **14.**

in town that sell healthy food!

CHAD: It seems there's junk food everywhere. Today at work everyone was eating cookies.

5 | EDITING: WORRIED MOM

Sandra is worried about her son, Joshua. Correct her conversation with Heather. There are nine mistakes. The first mistake is already corrected.

SANDRA: Hello, Heather. How's your ~~the~~ day going?

HEATHER: Good, thanks. How's yours?

SANDRA: OK, but I'm worried. Me and Chad talked about article in a paper today. There are a problem at Josh's school. It has lot of overweight students. Some parents say it's because they aren't any healthy food machines in the school.

HEATHER: Does Joshua buy a lot of junk food from the machines?

SANDRA: No, and we always give them healthy food.

HEATHER: Then don't worry about his. He's still young, and he's pretty thin.

Name _____   Date _____

Unit 23 Achievement Test

30 Items
Score: _____

1 | LISTENING: MOVING IN

🎧 **A.** *Patrick is moving into a new apartment. Listen to his conversation with the landlord, Robert. Complete the conversation by writing the words that you hear. You will hear the recording two times.*

ROBERT: ____Here's____ your key. Rent is due by the first of the month. If it's late,
                    0.

   _____ a $20 fee. There's a laundry room by the office.
              1.

   _____ mailboxes by the parking lot. There isn't anyone in the office on
              2.

   Sundays. Do you have any questions for me?

PATRICK: Yeah, _____ bank machines nearby?
                                3.

ROBERT: There aren't any very close, but there's one on Fourth Avenue. It's in the grocery store.

PATRICK: OK, I went _____ yesterday, so I know where it is.
                                    4.

B. *Reread the conversation. Find three affirmative contractions and two negative contractions. Write them in the table below. (Note: Only use words that are given in the conversation. Do not use any words that you wrote.) An example is given.*

AFFIRMATIVE CONTRACTIONS	NEGATIVE CONTRACTIONS
0. *it's*	1. _____
1. _____	2. _____
2. _____	
3. _____	

UNIT 23 ■ ACHIEVEMENT TEST   121

Name _____ Date _____

2 | PATRICK'S NEW APARTMENT

Match the beginnings of the statements about Patrick's new apartment with the endings. Make logical sentences.

Beginnings	Endings
_c_ 0. There are books	a. in the living room.
____ 1. There are paintings	b. in the kitchen. I wash dishes in the sink.
____ 2. There aren't any messages	~~c.~~ on the bookshelf.
____ 3. There's a sofa	d. on the third floor.
____ 4. There aren't any ice cubes	e. on the pillow.
____ 5. There's a bed	f. in the freezer. I used them all.
____ 6. There's a shower	g. on the walls.
____ 7. There isn't a dishwasher	h. in the bathroom.
____ 8. There are neighbors upstairs	i. on the answering machine.
	j. in the bedroom.

3 | MORE QUESTIONS

Patrick has more questions for Robert. Complete their conversation. Circle the correct words.

PATRICK: Are there a / (any) good places to eat nearby?
    0.

ROBERT: Sure. There are / is lots of little restaurants downstairs, and they isn't / aren't very
    1.   2.
expensive.

PATRICK: I saw those, but are there a / any others close to here?
    3.

ROBERT: Yeah, they're / there's a great Chinese buffet on Sixth Street. They're / It's really close.
    4.   5.

PATRICK: Great. Oh, one more question—are there a / any Internet cafés near here?
    6.

ROBERT: Yeah, there's / there are one on Fifth Street. There's / It's open until 11:00.
    7.   8.

122 | UNIT 23 ■ ACHIEVEMENT TEST

Name _____ Date _____

4 | EDITING: MOVIE NIGHT

Correct Patrick's conversation with his classmate Allen about seeing a movie. There are six mistakes. The first mistake is already corrected.

PATRICK: You know, there's nothing to do around here.

ALLEN: Is a movie tonight at 9:00. Do you want to go? Is a good movie.

PATRICK: Sure, but is there a movie theater near here?

ALLEN: Yeah, there is two theaters close by. The one on Sixth Street is nice, but it's small. There a candy counter, but there aren't any popcorn.

PATRICK: That's OK. I don't like popcorn anyway.

Name _____ Date _____

Unit 24 Achievement Test

30 Items
Score: _____

1 | LISTENING: NEW ROOMMATE

🎧 **A.** *Reiko is talking on the phone with her father. Listen to their conversation. Complete the conversation by writing the words that you hear. You will hear the recording two times.*

REIKO: Hello?

MR. ITO: Hi, Reiko! How are you?

REIKO: Oh hi, Dad. I'm great! Beth and ____I____ have a new roommate named
                                             0.

Federica. _____'s from Italy, and she knows how to cook.
              1.

MR. ITO: Oh, terrific!

REIKO: I know. She made spaghetti last night, and she gave us a lot. She gave

_____ three servings. I loved it.
  2.

MR. ITO: That sounds great. Is she teaching _____ any Italian?
                                                               3.

REIKO: Yes, and _____ wants to learn some Japanese, so I'm teaching
                             4.

_____. Oh, and this morning Federica and _____ went
  5.   **6.**

shopping. We bought Beth a few small things. We'll give them to her tomorrow. It's her

birthday, and we want to celebrate _____.
                                                     7.

MR. ITO: Well, it sounds like you're all getting along well.

REIKO: We are. I have to go to class now, but I'll talk to you later.

MR. ITO: OK, bye.

REIKO: Bye.

B. *Reread the conversation. Find two singular object pronouns and one plural object pronoun. Write them in the table below. (Note: Only use words that are given in the conversation. Do not use any words that you wrote.) An example is given.*

SINGULAR OBJECT PRONOUNS	PLURAL OBJECT PRONOUNS
1. _____	0. *us*
2. _____	1. _____

124 | UNIT 24 ■ ACHIEVEMENT TEST

Name _____   Date _____

2 | FEDERICA'S PHOTOS

Federica is showing three pictures to her friend Mark. Read the sentences. Write the name of the person or the thing that each pronoun replaces.

Picture 1:

0. ____Liliana____ This is a picture of my friend Liliana. <u>She</u>'s a teacher.

1. _____ And that's Liliana's cat. It was a gift to <u>her</u>.

2. _____ <u>She</u> loves cats!

Picture 2:

3. _____ This is a picture of my parents. Remember that I visited <u>them</u> last month?

4. _____ I have other pictures of my parents, but I don't like <u>them</u> as much as this one.

Picture 3:

5. _____ This is my brother, Tito. My dad gave <u>him</u> the car in the picture.

6. _____ Tito got <u>it</u> last year for his birthday.

7. _____ Unfortunately, he has to sell <u>it</u> because he needs money.

3 | REIKO'S PARENTS

Federica is talking to Mark about Reiko's parents. Read the sentences. Circle the direct objects and underline the indirect objects.

0. I want to show <u>you</u> my new (shirt).

1. Reiko's parents gave it to me.

2. They write me e-mails regularly.

3. They tell me stories.

4. I e-mail pictures to them once in a while.

5. I teach them words in Italian.

4 | EDITING: TOASTER

Correct Reiko and Federica's conversation about their toaster. There are four mistakes. The first mistake is already corrected.

REIKO: Where's our toaster?

FEDERICA: Our neighbor Julie has ~~him~~ *it*.

REIKO: Why does she have?

FEDERICA: Me and her were talking yesterday, and she wanted to borrow it. So I loaned her it.

UNIT 24 ■ ACHIEVEMENT TEST | 125

Name _____   Date _____

Unit 25 Achievement Test

30 Items
Score: _____

1 | LISTENING: STREET FAIR

🎧 **A.** Tim and Nicole are at a street fair. Listen to their conversation. Complete the conversation by writing the words that you hear. You will hear the recording two times.

NICOLE: I love street fairs. There are always interesting ___things___ for sale.
                                                                           0.

TIM: Yes, there are. Hey, I'm hungry. I want to get a sandwich and some soda at the restaurant over there.

NICOLE: Wait a minute, I want to buy some _____ here.
                                                                      1.

TIM: Why do you want to buy that? It smells strange.

NICOLE: No, it doesn't. I think it smells good. Besides, it's pretty, and it doesn't cost much money. There's a lot of nice _____ here, too. I bought a few shirts here once.
                                                                      2.

TIM: Well, I'm going over there to try some _____. I need a little food!
                                                                      3.

B. Reread the conversation. Find one indefinite article + a singular count noun, one definite article + a singular count noun, one quantifier + a plural count noun, and three quantifiers + non-count nouns. Write them in the table below. (Note: Only use words that are given in the conversation. Do not use any words that you wrote.) An example is given.

INDEFINITE ARTICLE + A SINGULAR COUNT NOUN	DEFINITE ARTICLE + A SINGULAR COUNT NOUN	QUANTIFIER + A PLURAL COUNT NOUN	QUANTIFIERS + NON-COUNT NOUNS
0. a sandwich 1. _____	1. _____	1. _____	1. _____ 2. _____

126 | UNIT 25 ■ ACHIEVEMENT TEST

Name _____ Date _____

2 | LUNCH INVITATION

The next day Tim wants to invite Nicole to lunch. Complete their conversation. Write the letter of the best answer on each line.

TIM: I'm getting hungry. I should go get __c__ (a. a b. much c. some) food. Do you have
0.

_____ (a. much b. a little c. a few) minutes for lunch?
1.

NICOLE: I don't have _____ (a. much b. many c. a little) time right now. I have _____
2.   3.

(a. some b. any c. much) essays to grade before I teach my class.

TIM: I think teachers do more homework than students! _____ (a. How much b. How many
4.

c. A lot of) essays do you have to read?

NICOLE: Six more.

TIM: Do you need _____ (a. a few b. a c. any) help?
5.

NICOLE: No, that's OK. Anyway, can we go for lunch tomorrow? I'll have _____ (a. any
6.

b. much c. a few) free hours in the afternoon.

TIM: Sure, tomorrow sounds great. But I'm still hungry now, so I'm going to go grab a

hamburger. Would you like me to pick up _____ (a. the b. a c. a few) coffee for you
7.

on my way back to the office?

NICOLE: Sure, if you have _____ (a. the b. a c. much) time.
8.

TIM: OK. Good luck grading!

3 | JOB DESCRIPTIONS

Complete this paragraph about Tim and Nicole's jobs. Circle the correct words.

Tim is (a) / an / the truck driver. He works for a / an / the big company. He has a / an / the
         0.   1.   2.

fun job. He travels around a / an / the country. He likes to see all a / an / the towns and meet
                            3.   4.

a / an / the people who live there. Nicole is a / an / the English teacher. She teaches students
5.   6.

from all over a / an / the world. She has a / an / the student from Turkey and a / an / the
              7.   8.   9.

student from Mongolia. All of a / an / the students in her class say Nicole is great.
                              10.

UNIT 25 ■ ACHIEVEMENT TEST   127

Name _____   **Date** _____

from all over <u>a / an / **the**</u> world. She has <u>**a** / an / the</u> student from Turkey and <u>**a** / an / the</u>
      7.   8.   9.

student from Mongolia. All of <u>a / an / **the**</u> students in her class say Nicole is great.
                               10.

4 | EDITING: AT LUNCH THE NEXT DAY

Correct this conversation between Tim and Nicole at lunch the next day. There are four mistakes. The first mistake is already corrected. (Note: There is often more than one way to correct a mistake.)

TIM: Did you finish grading ~~much~~ *many* essays yesterday?

NICOLE: Yes. I don't have some more essays to read until next week.

TIM: Good. What do you want to order?

NICOLE: I want hamburger and fries, with ketchup a lot.

TIM: That sounds good.

Name _____ Date _____

Part VII Achievement Test

60 Items
Score: _____

1 | LISTENING: LOUGH MELVIN

🎧 **A.** Amy and Heidi are friends. Listen to their conversation about Amy missing her home in Leitrim, Ireland. Complete the conversation by writing the words that you hear. You will hear the recording two times.

HEIDI: Do you miss Ireland?

AMY: I miss swimming. I love to swim, but ____there____ isn't any place to go swimming
 0.
in this town. In Leitrim, the town I grew up in, _____ a huge lake called
 1.
Lough Melvin.

HEIDI: Really? What's it like _____?
 2.

AMY: It's beautiful. Billy and _____ were engaged on Lough Melvin. Early in the
 3.
morning, he took _____ out on a boat and asked me to marry him.
 4.

HEIDI: Wow! That sounds romantic.

AMY: It was. Billy caught a big fish that day, and we ate _____ for lunch. I really
 5.
like to be on a boat, and I love to go fishing. Are there _____ places to fish
 6.
around here?

HEIDI: No. There aren't _____ lakes, but _____ grocery store in the
 7.   8.
center of town sells fresh fish.

AMY: Really? I'll have to check it out.

B. Complete these sentences based on the conversation. Circle the correct words.

0. Billy asked Amy to marry him on (a)/ an / the boat.

1. There's a / an / the huge lake in Leitrim.

2. Billy caught a / an / the big fish.

3. Amy is interested to hear that a / an / the grocery store sells fresh fish.

PART VII ■ ACHIEVEMENT TEST | 129

Name _____ Date _____

2 | MUFFINS

Read this conversation between Amy's husband, Billy, and his co-worker, Doug. Billy and Doug are discussing some muffins that a co-worker brought to share. Complete their conversation. Write the letter of the best answer on each line.

DOUG: __a__ (a. The b. Any c. Some d. Much) muffins are great! But they make me thirsty! I
 0.

need _____ (a. a b. some c. the d. a few) glass of milk.
 1.

BILLY: What muffins?

DOUG: Didn't you get _____ (a. some b. a c. the d. any) muffin? There _____ (a. is b. isn't
 2. 3.

c. 's d. are) different kinds of muffins in the lunchroom.

BILLY: Oh! Are there _____ (a. a little b. much c. any d. a) chocolate ones?
 4.

DOUG: Probably.

[later . . .]

BILLY: There _____ (a. aren't b. isn't c. is d. are) any more muffins. _____
 5. 6.

(a. They're b. They is c. There are c. There is) all gone.

DOUG: _____ (a. Me am b. I'm c. He's d. Him is) sorry. There were _____ (a. any b. much
 7. 8.

c. a little d. a lot of) muffins when I was there.

BILLY: I guess _____ (a. one b. much c. some d. a little) people took a lot. I see that you have
 9.

_____ (a. a few b. a little c. any d. much) muffins on your desk.
 10.

DOUG: Oh, uh, do you want _____ (a. the b. some c. a d. an) chocolate muffin? I have two. I
 11.

can give _____ (a. them b. her c. us d. you) one.
 12.

BILLY: That's OK. My wife, Amy, makes _____ (a. I b. me c. we d. them) muffins all the time.
 13.

I'm trying to lose _____ (a. a weight b. weight c. the weight d. many weight) anyway.
 14.

Name _____ Date _____

3 | LAMPS

Complete this conversation between Doug and his wife, Heidi. Use the words in the box. Some items may have more than one right answer.

a	an	is	price	them
a	any	it	some	they
a few	are	me	some	you
a few	cheese	me	some	
a few	X	money	the	

DOUG: Hi dear. What did you do today?

HEIDI: ____I____ went to the grocery store to buy some _____, and
          0.   1.
then I went to _____ hardware store downtown to look for a lamp. I saw
                   2.
one nice lamp with a good price, but they sold _____ to someone else. In
                                                     3.
general, they have _____ nice things, but their prices are too high. Look,
                        4.
here's their catalog.

DOUG: Hmm . . . these are nice. Aren't there _____ other lamps here that interest
                                                  5.
_____?
    6.

HEIDI: Yeah, there are _____ beautiful lamps in that store. There
                             7.
_____ two more lamps that interest _____ on this page. But
    8.   9.
look . . . _____ are just too expensive.
              10.

DOUG: I guess you're right. Well, _____ woman at work told _____
                                       11.   12.
she's having a yard sale tomorrow. She has _____ lamps to sell. Why don't
                                                 13.
we go?

HEIDI: OK.

Name _____   Date _____

4 | CHEATING AT SCHOOL

Amy and Billy are discussing a radio program about their son Jack's school. Complete their conversation. Circle the correct words or phrases.

AMY: Did you listen to the radio today?

BILLY: No, I didn't turn him / them /(it) on. Why?
　　　　　　　　　　　　　　　0.

AMY: I heard an interesting story this morning. They are / There's / There are a kid at Jack's
　　　　　　　　　　　　　　　　　　　　　　　　　　1.
school. Him / Them / He won a national contest for an essay he wrote. But some kids
　　　　　2.
say he didn't really write him / them / it. The reporter said that much / many / any
　　　　　　　　　　　　　　3.　　　　　　　　　　　　　　　　　4.
students find essays on the Internet and copy them. I hope Jack doesn't do that.

BILLY: Me, too. Do students have to pay many / any / a few money to get the essays?
　　　　　　　　　　　　　　　　　　　　5.

AMY: I don't know. I just don't understand why students want to steal the / many / a few work
　　　　　　　　　　　　　　　　　　　　　　　　　　　　　　　　　6.
of others. Why don't they just study, play, maybe listen to a / some / much music, like we
　　　　　　　　　　　　　　　　　　　　　　　　　　　　　　　7.
did when we were kids?

BILLY: Yeah, there really is / are / aren't a problem there. What should we do?
　　　　　　　　　　　　　　8.

AMY: Well, me / I / us called an / the / a school and talked to Jack's English teacher. I asked
　　　　　　9.　　　　　　　　10.
him / he / them if Jack copied any essays. He told me / I / us that there
11.　　　　　　　　　　　　　　　　　　　　12.
aren't / are / isn't any websites that Jack could go to because the students write ø / an / a
13.　　　　　　　　　　　　　　　　　　　　　　　　　　　　　　　　　　　14.
their essays in class.

BILLY: That's good.

Name _____ **Date** _____

5 | EDITING: WORRIED MOM

Amy is worried about her son, Jack. Correct her conversation with Heidi. There are nine mistakes. The first mistake is already corrected.

AMY: Hello, Heidi. How is your ~~a~~ day going?

HEIDI: OK, thanks. How are you?

AMY: Fine, but I'm a little worried.

HEIDI: Why?

AMY: Well, me and Billy talked about story on a radio yesterday. Lot of students at Jack's school copy their essays from the Internet.

HEIDI: Do you think Jack is copying his essays?

AMY: Jack's teacher said they aren't any websites that Jack can copy from. They write their essays in class. But I want to teach to do his own work.

HEIDI: You're right. They are many children who copy from the Internet. It's a good idea to teach his not to do it.

Name _____ Date _____

PART VIII Diagnostic Test

60 Items
Score: _____

1 | LISTENING: *ENTERTAINMENT NIGHTLY*

🎧 **A.** Pop stars Liza Russet and Jeremy Whithers are watching a nightly TV show. Listen to part of the show. Complete the show by writing the words that you hear.

Welcome to *Entertainment Nightly*. The romance between pop stars Liza Russet and Jeremy Whithers __seems to be__ heating up. The two are spending lots of time together, and they
_____ apart. They _____ to the press about their relationship, but
     1.   **2.**
they often appear in public hand in hand.

In fact, they are appearing in public a lot these days. Fans were surprised that they didn't appear at last night's awards ceremony.

And the singers _____ as good as they look together. They just released a new
                      3.
album, called *Dream World*, and their fans love it. How _____ in its first few
                                                                      4.
weeks on the charts? Well, it started out at number one, and after three weeks, it
_____ still the best-selling album in the country. _____ listen to Liza
     5.   **6.**
and Jeremy? Tell us what you think of their new album on our website, www.enshow.com.

B. Match the underlined verb in each sentence with the explanation of the verb form.

Sentences

_d_ 0. They <u>have</u> great voices.

____ 1. The two <u>are spending</u> lots of time together.

____ 2. The singers <u>sound</u> great.

____ 3. They often <u>go</u> places together.

____ 4. They <u>didn't appear</u> at last night's award ceremony.

Explanations

a. describes senses and appearances

b. expresses an action that is happening right now or these days

c. expresses a routine or regular occurrence

d̶. shows possession

e. expresses a past event

Name _____ Date _____

2 | LIZA AND JEREMY

Complete Liza and Jeremy's conversation after the show. Use the correct forms of the words in the box. Some items may have more than one right answer.

| ~~be~~ | eat | get | hear | listen | see | take | worry |
| be | eat | get | know | look | sound | taste | |

JEREMY: That ___was___ a terrible picture of me on TV tonight! Who
　　　　　　　　0.
_____ that photo? I _____ like I just woke up.
　　　1.　　　　　　　　　　　　　　2.

LIZA: Oh, you always _____ too much. Everybody _____ you're
　　　　　　　　　　　　　3.　　　　　　　　　　　　　　　　　　4.
cute! _____ you _____ all the fans screaming your name
　　　　　　　　　　　　　5.
on the show? We _____ the most popular couple in the world right now.
　　　　　　　　　　　6.
Come on, we need _____ some food. I'm hungry!
　　　　　　　　　　　　　7.

JEREMY: What do you want _____?
　　　　　　　　　　　　　　　　8.

LIZA: I don't know. Maybe something spicy.

JEREMY: Did you _____ that new Chinese place on the corner? Let's go there.
　　　　　　　　　　9.

LIZA: That _____ like a good idea!
　　　　　　　10.

3 | REPORTER'S QUESTIONS

Liza and Jeremy decide to talk to a reporter one day. Complete the interview. Circle the correct words or phrases.

REPORTER: Why did you decided / **decide** to record an album together?
 0.

LIZA: Even before I met him, I really admire / admired Jeremy's talent. I told Jeremy that I
 1.
wanted to sing with him.

REPORTER: How often do you see / are you seeing each other?
 2.

LIZA: Oh, we always see / are seeing each other if we're not traveling—every day, in fact.
 3.

REPORTER: How often do you talk / are you talking on the phone if you can't see each other?
 4.

JEREMY: It depends, but usually about three times a day.

REPORTER: How did you met / meet?
 5.

JEREMY: We met / meet at a party one night after we performed in a music video show.
 6.

REPORTER: Why didn't you go / went to Awards Night last week?
 7.

JEREMY: We decided / decide to have dinner together instead.
 8.

REPORTER: Where did you eat / ate?
 9.

LIZA: We went / go to a nice Italian restaurant.
 10.

REPORTER: Did you watch / watched Awards Night on TV?
 11.

JEREMY: We didn't see / not saw the show that night. We recorded / did record it and
 12. **13.**
watched it later.

REPORTER: Do you think about to get / getting married?
 14.

LIZA: We don't have / aren't having any plans to get married.
 15.

REPORTER: How many kids do you want to have / having if you get married?
 16.

LIZA: Well, like I said, we're not planning to get / getting married soon, so kids aren't part
 17.
of our plans right now.

136 | PART VIII ■ DIAGNOSTIC TEST

Name _____   Date _____

4 | MAGAZINE ARTICLE

Complete this magazine article about Liza and Jeremy. Write the simple present, simple past, present progressive, gerund, or infinitive form of each verb. Some items may have more than one right answer.

Liza Russet and Jeremy Whithers __*sounded*__ great together on their last album.
                                  0. (sound)
Their new album, *Dream World*, is on sale in stores now, and it _____ about $14.
                                                                    1. (cost)
An estimated 17 million people around the world already _____ the new album,
                                                              2. (own)
and sales _____ to rise.
            3. (continue)

Liza and Jeremy _____ a lot of time together these days. They usually
                   4. (spend)
_____ to talk to the media, but earlier this week they _____ outside
  5. refuse)   **6. (appear)**
a local club, and they _____ to answer a few questions from one of our reporters.
                         7. (agree)
In that interview, they _____ about their present and their future.
                          8. (talk)
There are rumors that Liza and Jeremy _____ getting married, but Liza
                                        9. (think about)
_____ for a wedding dress yet. According to Liza, they _____ any
 10. (look, not)   **11. (have, not)**
plans to get married soon. We asked them how many kids they plan _____ if they
                                                                   12. (have)
get married, but they had no comment. If they have plans for marriage and a family, they

_____ to keep quiet about them for now.
 13. (prefer)

5 | EDITING: FAN MAIL FOR LIZA AND JEREMY

Correct this fan's e-mail to Liza and Jeremy. There are 11 mistakes. The first mistake is already corrected. (Note: There can be more than one way to correct a mistake.)

Dear Liza and Jeremy,

    My name ~~be~~ *is* Michelle, and I probably your biggest fan! I write never to famous artists. But I buy your album last week, and I am wanting to tell you how much I love it! I listen every day to it. I don't thinking there is very much really good music nowadays. But you are always making wonderful, creative music. Your album were the best thing to happen to music today. I am loving it. Please, keep make music together!

Sincerely,

Michelle Sutter

Name _____ Date _____

Unit 26 Achievement Test

30 Items
Score: _____

1 | LISTENING: *LOVE MATTERS*

🎧 **A.** *Listen to part of a radio show. Complete the radio show by writing the words that you hear. You will hear the recording two times.*

DR. RICE: You ___'re listening___ to *Love Matters*. I'm your host, Dr. Naomi Rice.
              0.
We have 24-year-old Cara in Manhattan on the line with us. What's your question, Cara?

CARA: Hi, Dr. Rice. My question is, how _____ my dentist that I
                       1.
love him?

DR. RICE: Your dentist?

CARA: Yes! Every time I visit his office, I just _____ that he is the
                            2.
right man for me.

DR. RICE: Every time you visit his office? Most people go to the dentist about
_____. But it sounds like you see your dentist more
        3.
frequently. _____ visit him?
               4.

CARA: Every month.

DR. RICE: Wow! I imagine your teeth look great!

CARA: Yeah, they're pretty healthy.

DR. RICE: And what is this incredible dentist's name, just in case there are any listeners who need a dentist?

CARA: Dr. Adam West.

DR. RICE: OK, Cara, stay on the line. Let's talk some more after the break.
_____ with Cara in Manhattan who's in love with her
       5.
dentist. You're listening to *Love Matters* with me, Dr. Naomi Rice. Don't go away.

Name _____ Date _____

B. *Reread the radio show. Then read each statement and circle **T** (true) or **F** (false).*

T (F) 0. Dr. Rice has a television program.

T F   1. Cara loves her dentist.

T F   2. Dr. Rice is looking at Cara's teeth.

T F   3. Cara has healthy teeth.

T F   4. Cara sees the dentist once a year.

T F   5. Cara rarely visits her dentist.

2 | DURING THE BREAK

Cara's dentist, Adam West, is talking on the phone with his friend Peter. Complete their conversation. Write the letter of the best answer on each line.

PETER: Hello?

ADAM: Peter! What ___d___ (a. are you do b. is you doing c. don't you do d. are you doing) right now?
                        0.

PETER: I _____ (a. wash b. 'm washing c. 'm wash d. washes) dishes, why?
              1.

ADAM: Turn on your radio to 94.9. One of my patients _____ (a. is calling b. calling c. is calls
                                                                    2.
d. calls) that show *Love Matters*. She _____ (a. think b. is thinks c. is thinking d. thinks) that
                                              3.
she's in love with me!

PETER: _____ (a. Do you kid b. Do you kidding c. Do you kidded d. Are you kidding)?
         4.

ADAM: No, I'm not. She _____ (a. never b. rarely c. frequently d. all the time) comes into the office
                           5.
to get her teeth cleaned. In fact, I _____ (a. am seeing b. am see c. see d. do see) her every
                                         6.
month.

PETER: Really? Is she pretty?

ADAM: You know, I _____ (a. don't remember b. am remembering c. don't remembering d. am not
                      7.
remembering). I seldom notice my patients' faces, but I _____ (a. never forget b. forget
                                                              8.
once a week c. usually forget d. forget several times) their teeth. This patient's teeth are beautiful!

She _____ (a. always is b. almost never is c. is always d. is almost never) responsible about
       9.
keeping them clean.

Name _____ Date _____

3 | DR. RICE'S SUGGESTIONS

Love Matters *continues after a break. Complete the conversation. Write the simple present or present progressive form of each verb.*

DR. RICE: I __*'m speaking*__ with Cara in Manhattan who says she is in love with her
0. (speak)

dentist. Cara, are you there?

CARA: Yes.

DR. RICE: So, how often _____ you _____ in love?
1. (fall)

CARA: I almost never _____ this way! But I _____ about
2. (feel)   3. (think)

Dr. West all the time.

DR. RICE: OK, and how old is he?

CARA: I _____ for sure, but he's around my age.
4. (know, not)

DR. RICE: And _____ he _____ anyone these days?
5. (see)

CARA: I'm not sure.

DR. RICE: OK, Cara. You know that I usually _____ people advice on this show.
6. (give)

So _____ you _____ to me now? Here's my advice for
7. (listen)

you: Tell him your feelings. It's scary, but if you really love him, then it's important.

4 | EDITING: A NOTE TO DR. WEST

Correct Cara's note to Dr. West. There are five mistakes. The first mistake is already corrected. (Note: There can be more than one way to correct a mistake.)

Dear Dr. West,

    am writing
  I ~~write~~ to you today because I need to tell you something. You are the most intelligent, thoughtful, and handsome man I know. I almost never don't have feelings like this. In fact, I do things rarely like this. I don't expecting a relationship with you, but I wanting to get to know you better.

Sincerely,

Cara Jenkins

Name _____   Date _____

Unit 27 Achievement Test

30 Items
Score: _____

1 | LISTENING: GROCERY SHOPPING

🎧 **A.** *Paul and Rachel are grocery shopping. Listen to their conversation. Complete the conversation by writing the words that you hear. You will hear the recording two times.*

PAUL: We need to buy fruit for tonight's dessert with Aaron and Brenda. __*Do you want*__
       0.
to buy some apples?

RACHEL: Apples? Apples _____ boring. Let's get a pineapple instead.
                        1.

PAUL: Oh, I _____ pineapples, but they're usually expensive. How much do
             2.
they _____ here?
        3.

RACHEL: Only $2 each, and they _____ really good.
                                 4.

PAUL: Hey, do you remember the pineapple we ate in Hawaii?

RACHEL: Yeah. I want to go back there. I can almost _____ the tropical air.
                                                      5.

PAUL: You know, Connie at work has a son who lives in Hawaii. He _____ an
                                                                    6.
apartment on the beach. Maybe we can use his apartment sometime.

RACHEL: Hmm . . . that _____ a little strange. I don't want to bother him. I don't
                         7.
even know him! I think I prefer to stay in a hotel.

B. *The box below contains action and non-action verbs from the conversation. Circle three non-action verbs. An example is given.*

| buy | eat | (know) | live | need | remember | use | want |

Name _____ Date _____

2 | IN THE KITCHEN

Paul and Rachel are cooking. Complete their conversation. Use the simple present or present continuous forms of the verbs in the box.

| be | like | ~~look~~ | need | sound | taste | think | use |

PAUL: The chili ____looks____ good. Can I _____ it?
　　　　　　　　　0.　　　　　　　　　　　　1.

RACHEL: Sure.

PAUL: Mmm! It's delicious.

RACHEL: What _____ you _____? I want your opinion.
　　　　　　　　　　　　　　　　　2.
　　　_____ it _____ more salt?
　　　　　　　　　　　　3.

PAUL: No, it's perfect.

RACHEL: Great. The cornbread _____ almost ready.
　　　　　　　　　　　　　　　　　4.

PAUL: This dinner is going to be great. I really _____ chili and cornbread.
　　　　　　　　　　　　　　　　　　　　　　　　　　　　5.

3 | GUESTS

Aaron and Brenda are at Rachel and Paul's apartment for dinner. Complete the conversation. Use the simple present or present progressive form of each verb. Some items may have more than one right answer.

BRENDA: Sorry we ____'re____ late! There was a lot of traffic.
　　　　　　　　　　0. (be)

RACHEL: I _____. Come on in. How are you?
　　　　　　　1. (understand)

AARON: Well Brenda _____ a cold, so she _____ very well.
　　　　　　　　　　　　2. (have)　　　　　　　　　　3. (not feel)

BRENDA: Oh, I'm fine! You _____ a very nice apartment.
　　　　　　　　　　　　　　　　4. (have)

AARON: And dinner _____ delicious. What are you making?
　　　　　　　　　　　　　5. (smell)

PAUL: Chili.

BRENDA: Oh, Aaron _____ chili. _____ you _____
　　　　　　　　　　　　6. (love)　　　　　　　　　　　　　　　　7. (need)
　　　any help?

PAUL: No thanks. Everything _____ ready! Let's eat.
　　　　　　　　　　　　　　　　　8. (be)

AARON: That _____ wonderful. I'm starving!
　　　　　　　　　9. (sound)

142　UNIT 27 ■ ACHIEVEMENT TEST

Name _____ Date _____

4 | EDITING: ASK AARON

Aaron is an advice columnist for a local newspaper. Correct this letter to him, and correct his response. There are seven mistakes. The first mistake is already corrected.

Dear Aaron,

I ~~am having~~ *have* a big problem. My friend owe me a lot of money. I want to ask her for the money, but now she isn't returning my phone calls. I don't understanding why she's acting this way, and now I'm angry. I hates feeling this way! Please help!

Angry and helpless

Dear Angry and helpless,

    I understand your problem. I am disliking giving people money for that reason. The money belong to you, and your friend needs to pay you back. Go to her house to discuss the problem directly. Perhaps she can pay you some of the money each month. I having a rule to help avoid problems like this in the future: Don't give something that you're not ready to lose.

Aaron

Name _____ Date _____

Unit 28 Achievement Test

30 Items
Score: _____

1 | LISTENING: A PRESENTATION

🎧 **A.** Annie Silva is giving a presentation at a conference. Listen to part of her presentation. Complete the presentation by writing the words that you hear. You will hear the recording two times.

Good afternoon. Today I __want to show__ you the results of my study on students and
                         0.

procrastination. Procrastination means _____ something, usually because it is
                                              1.

boring or unpleasant. I decided to conduct this study because I'm interested in students'

motivations. All students _____ homework and study. But many of them dislike
                                 2.

doing schoolwork, and as a result, they procrastinate.

In my study, I compared students who procrastinate with students who _____
                                                                              3.

their schoolwork as early as possible. I found that students felt less stress when they

_____ their homework in the afternoon or early in the evening. Students who
      4.

procrastinated felt much more stress about their assignments.

Also, when students _____ their homework as soon as possible, they generally
                           5.

expected to receive higher grades, and they _____ to school more. But students
                                                    6.

who _____ their homework early generally didn't hope to get good grades. Now,
        7.

in the next part of my study . . .

B. Reread Annie Silva's presentation. Find one verb followed by a gerund and two verbs followed by infinitives. Write them in the table below. (Note: Only use words that are given in the presentation. Do not use any words that you wrote.) An example is given.

VERB + GERUND	VERB + INFINITIVE
1. _____	0. _decided to conduct_
	1. _____
	2. _____

144 | Unit 28 ■ Achievement Test

Name _____ Date _____

2 | DOING HOMEWORK

Luis and Jake are roommates in college. Complete their conversation. Circle the correct words or phrases.

LUIS: Do you want (to go) / going to a movie? I'm thinking about to leave / leaving in half an
     　　　　　　　　　 0.　　　　　　　　　　　　　　　　　　　 1.

     hour.

JAKE: Sorry, I need to finish / finishing my chemistry homework.
     　　　　　　　　　　 2.

LUIS: But your class isn't until Wednesday.

JAKE: I know, but I decided to get / getting all my homework done early.
     　　　　　　　　　　　　　 3.

LUIS: Why?

JAKE: Well, I keep on to get / getting in trouble with my professors. I procrastinate, and then I
     　　　　　　　　　　 4.

     have to hurry to finish my assignments on time. But I always regret to wait / waiting until
     　　　　　　　　　　　　　　　　　　　　　　　　　　　　　　　　　　　　　 5.

     the last minute because I don't get good grades. So I intend to do / doing my homework
     　　　　　　　　　　　　　　　　　　　　　　　　　　　　　　 6.

     early this semester.

LUIS: You know, that's a good idea. Maybe I'll stay in and finish to write / writing that paper
     　　　　　　　　　　　　　　　　　　　　　　　　　　　　　　　　 7.

     for my European history class. I can go to a movie another time.

3 | JAKE'S ADMIRER

Jake just arrived home. Complete his conversation with Luis. Write the gerund or infinitive form of each verb.

LUIS: You need ____to call____ Beverly back. She keeps _____.
     　　　　　　　　 0. (call)　　　　　　　　　　　　　　　　　　 1. (call)

JAKE: I don't want _____ to her.
     　　　　　　　　　 2. (talk)

LUIS: Well, don't avoid _____ to her. She is expecting _____ from
     　　　　　　　　　　　 3. (talk)　　　　　　　　　　　　　　　　　 4. (hear)

     you. Anyway, I thought you liked her. What happened?

JAKE: I like her, I just don't think she's right for me. At first, I enjoyed _____ time
     　　　　　　　　　　　　　　　　　　　　　　　　　　　　　　　　　　　　 5. (spend)

     with her. But now she wants to be with me all the time. I think she's planning

     _____ me or something.
      　6. (marry)

LUIS: Well, if you're not interested, you need to tell her.

JAKE: I know. I intend _____ with her soon.
     　　　　　　　　　　 7. (speak)

UNIT 28 ■ ACHIEVEMENT TEST

Name _____ **Date** _____

4 | EDITING: MOVIE TIME

Luis is inviting Jake to go to the movies again. Correct their conversation. There are seven mistakes. The first mistake is already corrected.

LUIS: Did you finish ~~to write~~ *writing* your paper?

JAKE: Yes, I just need to print it out.

LUIS: Great. I'm done with my homework, too. Adam and I are planning go see a movie. Do you want coming with us?

JAKE: Sure, what did you decide seeing?

LUIS: *Procrastination.*

JAKE: Oh, my friend keeps to tell me that it's good. I was hoping see it this weekend, and I don't want procrastinate. Let's go!

Name _____ Date _____

Unit 29 Achievement Test

30 Items
Score: _____

1 | LISTENING: HOCKEY PLAYER

A. *Listen to this conversation between two college friends. Complete the conversation by writing the words that you hear. You will hear the recording two times.*

SILVIA: I ____looked____ for your name on the school website, and I found your student
0.
profile. I _____ you played hockey when you were younger. That's
1.
really neat.

CARMEN: Oh, yeah! I _____ on a team in my hometown. It was a lot of fun.
2.

SILVIA: _____ for a long time?
3.

CARMEN: Six years.

SILVIA: Wow.

CARMEN: Yeah. I _____ playing. Our team won lots of awards. I
4.
_____ the Most Valuable Player award my last two years.
5.

SILVIA: Why _____ playing?
6.

CARMEN: Well, there are a few reasons. But mostly I'm too busy to play since I
_____ to college.
7.

B. *Reread the conversation. Match the questions with the answers.*

Questions

__d__ 0. Where did Carmen play hockey?

____ 1. How did Silvia learn about Carmen's interest in hockey?

____ 2. What did Carmen's team win?

____ 3. How many times did Carmen get the Most Valuable Player award?

Answers

a. lots of awards

b. from the school website

c. two

~~d. in her hometown~~

e. because she went to college

f. three years

Name _____ Date _____

2 | FAMILY HISTORY

Carmen is studying her family's history. Read her conversation with Silvia. Then write each word or phrase from the box below in the correct category. Three examples are given.

SILVIA: I didn't know that you were interested in your family history. Did you always want to study it?

CARMEN: No, I didn't care much about it until recently.

SILVIA: Why did you decide to study it, then?

CARMEN: My parents and I went on a trip last summer. We visited the houses where my grandparents grew up. I saw where they lived and worked. We had a wonderful time. I learned that my family history is really interesting.

~~saw~~	learned	Did you always want
didn't care	~~visited~~	went
Why did you decide	~~didn't know~~	had

AFFIRMATIVE REGULAR SIMPLE PAST VERB	AFFIRMATIVE IRREGULAR SIMPLE PAST VERBS	NEGATIVE SIMPLE PAST VERB	SIMPLE PAST YES / NO QUESTION	SIMPLE PAST WH- QUESTION
0. *visited*	0. *saw*	0. *didn't know*	1. _____	1. _____
1. _____	1. _____	1. _____		
	2. _____			

148 | UNIT 29 ■ ACHIEVEMENT TEST

Name _____ Date _____

3 | FREDRICK CLARK

Read this conversation about Carmen's great-great-grandfather, Fredrick Clark. Complete the conversation. Write the simple past form of each verb.

CARMEN: Look at what I ___found___ today. It's my great-great-grandfather's obituary.
                        0. (find)

SILVIA: An obituary? What's that?

CARMEN: An obituary is a newspaper article about someone who died. Look, here's his. It says, "Fredrick Clark, 84, _____ Thursday, March 30, 1989, in a North
                                                    1. (die)
Dakota hospital. Fredrick _____ born on January 4, 1905, on his
                          2. (be)
family's farm near Coulee, North Dakota. He _____ Lucille Alice Rose
                                            3. (marry)
on June 14, 1928. Fred _____ a clothing store, which later
                       4. (open)
_____ the United Clothiers Association. His hobbies included fishing
5. (become)
with his grandchildren."

SILVIA: That's cool. _____ he _____ many children?
                                     6. (have)

CARMEN: No, he _____ many for that time—only three.
               7. (not have)

SILVIA: What _____ to him? Did you ever meet him?
             8. (happen)

CARMEN: Yes, I was very young, but I remember him. He _____ to visit when I
                                                     9. (come)
was a child, and we _____ fishing together.
                    10. (go)

4 | EDITING: QUESTIONS TO ASK YOUR RELATIVES

Correct this paragraph from a family history website. There are five mistakes. The first mistake is already corrected.

           want
Did you ever ~~wanted~~ to know more about your family history? A good way to learn about your family's past is to talk to your relatives. Here are some questions you can ask:

Who did be your parents?

How did your parents met?

Where they come from?

What did do your father for a living?

What did you like to do as a child?

What were the best moments of your childhood?

UNIT 29 ■ ACHIEVEMENT TEST 149

Name _____ Date _____

Part VIII Achievement Test

60 Items
Score: _____

1 | LISTENING: NETWORK GLOBAL NEWS

🎧 **A.** *Listen to this radio report about an author-and-illustrator team. Complete the report by writing the words that you hear. You will hear the recording two times.*

You __'re listening__ to NGN, Network Global News. Author Lenore Penner and
    0.

illustrator Justin Cohen _____ to be changing the world of children's books. They
                              1.

are famous for their wonderful stories and illustrations. The two are working together a lot

nowadays, and you _____ their names separately anymore. Their series of
                         2.

children's books about Marty the Monster is very popular. Even adults _____ the
                                                                              3.

Marty books. Penner and Cohen _____ to the press, but their names are often in
                                        4.

the news. They didn't go to the annual Convention of Children's Books last week, which

_____ many people. After 12 weeks, their newest book, *Marty Finds a Friend,*
     5.

_____ still number one on the best seller list for children's books. Cohen's beautiful
     6.

illustrations look amazing, as always, and Penner's writing is inspired. Do you like the Marty

books? Tell us what you think at our website, www.networkglobalnews.org.

B. *Match the underlined verb in each sentence with the explanation of the verb form.*

Sentences | Explanations

__d__ 0. Penner and Cohen <u>have</u> incredible talent.   a. describes senses and appearances

____ 1. The two <u>are working</u> together a lot
        nowadays.   b. expresses an action that is happening
                                                                right now or these days

____ 2. Their names <u>are</u> often in the news.   c. expresses a routine or regular occurrence

____ 3. They <u>didn't go</u> to the annual convention.   d̶.̶ shows possession

____ 4. Cohen's illustrations <u>look</u> amazing.   e. expresses a past event

150 | PART VIII ■ ACHIEVEMENT TEST

Name _____ Date _____

2 | LENORE AND JUSTIN

Lenore and Justin listened to the radio report on Network Global News. Complete their conversation about the report later that day. Use the correct forms of the words in the box. Some items may have more than one right answer.

be	eat	go	leave	like	love	meet	~~think~~
eat	go	have	like	look	love	read	

JUSTIN: I ___thought___ that was a nice report on NGN! The story is on the NGN
     0.
website, too. In fact, I _____ it this morning.
                               1.

LENORE: Me, too. Your illustrations _____ great there. Everyone
                                            2.
_____ your pictures! You _____ probably the most
       3.   4.
popular artist in the world right now. I'm so glad I _____ you! Anyway,
                                                              5.
it's already noon. I _____ for lunch now. Do you want
                           6.
_____ with me?
        7.

JUSTIN: Sure. How about something from the deli across the street?

LENORE: Again? You _____ a sandwich there yesterday.
                          8.

JUSTIN: I know. But I _____ their sandwiches.
                             9.

LENORE: I guess so. You _____ there a couple times a week!
                                10.

Name _____ Date _____

3 | INTERVIEW WITH NGN

Lenore and Justin decide to talk to a NGN reporter. Complete the interview. Circle the correct words or phrases.

REPORTER: Why did you (decide) / decided to work together?
                                 0.

LENORE: I admire / admired Justin's work for a long time. I asked him to illustrate my books.
            1.

REPORTER: How often do you get / are you getting e-mail from people who love your books?
                      2.

LENORE: Oh, we getting / get it every day. We can't answer it all.
             3.

REPORTER: Justin, how often do you tell / are you telling Lenore "You should write about this"
                          4.
so that you can draw what you want?

JUSTIN: Oh, I frequently tell her / tell her frequently what I want to draw. Sometimes she
                 5.
changes the story for my pictures.

REPORTER: How did you meet / met ?
                 6.

JUSTIN: We met / meet at the Convention of Children's Books about nine years ago.
      7.

REPORTER: Why you didn't go / didn't you go to the convention this year?
              8.

JUSTIN: We needed to finish / finishing our latest Marty book.
           9.

REPORTER: Lenore, where you learned / did you learn how to write?
               10.

LENORE: I had / have some very wonderful English teachers in high school.
      11.

REPORTER: Justin, did you beginning / begin to paint in school, too?
              12.

JUSTIN: No, I painted / did paint at home. We didn't have an art teacher at my school.
       13.

REPORTER: When did you first think / thought about making the Marty books into movies?
               14.

LENORE: Well, actually, we don't have / aren't having any plans to do that.
           15.

REPORTER: Lenore, who were / was your favorite author when you were young?
             16.

LENORE: Well, I loved / love Lisa Gersten's books.
      17.

REPORTER: Did you ever think you were going to write so many books?

LENORE: Never! But now we're planning to write at least two more books together.

Name _____ Date _____

4 | NGN'S ARTICLE

Complete NGN's article about Lenore and Justin. Write the simple present, simple past, present progressive, gerund, or infinitive form of each verb.

Lenore Penner and Justin Cohen just __completed__ their seventh Marty the Monster
                                    0. (complete)
book. The book _____ $8.95. About 15 million people around the world
              1. (cost)
_____ Marty books, and Marty _____ to grow in popularity.
2. (own)   **3. (continue)**

Sometimes Penner and Cohen _____ hard to find. They usually refuse
                           4. (be)
_____ to reporters, but last week they _____ us into their office.
5. (talk)   **6. (allow)**
They _____ to talk with us about the future of the Marty series. We asked them
    7. (agree)
how many more books they plan _____. According to Penner, they
                              8. (write)
_____ for sure. Penner and Cohen also said they are not thinking about
9. (know, not)
_____ a movie yet, and they _____ for a producer right now. When
10. (make)   **11. (look, not)**
we spoke, they _____ any plans for a movie. If they have plans, they prefer
              12. (confirm, not)
_____ them quiet for now.
13. (keep)

5 | EDITING: FAN MAIL FOR LENORE AND JUSTIN

Correct this fan's e-mail to Lenore and Justin. There are 11 mistakes. The first mistake is already corrected.

Dear Lenore and Justin,

            is
My name ~~be~~ Michael, and you my favorite author-and-illustrator team. How do you get such wonderful ideas? You read a lot of children's books when you were young? Or did you learned from working together? I buy your first book six years ago, and now I buy every new book that you publish. I am wanting to tell you that I love them! My kids and I every day read them. I don't thinking there are a lot of good children's books, but Marty is an exception. In fact, because of you, now I am get inspired to write a book myself. Oh, and I am loving the art! Please keep work together!

Sincerely,

Michael Farber

Name _____ Date _____

PART IX Diagnostic Test

60 Items
Score: _____

1 | LISTENING: RICH LOIS

🎧 **A.** *Lois sold her business for a lot of money. Listen to her conversation with her friend Raquel about her plans for the money. Complete the conversation by writing the words that you hear. You will hear the recording two times.*

RAQUEL: Now that you sold your business, you won't need to worry about money. What

_____will you do_____ with all your money?
           0.

LOIS: I'm not sure. I may give it all away.

RAQUEL: Really?

LOIS: No. I _____ some of it away, but not all of it. I'm probably going to buy
           1.

a new house.

RAQUEL: _____ away from Springfield?
           2.

LOIS: Maybe I will, but I _____. I like it here. I'm going to talk about it more
           3.

with my husband.

RAQUEL: Do you think you're going to like staying at home instead of working?

LOIS: Well, I won't be so stressed, that's for sure. I _____ my friends from
           4.

work as often, but I sure will enjoy my time at home.

RAQUEL: That sounds very nice. I _____ my business soon so that I can join you.
           5.

B. *Read each numbered statement based on Lois and Raquel's conversation. Then circle the letter of the sentence that best explains the meaning of the statement.*

0. Lois won't need to worry about money.
   a. Lois might not need to worry about money.
   b. Lois is probably not going to need to worry about money.
   ⓒ Lois is definitely not going to need to worry about money.

1. Lois may give some of her money away.
   a. Lois might give some of her money away.
   b. Lois is probably going to give some of her money away.
   c. Lois will definitely give some of her money away.

Name _____ Date _____

2. Lois is probably going to buy a new house.
   a. Lois won't buy a new house.
   b. It's not definite that Lois will buy a new house.
   c. Lois will definitely buy a new house.

3. Maybe Lois will move away from Springfield.
   a. Lois might move away from Springfield.
   b. Lois is probably going to move away from Springfield.
   c. Lois is definitely going to move away from Springfield.

4. Lois is going to talk with her husband about moving.
   a. Lois may talk with her husband about moving.
   b. Lois will probably talk with her husband about moving.
   c. Lois will definitely talk with her husband about moving.

5. Lois is going to enjoy her time at home.
   a. Lois might enjoy her time at home.
   b. Lois will probably enjoy her time at home.
   c. Lois will definitely enjoy her time at home.

2 | MORE TIME AT HOME

Read this conversation between Lois and her husband, Carlos. Circle 13 verbs that refer to the future or to possibility. Be sure to circle the complete verb. An example is given.

LOIS: What (are we going to do) with all our money? Are you going to quit working?

CARLOS: I may not quit right away. Maybe I'm not going to quit until next year. I enjoy my job. Besides, it'll be good to get out of the house. But I might work fewer hours.

LOIS: I think working fewer hours is a good idea. Phillip is going to like having you home more. Will you spend more time with him?

CARLOS: Of course! I'm going to love that! His birthday will be this Friday. Do you know what he wants?

LOIS: No, he won't tell me. He says he doesn't need anything. Will you ask him? He might tell you.

CARLOS: I may get him a gift certificate. Then he can choose what he wants.

LOIS: That's a good idea.

Name _____ Date _____

3 | 16TH BIRTHDAY

Complete this conversation between Lois and Carlos's son Phillip and his friend Julian. Use the future be going to *forms of the verbs in parentheses.*

JULIAN: Isn't your birthday this month? When ____is____ your birthday

____going to be____ ?
0. (be)

PHILLIP: This Friday.

JULIAN: How old _____ you _____ ?
1. (be)

PHILLIP: I'll be 16, the same age as you.

JULIAN: What _____ you _____ for your birthday?
2. (get)

PHILLIP: Oh, I don't know. I _____ a party or anything.
3. (have, probably, not)

JULIAN: _____ your parents _____ you anything?
4. (give)

PHILLIP: They _____ me clothes or something.
5. (get, probably)

JULIAN: Maybe they'll give you a car!

PHILLIP: Of course they _____ me a car!
6. (buy, not)

JULIAN: Why not? You _____ 16. You _____ able to drive in this
7. (turn)   8. (be)

state.

PHILLIP: I know, but they _____ me a car.
9. (get, not)

JULIAN: _____ you _____ your own car?
10. (buy)

PHILLIP: Not soon. I _____ enough money for a car for a while. Until then, I
11. (have, not)

_____ the bus.
12. (ride)

Name _____ Date _____

4 | PLANS FOR THE DAY

Complete this conversation between Phillip's parents, Lois and Carlos. Use the future will *forms of the verbs in parentheses.*

LOIS: ____Will____ you ____get____ Phillip's gift certificate today?
                                  0. (get)

CARLOS: Yeah, I'll buy it this afternoon.

LOIS: _____ you _____ it at the mall?
                                    1. (buy)

CARLOS: Yes.

LOIS: _____ you _____ the station wagon there?
                                    2. (drive)

CARLOS: Probably. Why?

LOIS: Because I need to take it to the repair shop. But if you're going to use it today, I

_____ it tomorrow instead. By the way, while you're at the mall,
3. (take)

_____ you _____ a birthday card as well?
                                   4. (pick out)

CARLOS: Sure, and I _____ a cake, too.
                           5. (choose)

LOIS: That's fine. I'll probably get some chicken for dinner. I _____ his favorite
                                                                                                                                                               6. (make)

food: fried chicken.

CARLOS: OK, but I _____ any since I'm on a diet. Phillip told me this morning
                             7. (eat, not)

that he plans to go to Julian's house after school. He's not sure when he'll be home.

LOIS: I _____ dinner until he gets home.
              8. (start, not)

PART IX ■ DIAGNOSTIC TEST | 157

Name _____ Date _____

5 | WEEKEND PLANS

Complete the conversation between Phillip and Julian. Use the correct forms of the words in parentheses and the verbs in the box. Some items may have more than one right answer.

be	fail	go	~~hold~~	leave	return	stay	turn
do	finish	help	know	meet	start	study	write

PHILLIP: Hey, ____will____ you ____hold____ my book for a second?
                               0. (will)

JULIAN: Sure. So, what _____ you _____ this weekend?
                                              1. (be going to)

PHILLIP: I _____ a book I'm reading. I'm almost done. Oh, and I
             2. (be going to)

_____ for our math test.
   3. (will)

JULIAN: I'm afraid I _____ our math test. _____ you
                         4. (will)

_____ me study?
   5. (will)

PHILLIP: Sure.

JULIAN: _____ you _____ home on Saturday?
                              6. (be going to)

PHILLIP: I _____ home in the morning because I _____ work at the
           7. (will, not)   8. (will)

bookstore at nine o'clock, but I _____ home from work in the evening.
                                    9. (will)

JULIAN: _____ you _____ home around six o'clock?
                              10. (be going to)

PHILLIP: Yeah, I _____ you at my house then.
                  11. (will)

6 | EDITING: USED CAR

Philip saved enough money to buy a car. Correct his conversation with Julian. There are seven mistakes. The first mistake is already corrected. (Note: There can be more than one way to correct a mistake.)

PHILLIP: The next time I see you, I ~~am~~ *will* probably have a car.

JULIAN: Really? When are you get a car?

PHILLIP: I thinking I might get one soon. My dad and I will looking at some cars tomorrow.

JULIAN: What kind of car are you going get?

PHILLIP: I'm not sure yet. But I know that it'll a used car, and it won't be expensive. It maybe ugly, though. Have you seen Bill's used car? It runs well, but it looks terrible!

158 | PART IX ■ DIAGNOSTIC TEST

Name _____ Date _____

Unit 30 Achievement Test

30 Items
Score: _____

1 | LISTENING: GOING TO THE LAKE

🎧 **A.** Listen to the telephone conversation between Jeff and Dan. Complete the conversation by writing the words that you hear. You will hear the recording two times.

DAN: Hello?

JEFF: Hi, Dan. It's Jeff. Listen, are you ____going to____ be around tomorrow?
                                              0.

DAN: Yeah, I think so. Why? What's going on?

JEFF: Well, a group of us are going to go to the lake tomorrow. Do you want to come?

DAN: Sure! Who's going?

JEFF: Well, it's _____ Rebecca, my wife Angie, and me. Lloyd and
                        1.

Sharon aren't going because Lloyd's going to be working _____.
                                                                      2.

DAN: Yeah, I think I can go. When _____?
                                           3.

JEFF: We're going to leave around 9:00 tomorrow morning. Rebecca

_____ lunch.
         4.

DAN: Do you know what the weather's going to be like?

JEFF: Yeah, _____ be sunny and warm. Bring your swimsuit. We're
                    5.

_____ go swimming.
         6.

DAN: That sounds great! See you _____ at 9:00!
                                          7.

B. Reread the conversation. Then read each statement and circle **T** (true) or **F** (false).

(T) F 0. Dan, Rebecca, Angie, and Jeff are going to the lake tomorrow.

T F 1. Lloyd's not going to be working.

T F 2. Dan, Rebecca, Angie, and Jeff are going to leave around 7:00 tomorrow morning.

T F 3. Tomorrow morning the weather's going to be sunny and warm, according to Jeff.

T F 4. Dan, Rebecca, Angie, and Jeff are definitely going to go swimming.

Name _____ Date _____

2 | BARBECUE

Complete the sentences about Dan, Rebecca, Angie, and Jeff's day at the lake. Circle the correct words or phrases.

0. Everyone (is going to) / is going / going to have lunch.

1. Where are Dan and Rebecca going to finding / to find / finds a picnic table?

2. They 're going to tell / are go to telling / are going tell the others when they find one.

3. They going to have / go to having / 're going to have a barbecue.

4. They are probably going swim / are probably going to swim / are probably go swim after lunch.

5. They 're going to go / 're going go / 're go to go home around 6:00.

Name _____ Date _____

3 | AFTER GRADUATION

*Rebecca and Angie are discussing Angie's plans after her college graduation. Complete their conversation. Use the correct forms of **be going to** or the present progressive and the verbs in parentheses. Some items may have more than one right answer.*

REBECCA: It was nice to go to the lake because it ___'s going to be___ a busy week.
0. (be)

ANGIE: I know! I _____ a final exam on Tuesday. It _____ the
1. (take)   2. (be)

last exam of my college career.

REBECCA: How exciting! What _____ you _____ after you
3. (do)

graduate?

ANGIE: Well, I _____ to find a job.
4. (need)

REBECCA: _____ you _____ here? I mean you and your husband, of
5. (stay)

course.

ANGIE: No, we _____ here. We _____ to a bigger city.
6. (stay, not)   7. (probably, move)

REBECCA: Where _____ you _____ to?
8. (move)

ANGIE: I don't know yet. We _____ wherever I can find a job.
9. (go)

REBECCA: _____ you _____ right after school is over?
10. (leave)

ANGIE: No. We _____ until I get a job. I _____ to Washington,
11. (stay)   12. (fly)

D.C. on Thursday for a job interview.

REBECCA: Great! Good luck!

4 | EDITING: BEFORE THE INTERVIEW

Correct this conversation between Jeff and Angie. There are three mistakes. The first mistake is already corrected.

JEFF: Are you going ^to ask about the salary for the job during your interview?

ANGIE: I don't think so. I going to wait for them to talk about it. I'm kind of nervous.

JEFF: You're going do great!

Name _____   Date _____

Unit 31 Achievement Test

30 Items
Score: _____

1 | LISTENING: JEJU ISLAND, KOREA

🎧 **A.** *Pete and Tanya are planning a trip to Korea. Listen to their conversation with their travel agent, Lisa. Complete the conversation by writing the words that you hear. You will hear the recording two times.*

LISA: When ____*will*____ you go to Korea? Will it be in _____ ?
                     0.   **1.**

PETE: Yes, we'll be in Seoul for part of June, and we're also thinking about spending a week on Jeju Island.

LISA: I have a vacation package in Jeju that you'll love! _____ in a great resort hotel in Jeju.
                                                                  2.

TANYA: _____ to go swimming?
             3.

LISA: Sure, you'll be able to swim on Hyeopjae Beach.

PETE: _____ time to see Manjanggul Cave?
             4.

LISA: Yes. The cave is near Hyeopjae Beach.

TANYA: Will the First Full Moon Field Fire Festival take place while we're there?

LISA: No, it won't. That will be in February. Will you be there again _____ February?
                                                                      5.

TANYA: No, I don't think so. Will we be able to climb Hallasan Mountain this summer?

LISA: _____ . The trails are closed in the summer because they're dangerous. But you'll be able to ride in a helicopter over the mountain and see the crater lake.
       6.

TANYA: How much will the helicopter ride cost?

LISA: I don't know the exact price, but it probably won't cost a lot of money. I'll find out the price and let you know by tomorrow.

PETE: That sounds good. We'll probably go to Jeju, then. How much is the hotel? . . .

162 | UNIT 31 ■ ACHIEVEMENT TEST

B. Read each numbered statement based on the conversation. Then circle the letter of the sentence that best explains the speaker's meaning.

0. Pete says, "Yes, we'll be in Seoul for part of June."
   a. Pete is making a promise.
   (b.) Pete is making a prediction.
   c. Pete is making an offer.

1. Lisa says, "I have a vacation package in Jeju that you'll love!"
   a. Lisa is making a prediction.
   b. Lisa is stating a refusal.
   c. Lisa is asking for something.

2. Lisa says, "Sure, you'll be able to swim on Hyeopjae Beach."
   a. Lisa is making an offer.
   b. Lisa is making a prediction.
   c. Lisa is stating something that is not definite.

3. Tanya asks, "Will the First Full Moon Field Fire Festival take place while we're there?"
   a. Tanya is asking something.
   b. Tanya is offering something.
   c. Tanya is promising something.

4. Lisa says, "You won't be able to climb Hallasan Mountain."
   a. Lisa is giving assurance.
   b. Lisa is making an offer.
   c. Lisa is talking about something that is not going to happen.

5. Lisa says, "You'll be able to ride in a helicopter over the mountain and see the crater lake."
   a. Lisa is refusing a plan for the future.
   b. Lisa is stating a fact or plan for the future.
   c. Lisa is stating something that is not definite.

6. Lisa says, "I'll find out the price of the helicopter ride in Jeju for Pete and Tanya."
   a. Lisa is refusing to do something.
   b. Lisa is stating something that is not definite.
   c. Lisa is making a promise to do something.

7. Pete says, "We will probably go to Jeju."
   a. Pete is making a promise.
   b. Pete is stating a refusal.
   c. Pete is stating something that is not definite.

UNIT 31 ■ ACHIEVEMENT TEST

Name _____ Date _____

2 | TANYA'S SUMMER PLANS

Complete this conversation between Tanya and her friend Jenny. Use the correct future forms of the verbs in parentheses with will.

JENNY: _____Will_____ you _____be_____ in town over the summer?
　　　　　　　　　　　　　　　0. (be)

TANYA: No. We _____ in Korea.
　　　　　　　　　1. (be)

JENNY: Very nice! What _____ you _____ there?
　　　　　　　　　　　　　　　　　　　　　　2. (do)

TANYA: Well, Pete _____ in Seoul for about a month, but then we
　　　　　　　　　3. (work)

　　　　_____ a week in Jeju, which is an island in South Korea.
　　　　4. (spend)

JENNY: _____ you _____ me back some *kimchi*?
　　　　　　　　　　　　　　5. (bring)

TANYA: I _____ some for you if I can. Some airports _____ you
　　　　　6. (bring)　　　　　　　　　　　　　　　　　　　　　　　7. (let, not)

　　　　take food out of the country.

JENNY: Well, I'll have to tell you about my plans for the summer later. I have a dentist

　　　　appointment to go to right now. See you!

TANYA: OK, talk to you later!

Name _____ Date _____

3 | JENNY'S SUMMER PLANS

*Complete another conversation between Tanya and Jenny. Use the correct forms of the verbs with **will** to rewrite each phrase in parentheses.*

TANYA: Hi, Jenny! How'd your dentist appointment go?

JENNY: Great! My teeth are fine.

TANYA: Good. You didn't have time to tell me about your summer plans during our last conversation. __Will you be__ in town this summer?
         0. (Are you going to be)

JENNY: Yeah, Adam and I _____ anywhere. We _____ busy
         1. (aren't going)   **2. (are going to be)**
running the car wash—we're always busy during the summer. We _____
                                                              3. (are going to open)
another car wash in August. We _____ you if you want to work for
                                4. (are probably going to ask)
us again then. _____ time for that when you get back from Korea?
                5. (Are you going to have)

TANYA: I think so.

JENNY: OK. Call us when you get back.

TANYA: OK, I _____ you. And I _____ to bring you the *kimchi*!
            6. (am going to contact)   **7. (am going to try)**

4 | EDITING: ON JEJU ISLAND

Pete and Tanya are on Jeju Island. Correct their conversation. There are four mistakes. The first mistake is already corrected.

                be
PETE: It'll ^ hard to leave here.

TANYA: I know! It's so beautiful that I willn't want to go home.

PETE: Yeah, I'll being sad to leave, but it'll is nice to get home, too.

Name _____ Date _____

Unit 32 Achievement Test

30 Items
Score: _____

1 | LISTENING: WORRIED MOM

🎧 **A.** *Listen to Norm and Julie's conversation about their son Chris. Complete the conversation by writing the words that you hear. You will hear the recording two times.*

JULIE: I'm worried about Chris. Where is he?

NORM: He ___*might be*___ at a friend's house. He'll probably be home soon.
                0.

JULIE: But he's never this late! He _____ in trouble. He might be hurt.
                                              1.

NORM: He'll probably call. He may be in the library studying, or he may be doing homework with a friend.

JULIE: Oh, Norm! _____ look for him, please?
                       2.

NORM: Maybe I will a little later. It's still early. He _____ home after I leave.
                                                              3.

JULIE: I'm not going to wait for him to come home. I'll call the police.

NORM: It _____ a good idea to wait just a little longer. Don't panic.
           4.

B. *Read each numbered statement based on the conversation. Then circle the letter of the sentence that best explains the meaning of the statement.*

0. Chris will probably be home soon.
   a. It's possible Chris will be home soon.
   ⓑ. It's likely Chris will be home soon.
   c. Chris will definitely be home soon.

1. Chris might be hurt.
   a. It's possible Chris is hurt.
   b. It's likely Chris is hurt.
   c. Chris is definitely hurt.

2. Chris will probably call.
   a. It's possible Chris will call.
   b. It's likely Chris will call.
   c. Chris will definitely call.

3. Chris may be in the library studying.
   a. It's possible Chris is in the library studying.
   b. It's likely Chris is in the library studying.
   c. Chris is definitely in the library studying.

Name _____ Date _____

4. Chris may be doing homework with a friend.
   a. It's possible Chris is doing homework with a friend.
   b. It's likely Chris is doing homework with a friend.
   c. Chris is definitely doing homework with a friend.

5. Maybe Norm will look for Chris a little later.
   a. It's possible Norm will look for Chris a little later.
   b. It's likely Norm will look for Chris a little later.
   c. Norm will definitely look for Chris a little later.

6. Julie will call the police.
   a. It's possible Julie will call the police.
   b. It's likely Julie will call the police.
   c. Julie will definitely call the police.

2 | AT THE LIBRARY

*Complete the conversation between Chris and his friend Rob. Use the affirmative or negative of **may** or **might** and the words in the box. Some items may have more than one right answer.*

| ask | be | buy | ~~have~~ | look | need | research | stop | talk | tell | write |

ROB: I don't know which topic to choose for my history paper. Do you have any ideas?

CHRIS: I ___might have___ a few good ones. Are you interested in World War II?
              0.

ROB: I don't know. That _____ the best topic for me. I don't know a lot about it.
                            1.

CHRIS: OK. Here's another idea. You _____ about President Theodore Roosevelt.
                                      2.

ROB: But I _____ lots of help with that topic. It might be hard for me. Which
           3.
topic are you going to research?

CHRIS: I _____ the Great Depression of the 1920s and 30s.
         4.

ROB: Oh, that'll be interesting.

CHRIS: I _____ to Mr. Li tomorrow. I _____ him for some ideas.
         5.   **6.**

ROB: Be careful. He _____ you to write about the Vietnam War. That seems to
                    7.
be his favorite subject.

Name _____ Date _____

3 | CONVERSATION WITH THE HISTORY TEACHER

Complete this conversation between Chris and his history teacher, Mr. Li. Circle the correct words or phrases.

CHRIS: Mr. Li, (will) / may you help me choose a topic for my paper?
0.

MR. LI: Sure. Here's one possibility: You might like / will like to write about the Vietnam War.
1.
There's a lot of information about it. I'm sure it may be / will be interesting.
2.

CHRIS: Rob thought you might tell / will tell me to write about the Vietnam War. But I'm not
3.
really interested in it. Can I write about something else?

MR. LI: Certainly. You won't / may not think you have any good ideas, but I bet you do. What
4.
topics are you thinking about?

CHRIS: Well, I'm considering writing about the Russian Revolution, but I might not / will be
5.
able to find enough information about it. What do you think?

MR. LI: Our library may not have / will not have lots of information on that. I'm not really
6.
sure. Ask a librarian. Also, you might not / probably not want to focus on the entire
7.
Russian Revolution. Might / Will you focus on a specific part?
8.

CHRIS: I might focus on Stalin's role.

MR. LI: Great.

4 | EDITING: PLANS FOR THE EVENING

Correct this conversation between Julie and her son Chris. There are six mistakes. The first mistake is already corrected. (Note: There is often more than one way to correct a mistake.)

                              Maybe
CHRIS: Bye, Mom. ~~May be~~ I'll see you tonight.

JULIE: Maybe? Will you be going to your friend Rob's house again?

CHRIS: I maght go there, or I maybe go to the library.

JULIE: Well, we like to know where you are. I was worried about you the other day. Your father not worry very much, but I do. Do you think you'll be home for dinner?

CHRIS: I not might make it in time for dinner. I'll be working on my paper, and I think it might takes a long time.

168 | UNIT 32 ■ ACHIEVEMENT TEST

Name _____ Date _____

Part IX Achievement Test

60 Items
Score: _____

1 | LISTENING: NEW JOB

🎧 **A.** *Listen to Lyle's conversation with his friend Rick about his new job. Complete the conversation by writing the words that you hear. You will hear the recording two times.*

RICK: I heard that you got a new job. Congratulations! ____Will____ you have a long
         0.
commute?

LYLE: No, I won't. I got a job at Wilson's Furniture Factory on Highway 1. I'm going to start tomorrow.

RICK: Interesting. _____ me a table?
                          1.

LYLE: Sorry, I'm not going to make the furniture. I'm going to be an advertising specialist. I _____ to buy the furniture more cheaply, though. Come take a look at it
        2.
sometime.

RICK: _____ go look at it, but I _____ anything. I don't have much
        3.   **4.**
money right now. I'm going to save money for a while.

LYLE: That's fine. When can you come?

RICK: I _____ to go this week. I'll probably be able to stop by next week on
         5.
Tuesday. But if I can't go on Tuesday, then I might go on Thursday during my lunch break.

LYLE: OK. Any day is fine with me.

B. *Read each numbered statement based on the conversation. Then circle the letter of the sentence that best explains the meaning of the statement.*

0. Lyle will work at a furniture factory.
   a. Lyle might work at a furniture factory.
   b. Lyle is probably going to work at a furniture factory.
   ⓒ Lyle is definitely going to work at a furniture factory.

1. Lyle is going to start the new job tomorrow.
   a. Lyle might start the new job tomorrow.
   b. Lyle will probably start the new job tomorrow.
   c. Lyle will definitely start the new job tomorrow.

PART IX ■ ACHIEVEMENT TEST | 169

Name _____ Date _____

2. Lyle is going to be an advertising specialist.
   a. Lyle might be an advertising specialist.
   b. Lyle will probably be an advertising specialist.
   c. Lyle will definitely be an advertising specialist.

3. Rick is going to save money for a while.
   a. Rick might save money for a while.
   b. Rick will probably save money for a while.
   c. Rick will definitely save money for a while.

4. Rick will probably stop by the furniture factory on Tuesday.
   a. Rick might stop by the furniture factory on Tuesday.
   b. It's likely that Rick is going to stop by the furniture factory on Tuesday.
   c. Rick will definitely stop by the furniture factory on Tuesday.

5. Rick might go to the furniture factory on Thursday.
   a. Rick may go to the furniture factory on Thursday.
   b. Rick will probably go to the furniture factory on Thursday.
   c. Rick will definitely go to the furniture factory on Thursday.

2 | MORE MONEY

Read this conversation between Lyle and his wife, Cathy. Circle 13 verbs that refer to the future or to possibility. Be sure to circle the complete verb. An example is given.

CATHY: I'm so excited about your new job! But it (will be) different from your old one. Are you going to like the new company?

LYLE: I don't know. I might miss my old job, but I hope I'm going to like my new one. I may not like it at first. I won't know until tomorrow when I start. It might be a nice change from what I was doing. At least I'll make more money.

CATHY: And we're going to be able to save money for a new house. Will you work longer hours though?

LYLE: No. I'm going to be home at 6:00, just like with my old job.

CATHY: That's great. Will you have weekends off?

LYLE: I might work some weekends. I'll ask my boss about it tomorrow.

Name _____ Date _____

3 | MOVING

Penny is Lyle and Cathy's daughter. Complete this conversation with her friend Jane. Use the future **be going to** forms of the verbs in parentheses.

JANE: _____Are_____ you ___going to be___ here next school year?
　　　　　　　　　　　　　　　0. (be)

PENNY: I hope so, but I _____ for sure until the end of the week.
　　　　　　　　　　　　　　1. (know, not)

JANE: _____ you _____ in town?
　　　　　　　　　　　　　　　　　2. (stay)

PENNY: Yeah, we _____ here. I hope I _____ schools.
　　　　　　　　　　3. (stay)　　　　　　　　　　　　4. (change, not)

JANE: Maybe your parents _____ you the old house!
　　　　　　　　　　　　　　　5. (give)

PENNY: Of course they _____ that! They'll sell it to buy their new house.
　　　　　　　　　　　　6. (do, not)

JANE: This will be the first time you move. _____ you _____ sad?
　　　　　　　　　　　　　　　　　　　　　　　　　　　　　　　　　　　　　　7. (be)

PENNY: I _____ some things, but I _____ used to the new house.
　　　　　　8. (miss)　　　　　　　　　　　9. (get, probably)

JANE: When _____ you _____?
　　　　　　　　　　　　　　　　　10. (move)

PENNY: I don't know yet, but it will probably be next month.

JANE: How _____ you _____ your things when you move?
　　　　　　　　　　　　　　　　　11. (transport)

PENNY: My parents _____ a huge truck, and then we'll load it ourselves.
　　　　　　　　　　　12. (rent)

4 | EVENING PLANS

Complete this conversation between Lyle and Cathy about their plans for the evening. Use the future **will** forms of the verbs in parentheses.

CATHY: Today is Penny's soccer game. I ___'ll skip___ my meeting to go.
　　　　　　　　　　　　　　　　　　　　0. (skip)

_____ you _____ able to go?
　　　　　　　　　　　1. (be)

LYLE: Yeah, I _____ time off this afternoon.
　　　　　　　2. (take)

CATHY: After the game _____ you _____ our clothes at the dry
　　　　　　　　　　　　　　　　　　　　3. (get)

cleaner? And _____ you _____ some milk?
　　　　　　　　　　　　　　　　4. (buy)

LYLE: Sure. I _____ some bread, too.
　　　　　　5. (get)

CATHY: OK. I _____ Penny shopping after her game, so I _____
　　　　　　6. (take)　　　　　　　　　　　　　　　　　　　　　　　7. (be, not)

home to make dinner. We _____ home until after 8:00.
　　　　　　　　　　　　　　8. (come, not)

Name _____   Date _____

5 | WEEKEND PLANS

Complete the conversation between Penny and her friend Jane. Use the correct forms of the words in parentheses and the words in the box. Some items may have more than one right answer.

be	do	finish	have	~~need~~	shop	study	watch
come	drive	give	know	see	stay	turn	use

JANE: I ___'ll need___ to work on my serve for the tennis championship next month.
              0. (will)

The tennis courts _____ open this weekend. What _____
                          1. (will)

you _____ this weekend?
     2. (be going to)

PENNY: I _____ for a biology test, and I _____ TV.
       3. (be going to)   4. (will, probably)

JANE: _____ you _____ time to play tennis with me?
                 5. (will)

PENNY: Sure. _____ you _____ in town on Sunday?
                    6. (be going to)

JANE: No, my parents _____ us to Minneapolis to visit my grandmother on
                 7. (will)

Sunday.

PENNY: _____ you _____ at the mall there? There are some great
             8. (be going to)

sales!

JANE: Probably, but I won't get to buy a lot because my parents _____ me any
                              9. (will, not)

more money this week.

PENNY: That's too bad. Well, can you play tennis with me on Saturday?

JANE: Sure, I'll meet you on Saturday at noon.

PENNY: Sorry, but I can't meet at noon because I have to work at the library. I

_____ work at 1:00, though.
10. (will)

JANE: How about 2:00 then?

PENNY: That's fine. I _____ you at the tennis courts at 2:00.
           11. (will)

Name _____ Date _____

6 | EDITING: NEW HOUSE

Penny and her parents are going to move. Correct this conversation between Penny and Jane. There are seven mistakes. The first mistake is already corrected. (Note: There can be more than one way to correct a mistake.)

PENNY: I think I'll ~~starting~~ *start* to pack tomorrow.

JANE: Really? When are you move into your new house?

PENNY: I thinking we might move this week. My parents will signing the papers tomorrow.

JANE: Where are you going move to?

PENNY: It'll pretty close to our old house, and I won't change schools! My parents might lets me have a pet, too!

JANE: Great!

Name _____ Date _____

PART X Diagnostic Test

60 Items
Score: _____

1 | LISTENING: SCHOOL BOOKS

🎧 **A.** Lisa is visiting her friend Wendy. Listen to their conversation about buying books for college. Complete the conversation by writing the words that you hear. You will hear the recording two times.

WENDY: I'm going to have ___*some juice*___ . Would you like _____?
                            0.   **1.**

LISA: Sure. That sounds great. Do you have _____?
                                              2.

WENDY: Of course.

LISA: So, I had to buy five books for my classes, and they were really expensive. _____ did you buy?
                                                                                   3.

WENDY: I bought five, too.

LISA: Oh, really? _____ did you spend?
                  4.

WENDY: Let me think . . . about $180, I guess.

LISA: Wow, _____ were much cheaper than mine.
           5.

WENDY: Well, I bought them online from <u>bookdeals.com</u>. Their prices aren't as bad as the prices at our campus bookstore.

LISA: Maybe I need to check that out. I won't have _____ for the rest of the
                                                    6.
semester if I shop at the campus bookstore again. Its prices are really high.

WENDY: I know. My friend Jeremy bought his books online, too, and he saved about $50. But he used <u>cheapcheapbooks.com</u>. He says _____ discounts are really good.
                                                                                7.

LISA: Were his cheaper than yours?

WENDY: I think ours were about the same price.

LISA: Wow, I'll have to check out both websites.

174 | PART X ■ DIAGNOSTIC TEST

Name _____ Date _____

B. *Reread the conversation. Find five possessive adjectives and four possessive pronouns. Write them in the table below. (Note: Only use words that are given in the conversation. Do not use any words that you wrote.) An example is given.*

POSSESSIVE ADJECTIVES	POSSESSIVE PRONOUNS
0. my	1. _____
1. _____	2. _____
2. _____	3. _____
3. _____	4. _____
4. _____	
5. _____	

2 | COMPLAINTS

A. *Wendy, Glen, and Betty love to complain. Read their conversation at a restaurant. Then read each statement and circle* **T** *(true) or* **F** *(false).*

GLEN: This place is terrible. The waiter is too slow, and the pizza is too expensive. Also, my soda has too few ice cubes.

WENDY: I know, it's not very good at all. The breadsticks are too dry, and my pizza has too much cheese.

BETTY: Well, my pizza has too many olives.

GLEN: Mine does, too.

WENDY: Mine has too few olives. And it has too much sauce.

BETTY: Let's complain to the manager. This place really *is* terrible!

T (F) 0. The waiter is fast.
T F 1. The pizza is a good price.
T F 2. Glen's soda has more than the right number of ice cubes.
T F 3. The breadsticks are perfect.
T F 4. Wendy's pizza doesn't need more cheese.
T F 5. Wendy's pizza doesn't have enough olives.
T F 6. Wendy's pizza has more than the right amount of sauce.

Name _____ Date _____

B. *Read these sentences based on the conversation. Match each underlined word with the phrase it replaces.*

_b_ 0. <u>Theirs</u> have too many olives.   a. Glen's soda

____ 1. <u>Mine</u> has too many olives.   ~~b.~~ Betty and Glen's pizzas

____ 2. <u>Hers</u> has too much sauce.   c. The waiter

____ 3. <u>His</u> has too little ice.   d. Betty's soda

____ 4. <u>Theirs</u> is not very good.   e. Wendy's pizza

f. Wendy, Betty, and Glen's pizzas

g. Betty's pizza

h. The waiter's soda

3 | BAD FOOD

A. *Read Glen's complaints about a hamburger and salad from a fast-food restaurant. Write* **C** *if the underlined word is a count noun,* **N** *if it is a non-count noun, and* **A** *if it is an adjective.*

0. _A_   The hamburger was too <u>small</u>.

1. ____ It had too little <u>ketchup</u>.

2. ____ There were too few <u>pickles</u> on my hamburger.

3. ____ The bun was too <u>old</u>.

4. ____ The tomatoes were too <u>soft</u>.

5. ____ My salad had too few <u>carrots</u>.

6. ____ There was too little <u>chicken</u> on the salad.

Name _____ **Date** _____

B. Glen has more complaints about his meal. Complete each sentence with **too much, too many, too few,** or **too little**.

0. My hamburger had _____too much_____ mustard. I don't like a lot of mustard, so I took some of it off.

1. My hamburger had _____ mayonnaise. I asked for more.

2. There were _____ onions on my hamburger. I only wanted a few, but they gave me a lot.

3. My salad had _____ lettuce. I didn't eat all of it.

4. My salad had _____ tomatoes. I wanted more than they gave me.

5. The salad had _____ salad dressing. They gave me more than I wanted.

6. The salad dressing had _____ oil. It was really oily.

4 | APPLE PIE

Lisa ate dinner at Wendy's house. Complete their conversation about dessert. Circle the correct words or phrases.

LISA: That was any / an /(a) wonderful dinner.
            0.

WENDY: Thank you. Would you like a few / some / a roll of dessert? I made an / a / any apple
                                      1.   2.
pie.

LISA: Sure, it looks great! How did you make the top of the pie shiny?

WENDY: I used a / an / any egg.
              3.

LISA: That's a / an / any great idea.
           4.

WENDY: How many / How much / How few pieces do you want? They're really small.
         5.

LISA: One is fine. . . . Mmm, it tastes delicious. Did you use any / a little / a red apples?
                                                                6.

WENDY: No, I used three green apples and two yellow ones.

LISA: It makes a great combination. And it's not too sweet. Did you use a few / any / a
                                                                         7.
sugar?

WENDY: Yes, I added a little / a few / one sugar. I also added a few / a little / any salt for extra
                      8.   9.
flavor.

Name _____ Date _____

LISA: Did you use <u>a few / an / any</u> special salt—like sea salt or kosher salt?
                    10.

WENDY: No, just regular table salt. <u>A few / Half a teaspoon of / A</u> salt is enough. And I used
                                     11.

some / a few / a butter.
12.

LISA: Oh really? <u>How many / How much / How few</u> butter did you use?
                  13.

WENDY: Two tablespoons.

LISA: Did you use <u>a / an / any</u> milk?
                   14.

WENDY: No. But I used <u>a few / any / a little</u> teaspoons of cold water.
                        15.

LISA: It's delicious!

5 | EDITING: PHONE CONVERSATION

Correct Lisa's phone conversation with her mother. There are eight mistakes. The first mistake is already corrected. (Note: There can be more than one way to correct a mistake.)

MOM: Hi, it's Mom. How are ~~yours~~ *your* first few weeks at college?

LISA: Things are going well.

MOM: What are you doing right now?

LISA: Not much. Just drinking a bottle soda and studying.

MOM: So, how do you like college so far?

LISA: I'm very happy with mine choice of schools. The college is great. Its campus is really beautiful.

MOM: How are your classes?

LISA: Well, I like them all, except for chemistry. My friend Wendy is taking chemistry too, and hers professor is really easy. But my is so difficult! He gives us too much homework, and the book is to hard.

MOM: Do you have time enough to study?

LISA: Actually, I'm too very busy with chemistry. I hardly have time for my other classes.

MOM: OK, I'll let you get back to studying. I just wanted to say hi.

LISA: All right. Thanks for calling. Bye.

Name _____ Date _____

Unit 33 Achievement Test

30 Items
Score: _____

1 | LISTENING: ARLINGTON, TEXAS

🎧 **A.** Tom is having dinner at his girlfriend Christie's house. He is meeting Christie's parents, Lori and Stan, for the first time. Listen to their conversation. Complete the conversation by writing the words that you hear. You will hear the recording two times.

LORI: Where are you from, Tom?

TOM: I'm from ____*a city*____ in Texas called Arlington.
                    0.

LORI: Oh, interesting. _____ live there?
                              1.

TOM: About 400,000.

STAN: Hmm. I didn't realize Arlington was that big. So, with a population of that size, does the city have _____ ?
                                                                                                          2.

TOM: No. Arlington isn't far from Dallas and Fort Worth, which have _____ airports—three actually. And there aren't _____ in Arlington for it to have its own airport.
                                                                       3.   **4.**

STAN: I see. And how far is it from downtown Arlington to downtown Dallas?

TOM: About 20 miles. But Arlington is actually considered part of the Dallas–Fort Worth metropolitan area. The whole area is growing a lot.

LORI: So is crime a problem since the city is part of a big metropolitan area?

TOM: There are _____ every year, but it's pretty safe. A big part of the growing population is older people who retire there because they like the climate.
              5.

LORI: Yeah, I bet it doesn't get cold there like it does here. Do you ever get snow?

TOM: We usually don't get _____. I remember that it snowed once when I was a kid, but not a lot. There wasn't even _____ to make a snowball.
                          6.   **7.**

STAN: Well, that's a big difference from here. Arlington sounds like a nice place.

TOM: It is. I'm glad to call it home.

UNIT 33 ■ ACHIEVEMENT TEST   179

Name _____ Date _____

B. *Complete these questions based on the conversation. Circle the correct words.*

0. How many (residents) / population / person are there in Arlington?

1. How much people / snow / airport is there in Arlington?

2. How many distance / time / miles is it from Arlington to Dallas?

3. How much crime / people / snowballs is there in Arlington?

2 | DINNER

Read the questions and answers. Write **S** *if the underlined noun is a singular count noun,* **P** *if it is a plural count noun, and* **N** *if it is a non-count noun.*

0. __P__ Q: Are there any <u>forks</u>?

   A: Sure. Here's one.

1. ____ Q: How much <u>spaghetti</u> do you want?

   A: That's enough. Thank you.

2. ____ Q: Do you want a <u>napkin</u>?

   A: Yes, I think I need one.

3. ____ Q: Can I have some <u>cheese</u>, please?

   A: Sure, here it is.

4. ____ Q: How many <u>rolls</u> would you like?

   A: Just one, thanks.

5. ____ Q: Would you like some <u>milk</u>?

   A: No, thank you.

6. ____ Q: Do you want some <u>juice</u>?

   A: Yes, please.

7. ____ Q: Do you want a few <u>vegetables</u>?

   A: Sure.

8. ____ Q: Did you have any <u>ice cream</u>?

   A: Yes, I did.

9. ____ Q: Did you get any <u>candy</u>?

   A: Not yet.

Name _____ Date _____

3 | GOING TO THE STORE

Complete Tom and Christie's conversation about buying some things from the store. Circle the correct words or phrases.

TOM: Oh, the light bulb just burned out. Do you have a / (an) / some extra one?
　　　　　　　　　　　　　　　　　　　　　　　　　　　　　　　　　0.

CHRISTIE: Let me look. . . . I thought I had one / an / some light bulb in the closet. No, it looks
　　　　　　　　　　　　　　　　　　　　1.

like I don't have any / some / a little extras. I have a / an / some idea. Why don't I
　　　　　　　　　　2.　　　　　　　　　　　　　　3.

walk to the store? I need a little / much / a few other things anyway. I need
　　　　　　　　　　　　　　　　4.

a quart of / a piece of / many milk and a package of / a few / a spinach.
　　　　　　5.　　　　　　　　　　　　　　　　6.

TOM: OK. Can you also buy me a few / a little / much eggs? I'm all out.
　　　　　　　　　　　　　　　　　7.

CHRISTIE: Sure. Do you want a few / a little / much bottles of water, too?
　　　　　　　　　　　　　　　8.

TOM: Yes, please, but you should probably take your car. You can't carry all of that stuff.

4 | EDITING: THIRSTY

Christie is at Tom's house. Correct their conversation. There are four mistakes. The first mistake is already corrected.

　　　　　　　　　　　　some
CHRISTIE: Can I have ~~any~~ water?

TOM: Sure. I have little juice, also, or do you prefer water?

CHRISTIE: Water, please.

TOM: Do you want any ice?

CHRISTIE: No, thanks. I didn't drink water enough today. I think I only had one glasses of water

all day. I really need to drink more.

Name _____   Date _____

Unit 34 Achievement Test

30 Items
Score: _____

1 | LISTENING: FOOD CRITIC

🎧 **A.** *Listen to this radio report about a new restaurant called Simply Spaghetti. Complete the report by writing the words that you hear. You will hear the recording two times.*

Hello, I'm Avery Hudson from the Food Critic's Corner. This week I'm reviewing Simply Spaghetti, a new Italian restaurant on the east side of town.

The first thing you notice when you enter the restaurant is that everything is crowded. There are __*too many tables*__, and there's too little space between them. The restaurant was also
      0.
uncomfortable because it was _____. There are too few windows to let cool air in.
                                     1.
They play lively Italian music, which is nice, but sometimes it's too loud. So, in general, the restaurant doesn't have a very good atmosphere.

The service is pretty good. The waiters are friendly, but they come to the table

_____ during the meal. And I suggest making a reservation. I waited too long to
  2.
get a table.

And, unfortunately, the food wasn't worth the wait. I tried the vegetable soup, but it was too salty. I can't recommend the spaghetti and meatballs, either. The dish had _____
                                                                                    3.
and too few meatballs.

The prices are too expensive for the experience that you get. Overall, Simply Spaghetti was simply awful, and I do not recommend it.

Name _____ Date _____

B. *Reread the report. Then circle the letter of the sentence that best describes each situation.*

0. ⓐ. There are more than enough tables in the restaurant.
   b. There are not enough tables in the restaurant.
   c. There is a good amount of tables in the restaurant.

1. a. There is not enough space in the restaurant.
   b. There is extra space in the restaurant.
   c. There is the right amount of space in the restaurant.

2. a. There are more than enough windows in the restaurant.
   b. There are not enough windows in the restaurant.
   c. There is a good amount of windows in the restaurant.

3. a. There was a good amount of salt in the soup.
   b. There was not enough salt in the soup.
   c. There was more than enough salt in the soup.

4. a. There were not enough meatballs.
   b. There was the right number of meatballs.
   c. There were more than enough meatballs.

C. *Reread the report. Then read each statement and circle* **T** *(true) or* **F** *(false).*

Ⓣ F   0. There are extra tables in the restaurant.
T F   1. The music is too quiet.
T F   2. People wait a long time to get a table.
T F   3. The prices are too low.

UNIT 34 ■ ACHIEVEMENT TEST

Name _____ Date _____

2 | MOVIE REVIEW

A. Read each sentence from a review of the movie Calling Card. Write **C** if the underlined noun is a count noun and **N** if it is a non-count noun.

0. _N_ The movie is a complete waste of time. The beginning of the movie has too little <u>action</u>, and it's too slow.

1. ____ Even though the beginning of *Calling Card* is boring, there is too much <u>violence</u> in the second half of the movie.

2. ____ There are too few good <u>actors</u>, and Howard Gleason, who plays someone in his 20s, is too old for the part.

3. ____ There are also too many <u>problems</u> with the story itself.

4. ____ There are too many <u>characters</u>. It's too hard to follow who everyone is.

5. ____ The dialogue isn't very interesting. There are too few good <u>lines</u>.

6. ____ There is too much <u>attention</u> on special effects and too little focus on the story. The makers of this movie were too interested in the special effects.

7. ____ In general, there was too little <u>effort</u> to make this a quality movie. I give *Calling Card* a "zero" rating.

B. Complete these sentences based on the movie review. Circle the correct words or phrases.

0. There are <u>few/(many)</u> problems with the story.

1. The beginning of the story is <u>very slow / very fast</u>.

2. Howard Gleason is <u>the right age / not the right age</u> for his part.

3. The characters are <u>easy / difficult</u> to follow.

4. The makers of this movie <u>were / weren't</u> very interested in the special effects.

Name _____ Date _____

3 | ADVERTISEMENT

Complete this advertisement for a new book. Write **too many**, **too much**, **too few**, **too little**, *or* **too**.

Nowadays people are busier than ever, and that means we're getting ___too___ stressed by our jobs and other activities. It's a situation that many of us know, and it's a problem that's becoming _____(1)_____ common. If you're like most people, you have _____(2)_____ things to do each day. And that means that you probably have _____(3)_____ time to relax and do things you enjoy. But now there's help! In her new book, *Time for Me*, Shirley Finnegan teaches readers to create free time within their busy schedules. Finnegan explains that _____(4)_____ work isn't good for us. She says that free time is important. Are you _____(5)_____ busy to go to the store and buy the book? Then order it online. But do it today, so that you can start enjoying your free time and your life.

4 | EDITING: WEDDING

Correct the conversation between Larissa and Barbara. There are five mistakes. The first mistake is already corrected.

LARISSA: How was the wedding?

BARBARA: It was nice, but the party afterward wasn't great. It lasted too ~~much~~ *many* hours, and there were too speeches.

LARISSA: Oh, that's too bad.

BARBARA: Also, the bride and groom invited too little friends and family members for the size of the hall. So it felt really empty. The lights were too bright, and the music was too old-fashioned.

LARISSA: Oh, no!

BARBARA: But it wasn't all bad. The food was delicious. And since there was too many food and too little guests to eat it all, I ate a lot!

Name _____   Date _____

Unit 35 Achievement Test

30 Items
Score: _____

1 | LISTENING: FAMILY PHOTO

🎧 **A.** *Listen to the conversation between two co-workers. Complete the conversation by writing the words that you hear. You will hear the recording two times.*

KEN: I noticed the pictures on _____your_____ desk. Are they pictures of your family?
                                                       0.

JULIE: Yeah, that's _____ husband in the picture on the left. And those are
                            1.

      _____ children in the other one. Emma is 10, Kristen is 8, and Mark is 5.
         2.

KEN: They're very good-looking kids.

JULIE: Thanks. And you can see they don't look anything alike! Well, Emma and Kristen both

      have blond hair, and _____ eyes are blue. But Mark's hair is brown, and
                                          3.

      _____ eyes are green.
         4.

KEN: And none of them have the same kind of hair, either.

JULIE: Yeah, Emma's hair is straight. But Kristen and Mark have totally different hair. Theirs is

      so curly.

KEN: Mark looks a lot like you.

JULIE: True. His body is tall and thin like mine.

KEN: You know, my wife and I have three children, too. But ours are much older than yours.

JULIE: Really? Do you have a picture?

B. *Reread the conversation. Find two possessive adjectives and four possessive pronouns. Write them in the table below. (Note: Only use words that are given in the conversation. Do not use any words that you wrote.) An example is given.*

POSSESSIVE ADJECTIVES	POSSESSIVE PRONOUNS
0. *your*	1. _____
1. _____	2. _____
2. _____	3. _____
	4. _____

Name _____ Date _____

2 | WHOSE IS IT?

Complete the sentences. Circle the correct words.

0. Julie has a picture. It is (her) / she / hers picture.

1. My husband and I have one son. Mark is us / ours / our son.

2. Emma and Kristen are ours / us / our, too. They're girls.

3. Emma and Kristen have blond hair. Theirs / Their / They hair is blond.

4. Mark's hair isn't like their / they / theirs. His is brown.

5. I also have a dog. The dog is me / my / mine.

6. Look, I have a picture. This is my / mine / me dog.

7. You have a dog, too, right? Do you have a picture of you / your / yours?

8. Oh, your / yours / you dog is really cute.

3 | BOOK COLLECTION

*Julie is visiting Ken's house. Read their conversation. Write **A** if the underlined word is a possessive adjective and **P** if it is a possessive pronoun.*

        KEN: Hi, Julie, come in.

0. _A_ JULIE: Thank you. . . . Oh, <u>your</u> living room is beautiful.

1. ____ KEN: Thanks. It's <u>our</u> favorite room in the house.

2. ____ JULIE: You have so many books! Are all these books <u>yours</u>?

3. ____ KEN: Well, some of them are <u>my</u> books, and some are my wife's books. Take a look at them if you're interested.

4. ____ JULIE: OK, thanks. . . . Oh, I love this book! Is it <u>yours</u> or your wife's?

5. ____ KEN: That one is <u>mine</u>, but my wife likes it more than I do.

6. ____ JULIE: So it's kind of <u>hers</u> now?

        KEN: Yeah, I guess so.

7. ____ JULIE: My husband and I have a copy of that book, too. We love it. But <u>ours</u> is really old, so I want to buy a new copy.

4 | EDITING: FAMILY PICTURES

Julie is still at Ken's house. Correct their conversation. There are six mistakes. The first mistake is already corrected. (Note: There is often more than one way to correct a mistake.)

JULIE: Are these ~~yours~~ *your* pictures? I'd like to see them.

KEN: Yes, they're our. This is a picture of my daughter and her husband. They're standing in front of theirs house. This dog is their, but this one is my.

JULIE: That dog is your? But you don't have a dog.

KEN: Well, he lives with my daughter now, but I still think he belongs to me.

Name _____   Date _____

Part X Achievement Test

60 Items
Score: _____

1 | LISTENING: NEW SHOES

🎧 **A.** *Leslie and Winona are roommates in college. Listen to their conversation. Complete the conversation by writing the words that you hear. You will hear the recording two times.*

WINONA: I'm going to make __*some lunch*__. Would you like _____?
                                               0.   **1.**

LESLIE: That sounds great. I'm really hungry. But do we have _____?
                                                                                     2.

WINONA: My dressing is gone, but we still have some of yours.

LESLIE: What kind is _____? I always forget what I buy.
                                   3.

WINONA: Let me look. . . . It's _____ ranch dressing.
                                 4.

LESLIE: Oh, good, I like that kind. Its flavor is delicious. Hey, by the way, do you want to go shopping with me later today?

WINONA: I can't. You know I have to work on a paper.

LESLIE: Yes, I know. And _____ do I have to tell you: You can work on your paper later! Come with me!
                              5.

WINONA: What are you shopping for?

LESLIE: Shoes. I want to buy some sandals like the black pair Ericka has. Hers are so pretty.

WINONA: Where are you going?

LESLIE: To City Savers. It's the best shoe store in the world. A friend's brother first told me about it, believe it or not. He buys all his shoes there. Anyway, City Savers is great because _____ prices are very reasonable. I think maybe Ericka got her black sandals there.
                            6.

WINONA: I really like those sandals, too. _____ do you think she paid for them?
                                                      7.

LESLIE: Not a lot at City Savers. Their discounts are really good. Nobody has prices like theirs.

WINONA: Well, if the prices can fit budgets like ours, then I'll go, but not for too long.

Name _____ **Date** _____

B. Reread the conversation. Find five possessive adjectives and four possessive pronouns. Write them in the table below. (Note: Only use words that are given in the conversation. Do not use any words that you wrote.) An example is given.

POSSESSIVE ADJECTIVES	POSSESSIVE PRONOUNS
0. My	1. _____
1. _____	2. _____
2. _____	3. _____
3. _____	4. _____
4. _____	
5. _____	

2 | COMPLAINTS ABOUT THE CAFETERIA

*Winona and Leslie are eating lunch at the campus cafeteria. Read their conversation. Then read each statement and circle **T** (true) or **F** (false).*

WINONA: This cafeteria is horrible. My soup is too hot. I can't even eat it.

LESLIE: What kind did you get?

WINONA: Well, they say it's chicken noodle soup. But it has too few pieces of chicken, and there are too many beans. How's yours?

LESLIE: Not very good. It has too much rice, and it's too salty. I need to drink some water. . . . My water isn't even cold! They gave me too few ice cubes.

WINONA: Here, have a roll. At least we can eat these.

LESLIE: Yeah, but they're too small. Why do we eat here? The food isn't good, and it's too expensive.

T (**F**) 0. The temperature of Winona's soup is good.

T **F** 1. Winona's soup doesn't have enough chicken.

T **F** 2. Winona's soup doesn't have enough beans.

T **F** 3. Leslie's soup has less than the right amount of rice.

T **F** 4. Leslie's soup has less than the right amount of salt.

T **F** 5. Leslie wants more ice cubes in her water.

T **F** 6. The food at the cafeteria costs too much money.

Name _____ Date _____

3 | BAD FOOD

A. *Read Winona's complaints about another meal at the campus cafeteria. Write* **C** *if the underlined word is a count noun,* **N** *if it is a non-count noun, and* **A** *if it is an adjective.*

0. _A_ The meat in my sandwich was too <u>dry</u>.

1. ____ My sandwich had too little <u>ketchup</u>.

2. ____ The bread for my sandwich was too <u>old</u>.

3. ____ There were too few <u>onions</u> on my sandwich.

4. ____ My soup was too <u>spicy</u>.

5. ____ There was too little <u>meat</u> in my soup.

6. ____ My soup had too few <u>carrots</u>.

B. *Winona has more complaints about her meal. Complete each sentence with* **too much**, **too many**, **too little**, *or* **too few**.

0. My sandwich had ____too much____ mayonnaise. I took some of it off.

1. My sandwich had _____ pickles. I asked for more.

2. My sandwich had _____ cheese. There was more than I wanted.

3. My sandwich had _____ mustard. I love mustard, and I wanted more.

4. My soup had _____ potatoes. I didn't eat all of them.

5. My soup had _____ salt, so I added some.

6. My iced tea had _____ water. It didn't have any flavor.

4 | ORANGE CAKE

Winona cooked dinner for Leslie. Complete their conversation about dessert. Circle the correct words or phrases.

LESLIE: That was an /(a)/ any wonderful dinner.
　　　　　　　　　　0.

WINONA: Thank you. Would you like some / a few / an dessert? I made an / a / a bottle of
　　　　　　　　　　　　　　　　　　　　1.　　　　　　　　　　　　　2.
orange cake.

LESLIE: Sure, it looks wonderful! Do we have a few / any / a milk?
　　　　　　　　　　　　　　　　　　　　　　　　3.

WINONA: Yes, we do. And I think I'll have a few / a / a glass of milk with my cake, too.
　　　　　　　　　　　　　　　　　　　　　　　4.

Name _____ Date _____

LESLIE: Mmm, it's delicious. My mom makes orange cake, but <u>she's / hers / her</u> isn't this
5.
good.

WINONA: Thanks. I'm glad you like it. I call it "Dad's cake" because it's my dad's favorite kind
of cake. I make it for <u>he / him / his</u> birthday every year.
6.

LESLIE: Well, I love it, too. You can make it for <u>my / me / mine</u> birthday! It's July 19th.
7.
Speaking of birthdays, when is <u>your / you / yours</u>?
8.

WINONA: November 11th.

5 | ORANGE CAKE INGREDIENTS

*A few weeks later, Leslie wants to make Winona's orange cake. Complete their conversation.
Circle the correct words or phrases.*

LESLIE: Hey, do you have <u>a /(a few)/ an</u> minutes? I want to make the orange cake you made a
0.
few weeks ago, and I need to make a list of things to buy.

WINONA: No problem. You just need <u>a little / a few / any</u> things.
1.

LESLIE: Thanks. So, I guess I need some oranges. <u>How much / How many / How little</u>
2.
oranges do you use?

WINONA: You just need <u>one / a / any</u> orange. And we have <u>a few / a quart of / a</u> orange juice in
3.   **4.**
the refrigerator, so you don't need to get more of that. Do we have <u>a / a few / any</u>
5.
vegetable oil?

LESLIE: Let me look. . . . Yes, here's <u>a few / an / a little</u> oil.
6.

WINONA: That's enough. Oh, and you need <u>a / one / any</u> egg.
7.

LESLIE: OK, I can buy eggs. <u>How much / How many / How little</u> butter do I need?
8.

WINONA: Not a lot. We have enough. Oh, is there <u>a few / any / a</u> salt around here? You need
9.
<u>a teaspoon of / a few / a</u> salt.
10.

LESLIE: Yes, here it is. Do I need to buy <u>an / any / a few</u> sugar?
11.

WINONA: No, we have a lot of sugar and flour. I think that's all you need.

LESLIE: Great. Now, I might need your help again later when I start to bake the cake!

WINONA: That's fine. I can help you.

Name _____ Date _____

6 | EDITING: CALL FROM MOM

Correct this phone conversation between Winona and her mother. There are eight mistakes. The first mistake is already corrected. (Note: There can be more than one way to correct a mistake.)

WINONA: Hello?

MOM: Hi, it's your mom. I wanted to see how ~~yours~~ *your* week is going. Am I interrupting you?

WINONA: No, I'm just eating a piece pizza for dinner.

MOM: That doesn't sound too good for you.

WINONA: Well, my roommate Leslie bought the pizza, and she gave some of it to my. She's really nice about sharing hers things.

MOM: I'm glad. So, how are your classes? Are they too very difficult?

WINONA: Not really. I think mine Spanish level is to low for the class I'm in. But I like the language department and its teachers.

MOM: Are you learning vocabulary enough?

WINONA: Actually, I have a vocabulary quiz tomorrow. I need to study for it.

MOM: OK. I'll let you go study. I just wanted to say hi.

WINONA: All right. Thanks for calling. Bye.

Name _____ Date _____

PART XI Diagnostic Test

60 Items
Score: _____

1 | LISTENING: TINA'S PLANT STORE

🎧 **A.** Robin works at Tina's Plant Store. Listen to Robin's conversation with a customer. Complete the conversation by writing the words that you hear. You will hear the recording two times.

TINA: Robin, here comes a customer. __Can you help__ him, please?
                                         0.

ROBIN: Sure! Good morning. _____ any help this morning?
                                1.

CUSTOMER: Yes. Can you show me some indoor plants? I like that one in the window. May I see it?

ROBIN: Of course. . . . Here you go.

CUSTOMER: Yeah, I like it. But I don't like the pot it's in.

ROBIN: You can change it for another one. Would you like to see one of these?

CUSTOMER: Maybe. . . . This pot looks nice.

ROBIN: Here. You can take a closer look at it.

CUSTOMER: Hmmm. OK, I'll take it.

ROBIN: Great. Would you like anything else today? You may take a look around the store if you like.

CUSTOMER: Actually, _____ me choose some flowers for my girlfriend?
                        2.

ROBIN: Sure. . . . How about these yellow roses?

CUSTOMER: Um . . . _____ the red ones instead?
                      3.

ROBIN: No problem. They're a good choice, too.

CUSTOMER: Great. I think that's everything. Do you take checks?

ROBIN: Sure.

194 | PART XI ■ DIAGNOSTIC TEST

Name _____   Date _____

B. Reread the conversation. Find three statements or questions with can or may for permission and two questions that are offers. Write them in the table below. (Note: Only use words that are given in the conversation. Do not use any words that you wrote.) An example is given.

CAN OR MAY FOR PERMISSION	OFFERS
0. May I see it?	1. _____
1. _____	2. _____
2. _____	
3. _____	

2 | PLANT INFORMATION

A. Match the facts about plants with the conclusions.

Facts

_b_ 0. Cats like to eat this plant, but it's not good for them.

____ 1. Singing to your plants probably helps them grow.

____ 2. This plant doesn't need a lot of water.

____ 3. This plant grows inside and outside.

____ 4. Last month my neighbors went on vacation.

____ 5. Dead leaves on your plant can make it sick.

____ 6. Your plant needs a bigger pot.

Conclusions

a. He had to work on it yesterday.

~~b.~~ You shouldn't leave it where a cat can get it.

c. You have to remove dead leaves.

d. I had to water their plants.

e. You should water it often.

f. You ought to put it in something bigger.

g. You should sing to your plants.

h. It doesn't have to be outside.

i. You should put it in something smaller.

j. You shouldn't water it often.

Name _____ Date _____

B. *Match these additional facts about plants with the conclusions.*

Facts

_c_ 0. This plant grows best outside.

____ 1. If this plant gets a lot of water, it will die.

____ 2. This plant is easy to take care of.

____ 3. This plant needs a lot of light.

____ 4. This plant likes warm temperatures.

____ 5. Animals can eat this plant if it's outside.

____ 6. This plant must not get direct sunlight.

Conclusions

a. You had better not leave this plant outside.

b. You had better not keep it in a sunny place.

c. You should keep it outdoors.

d. You shouldn't let it get very cold.

e. You have to remove dead leaves.

f. You must not give this plant too much water.

g. The only thing you have to do is add water.

h. You should put it in something bigger.

j. You must keep it in a sunny place.

Name _____ Date _____

3 | CONVERSATIONS IN THE STORE

Complete Tina and Robin's short conversations. Circle the correct words or phrases.

TINA: (Can you) / You can / Can clean the floor today?
　　　　　　0.

ROBIN: Sure. I'd like / I would / I'd want to wash the windows, too. I hate dirt!
　　　　　　　　1.

ROBIN: I may have / I've / May I have the day off on Saturday?
　　　　　2.

TINA: Sure. May you / Could you / You'd better work Sunday instead?
　　　　　　　3.

TINA: Want you / Would you like / You'd like this plant? I don't think anyone will buy it.
　　　　　　　4.

ROBIN: Sure, I'd like / I like / I'd want to put it in my bedroom. Thanks!
　　　　　　　5.

ROBIN: I should / I must / Should I put price tags on these flower pots?
　　　　　6.

TINA: No, would I like / I'd like / I had to clean them first.
　　　　　　7.

ROBIN: Where can I / Where I can / Can I put these flower pots?
　　　　　8.

TINA: I'd like / Would I like / I'd to like them in a safe place so people won't break them.
　　　　　9.

ROBIN: I should / Where I / Should I go to the bank?
　　　　　10.

TINA: No, you don't have to / do haven't to / have to go. I went this morning.
　　　　　　　11.

ROBIN: I can / Can I / When can I take my lunch break now?
　　　　　12.

TINA: Of course. / I'd be glad to. / Sorry you can't. Enjoy your lunch!
　　　　　13.

Name _____ Date _____

4 | ANOTHER CUSTOMER

Complete Tina's conversation with a customer. Write the letter of the best answer on each line.

ROBIN: Tina, ___a___ (a. can you wait b. I'd wait c. may you wait d. I'd like to wait) on this man?
0.

TINA: Sure. . . . Good afternoon. _____ (a. May you help b. Can I help c. Would you help
1.
d. Can you help) you, sir?

CUSTOMER: Yes, my friend's birthday is today, and I'd like to buy her a plant. _____
2.
(a. May you b. Can you c. Should you d. May I) recommend something?

TINA: Well, do you know what kind of plant you want?

CUSTOMER: _____ (a. I had better like b. I can like c. I can't like d. I'd like) something that grows
3.
quickly. _____ (a. Would you like to see b. Could you see c. Can you see d. May I see) your
4.
selection?

TINA: Sure. _____ (a. I may show b. Can I show c. Can you show d. May you show) you this
5.
plant? It grows quickly, and it's easy to care for. You _____ (a. shouldn't
6.
b. oughtn't c. had better d. mayn't) give it a lot of water. It just needs a little water a few

times a week. And it's a houseplant, so you _____ (a. can't to b. would like to c. may
7.
not d. should) leave it outside. Keep it inside by a window.

CUSTOMER: OK, _____ (a. I would b. I'd like to c. you would like to d. you have to) get it. But I have a
8.
question. _____ (a. I should b. Would you like to c. Can I d. Do I have to) leave it in my
9.
car for a few hours before I go to my friend's apartment? Is that OK?

TINA: Sorry, _____ (a. you shouldn't b. you should c. you had better d. you may) leave it in
10.
there, because the warm air isn't good for it. Let me ring you up. _____ (a. Could
11.
you give me b. May I please get c. Can I have d. Would you like) a bag for the plant?

CUSTOMER: Yes, please.

TINA: Here's your receipt. _____ (a. Can I b. Would you please c. Where should I d. Where may I)
12.
put it in your bag?

CUSTOMER: That's fine. _____ (a. Would you like b. May you please c. Could you please d. May I please)
13.
help me carry the bag to the car?

TINA: Of course.

Name _____ Date _____

5 | CACTUS GARDEN

Tina writes a weekly article about growing plants for a newspaper. Complete each sentence with a word or phrase to indicate advice or necessity. The first letter of each word or phrase is provided. Some items may have more than one right answer.

If you want inexpensive and easy plants, you s__**hould**__ (0.) think about growing cactus plants. Cactuses are attractive, and they're easy to care for. They don't need a lot of water, so you d_____ (1.) spend a lot of time watering them.

Cactuses grow well with a lot of sunlight. So, you s_____ (2.) put your cactus plants in a place that gets direct sunlight. Cactuses also need nutrients. Many plant specialists agree that you h_____ (3.) give them nutrients every other week.

One big mistake people make is giving cactuses more water than they need. You'd b_____ (4.) water your cactus plants very often. If you do, they might die. You o_____ (5.) give your cactuses water only when the plants begin to look dry.

For more information on caring for your cactus plants, visit www.tinasplantstore.com.

6 | EDITING: TINA'S WEBSITE

Correct this page from Tina's website about plants. There are 10 mistakes. The first mistake is already corrected.

If you have a pond, you should ~~to~~ think about adding water plants. These are plants that live on or in the water. Many water plants have to beautiful flowers.

But before you start your water garden, you better had plan your planting schedule. Usually, you have start water gardens in the spring.

Once you have water plants, you better not change the water in your pond often because it's not good for the plants. Instead, you have to finding a way to clean the water. You haven't to have fish, but they can help keep your pond clean. The fish eat tiny insects in the water, and you don't have feed them anything else.

Water plants should not to cover more than half of your pond. If your plants cover more than half the water, you have remove some of them. Click here to see photos of water plants.

Name _____ Date _____

Unit 36 Achievement Test

30 Items
Score: _____

1 | LISTENING: SHOPPING FOR A DIGITAL CAMERA

🎧 **A.** *Listen to Marty's conversation with a salesperson. Complete the conversation by writing the words that you hear. You will hear the recording two times.*

MARTY: Excuse me. Can I ask you a question?

SALESPERSON: Sure you can.

MARTY: May I look at those digital cameras behind the glass?

SALESPERSON: Certainly. Which one do you want to look at first?

MARTY: ____Can I see____ the small black one? Oh, and may I see the one next to it, too?
　　　　　　0.

SALESPERSON: Sure. Here you are. _____ you decide between them?
　　　　　　　　　　　　　　　　　　　　　1.

MARTY: I'm not sure. Can I take a picture with this one?

SALESPERSON: That's fine, but you may not take more than a few.

MARTY: _____ take the pictures?
　　　　　　2.

SALESPERSON: Anywhere in the store.

MARTY: I want to try photographing people. Can I take your picture?

SALESPERSON: Sure.

MARTY: Thanks. May I take the camera outside to try it there?

SALESPERSON: I'm sorry, but you can't take anything out of the store without buying it. But you can try it outside if you buy it.

MARTY: If I'm not happy with the camera, may I return it?

SALESPERSON: Yes. You may return it within 30 days. Just keep your receipt.

MARTY: OK. _____ the instructions for this camera?
　　　　　　　　3.

SALESPERSON: Of course.

200 | UNIT 36 ■ ACHIEVEMENT TEST

Name _____ Date _____

B. *Reread the conversation. Complete these sentences. Circle the correct words or phrases.*

0. (It's OK to)/ Marty can't ask the salesperson a question.

1. Marty has permission to / can't see the small black camera.

2. The salesperson gives / doesn't give Marty permission to take a picture with a camera.

3. It's OK to / Marty can't take a lot of pictures with the camera.

4. Marty has permission to / can't take the salesperson's picture.

5. It's OK / not OK to take the camera outside without buying it.

6. Marty can / can't return the camera if he is not happy with it after buying it.

2 | AT THE ART MUSEUM

Marty and his friend Shannon are at an art museum. Complete Marty's conversation with a museum worker. Use the sentences and questions in the box.

> Can I take my camera in with me?
> May I have change for a dollar?
> Can I leave it somewhere?
> But you may not take food in the museum.
> May we go into the modern art section?
> Can I take my bottle of water with me?
> ~~May I have two tickets, please?~~
> Can I take food in with me?
> But you may not take any photos with a flash.
> Can I have one, please?
> You can visit any section of the museum that you like.
> You can leave your bag in the lockers downstairs.
> Can I have a map, please?

Name _____   Date _____

MARTY: <u>May I have two tickets, please?</u>
0.

MUSEUM WORKER: Certainly. That'll be $14 dollars for two.

MARTY: Here you go. Oh, and I need a receipt. _____
1.

MUSEUM WORKER: Sure. Here are your tickets and your receipt.

MARTY: Thank you. I have a couple questions. My bag is really heavy, so I don't want to carry it. _____
2.

MUSEUM WORKER: Yes. _____
3.

MARTY: Great. And I want to take some photos of the art. _____
4.

MUSEUM WORKER: Yes, it's OK to take your camera. _____
5.
The flash damages the artwork.

MARTY: I understand. _____ Or is that section
6.
still closed?

MUSEUM WORKER: No, it's not closed anymore. _____
7.

MARTY: That's great. But this museum is so big that I'm afraid of getting lost.
_____
8.

MUSEUM WORKER: Sure, here you go.

MARTY: Sorry, one more question. _____
9.

MUSEUM WORKER: No, but there are water fountains throughout the building.

MARTY: OK, thank you.

Name _____ Date _____

3 | THE MUSEUM CAFÉ

*Marty and Shannon are still in the museum, and they want to get some lunch. Read their conversations with a museum worker and a waiter at the museum café. Then read each statement and circle **T** (true) or **F** (false).*

[In the museum]

SHANNON: I'm getting hungry. Can we go to the café for lunch?

MARTY: Sure, but I don't know where it is. Let me ask that woman. Excuse me.

MUSEUM WORKER: Can I help you?

SHANNON: Yes. We're looking for the café.

MUSEUM WORKER: Sure. The café for visitors is on the third floor. You might also notice that there's a café on the second floor, but you can't eat there because it's only for employees.

SHANNON: Can we take this elevator here?

MUSEUM WORKER: I'm sorry, but you can't take the south elevator because it's closed right now. But the north elevator is working. Or you may use the stairs. If you like, you may also leave the museum and go to a restaurant and then come back.

MARTY: Great. Thank you.

[In the museum café]

WAITER: May I bring you something to drink, or do you want to look over the menu first?

SHANNON: I'll have a lemonade, please. But can we move to a different table? This one is too near the restrooms.

WAITER: Sure. I'll clean that table over there for you in a minute. Can I get something for you to drink, sir?

MARTY: I'll have an iced tea, please. But can I get it without sugar? I can't have sugar on my diet, but I can have sugar substitute.

WAITER: Sure, I'll be right back.

T (F) 0. Marty asked Shannon if it was OK to go to the café for lunch.

T F 1. The museum worker offered help to Marty and Shannon.

T F 2. It's OK for Marty and Shannon to eat in the café on the second floor.

T F 3. It's not OK for Marty and Shannon to take the south elevator.

T F 4. It's not OK for Marty and Shannon to use the stairs.

T F 5. It's not OK for Marty and Shannon to go to a restaurant for lunch.

T F 6. The waiter offered to bring Shannon and Marty something to drink.

T F 7. It's OK for Marty and Shannon to move to a different table.

T F 8. It's OK for Marty to have sugar substitute.

Name _____   Date _____

4 | EDITING: CALLING THE DOCTOR

Marty ate something bad at the museum café, and his stomach hurts a lot. Correct his telephone conversations as he tries to communicate with his doctor. There are five mistakes. The first mistake is already corrected. (Note: There can be more than one way to correct a mistake.)

DIRECTORY ASSISTANCE: Directory Assistance, what city and listing please?

MARTY: Seattle. Can you ~~gives~~ *give* me the number for Dr. Jacob Stephen?

DIRECTORY ASSISTANCE: Sure. The number is 555-3094. Hold on, I'll connect you. . . .

SECRETARY: Dr. Stephen's office. May I helping you?

MARTY: Yes, may I to speak with Dr. Stephen, please?

SECRETARY: I'm sorry, he's not available now. Can I help you?

MARTY: No, thanks. I really need to talk to the doctor. I can have his cell phone number?

SECRETARY: I'm sorry, you mayn't have his cell phone number. But if you give me your name and number, Dr. Stephen can call you back.

Name _____ Date _____

Unit 37 Achievement Test

30 Items
Score: _____

1 | LISTENING: DINNER PLANS

Listen to Dustin's conversation with Carla. Complete the conversation by circling the words that you hear. You will hear the recording two times.

DUSTIN: Hey, Carla. (Would you like to)/ Can you / Could you go to lunch with me?
                                     0.

CARLA: Sorry, I can't. I have a lot of work right now, but I'd like to / I'd be glad to / could you
                                                                                                                              1.

go another time.

DUSTIN: OK. Well, I don't have any plans for this evening.

Can you / Would you like to / Do you want to go to dinner tonight?
                                2.

CARLA: Yes. That's perfect. Would you / Could you / Can you pick me up at 6:00?
                                                        3.

DUSTIN: Sure. Where do you want to go?

CARLA: Would you like / You'd like / I'd like to try that new sushi restaurant downtown. How
                      4.

does that sound?

DUSTIN: Well, I'd like to eat / sorry, I can't eat / would like to eat sushi, but I'm allergic to
                                              5.

seafood. Can you think of another place?

CARLA: Let me see. . . . Oh, I know! How about the Mexican restaurant on Broadway?

You'd like / Would you like / I'd like that a lot.
                              6.

DUSTIN: Yeah, that sounds great. So, I'll see you at 6:00.

CARLA: Actually, could you / would you like to / can you make it 6:30 instead? That way you
                                            7.

won't have to hurry to get there.

DUSTIN: All right. I'll see you at 6:30.

CARLA: And would you / can you / could you please do me a favor and call me a few minutes
                               8.

before you get to my apartment?

DUSTIN: No problem, but can you / would you like to / could you remind me where you live?
                                                  9.

CARLA: 301 Chestnut Street. It's the red building on the corner.

Name _____ **Date** _____

2 | AT THE RESTAURANT

Dustin and Carla are ordering dinner at the Mexican restaurant. Complete their conversation with the waiter. Circle the correct words or phrases.

WAITER: Hello, I'm Michael. I'll be your waiter. (Can you tell) / tell you / would you me what
 0.
you'd like to drink?

CARLA: Sure / I be glad to / No thanks. Could you bring me a glass of *horchata*?
 1.

WAITER: OK, and for you, sir?

DUSTIN: I like / what / I'd like some water. You can / Can you / Do you want bring some lemon
 2. 3.
with that?

WAITER: Of course. Would you like / Want you / Would like some more time to look at the
 4.
menu?

DUSTIN: No, we could like / we'd like / we would to order now.
 5.

WAITER: OK. Go ahead.

CARLA: You would / Want you / Would you please bring me the chicken enchiladas?
 6.

WAITER: Sure. Would you like / Want you / You'd like a side salad?
 7.

CARLA: Yes, that sounds good.

WAITER: OK. And for you, sir?

DUSTIN: I like / I'd like / I'd want the *carne asada*.
 8.

WAITER: And would you like / you'd like / want you a salad as well?
 9.

DUSTIN: Yes, please.

Name _____ Date _____

3 | DESSERT

Dustin and Carla are ordering dessert. Complete their conversation with the waiter. Write the letter of the best answer on each line.

DUSTIN: I'm still a bit hungry. __a__ (a. I'd like b. I'd liking c. Would I like d. I like would) some
0.
dessert. What about you? _____ (a. Would you like b. You'd like c. Like you'd d. You'd)
1.
anything?

CARLA: Yes, _____ (a. I'd liking b. I like would c. I'd like d. Would I like) some fried ice cream. It's
2.
supposed to be really good here.

DUSTIN: That sounds great. I'll get the waiter. Excuse me. _____ (a. Can you to bring
3.
b. Can you bring c. You can bring d. Can bring) us a dessert menu, please?

WAITER: Of course. Here you are. _____ (a. You'd b. Would you like c. You'd like d. Like you'd) to try
4.
our famous fried ice cream?

DUSTIN: _____ (a. Yes, thank you. b. Yes, we'd to like some. c. No, would we not. d. No, we not would like
5.
any.)

WAITER: OK, we have two choices: chocolate and vanilla.

CARLA: _____ (a. I'd like b. Would I like c. I'd liking d. I would to like) the vanilla.
6.

DUSTIN: _____ (a. Can get you me b. Can you me c. Can you get me d. You can get me) the same thing,
7.
please?

WAITER: OK, I'll bring those right out for you. _____ (a. Would you to like b. You would like
8.
c. Would you like d. Would you liking) some coffee with your dessert?

DUSTIN: Yes, please.

CARLA: I would too, please.

DUSTIN: And _____ (a. You would bring b. Bring you would c. Would you d. Would you bring) us the
9.
check as well?

WAITER: No problem.

4 | EDITING: AFTER DINNER

Correct Dustin and Carla's conversation after dinner. There are four mistakes. The first mistake is already corrected.

DUSTIN: Oh, Carla, ~~you can~~ *can you* do me a favor?

CARLA: Sure, what is it?

DUSTIN: Could you to lend me some money? Since we're on this side of town, I'd like to stop by the pharmacy. I want to get a few things, but I don't have enough money.

CARLA: Of the course.

DUSTIN: Would you like come in with me?

CARLA: Sure.

Name _____ Date _____

Unit 38 Achievement Test

30 Items
Score: _____

1 | LISTENING: CAREER ADVICE

🎧 **A.** *Listen to this radio show about career advice. Complete the show by writing the words that you hear. You will hear the recording two times.*

EDDIE: Welcome back to the show. I'm Employment Eddie. Our next caller is in Santa Fe, New Mexico. Hi, Ron. What's up?

RON: Hi, Eddie. Here's my question: What ___*should I do*___ about my career? Right
                                              0.
now, I'm the manager of a pet store. I make good money, but I think I ought to do something different with my life. I think I ought to become a teacher. My wife says I _____ it, but I'm afraid. I don't know what to do. Should I keep my
          1.
present job? Or _____ my dream and become a teacher? It's something
                      2.
I've been thinking about for a long time.

EDDIE: Well, Ron, you _____ in a job just because you're afraid to change. But
                              3.
you shouldn't be irresponsible, either. Do you know much about teaching?

RON: No, not a lot.

EDDIE: Well, _____ a decision without all the facts. Talk to some teachers. And
              4.
you shouldn't talk to just one or two. Talk to as many different teachers as you can. Find out what their jobs are really like. And you'd better make sure your wife supports you.

RON: Oh, she does.

EDDIE: Great. But you'd better not quit your job yet. Take a couple of night classes while you work, and see how you feel about teaching. Then you can make an educated decision.

RON: OK, Eddie. Thanks for the advice.

Name _____ Date _____

B. *Reread the conversation. Find one question about advice and five statements of advice. Write them in the table below. (Note: Only use sentences that are given in the conversation. Do not use any sentences that you wrote.) An example is given.*

QUESTION ABOUT ADVICE	STATEMENTS OF ADVICE
1. _____	0. *I ought to do something different with my life.*
	1. _____
	2. _____
	3. _____
	4. _____
	5. _____

2 | PET ADVICE

Read each numbered statement about the pets at Ron's pet store. Then circle the letter of the sentence that best describes each situation.

0. The cat needs to have its shots.
   a. The cat should have its shots. *(circled)*
   b. The cat shouldn't have its shots.
   c. The cat had better not have its shots.

1. That dog is too fat.
   a. We'd better put that dog on a diet.
   b. That dog had better eat more.
   c. That dog should gain weight.

2. Chocolate isn't good for dogs.
   a. Dogs had better eat chocolate.
   b. Dogs ought to eat chocolate.
   c. Dogs shouldn't eat chocolate.

3. This dog needs to exercise.
   a. This dog ought to walk less.
   b. This dog had better not walk too much.
   c. This dog should walk more.

4. This cat needs its medicine regularly.
   a. We shouldn't remember to give this cat its medicine.
   b. We'd better not forget to give this cat its medicine.
   c. This cat had better not take its medicine.

Name _____ Date _____

3 | RON'S CAREER

Read each numbered statement about Ron's career. Then circle the letter of the sentence that best describes each situation.

0. Ron needs to think about his decision.
   a. Ron had better not think about his decision.
   (b.) Ron ought to think about his decision.
   c. Ron shouldn't think about his decision.

1. Ron doesn't like working at the pet store anymore.
   a. Ron ought to keep working at the pet store.
   b. Ron shouldn't continue to work at the pet store.
   c. Ron should buy some pets.

2. Ron wants to teach science.
   a. He shouldn't teach science.
   b. He shouldn't enjoy science.
   c. He'd better learn to teach science.

3. Ron doesn't know a lot about teaching.
   a. He should find out more about teaching.
   b. He'd better be a teacher.
   c. He should be a teacher.

4. The last day for Ron to sign up for classes is June 1.
   a. He shouldn't sign up before June 1.
   b. He had better sign up after June 1.
   c. He ought to sign up before June 1.

5. Ron thinks he will love teaching, but he doesn't have teaching experience.
   a. He should get some teaching experience.
   b. He ought to stop teaching.
   c. He'd better not get teaching experience.

Name _____ Date _____

4 | BASIC TIPS FOR DOG OWNERS

Complete Ron's list of basic tips for dog owners. Use the words in parentheses and the verbs in the box.

~~brush~~	forget	go	let	put	take
fill	give	leave	play	return	

0. You __*should brush*__ your dog's teeth at least once a week.
   (should)

1. You _____ with your dog often. Dogs need to have fun and exercise every day.
   (ought to)

2. You _____ fresh water in your dog's water bowl several times each day. Dogs
   (should)
   need a lot of water to stay cool and healthy.

3. You _____ your dog alone in a car. Even if the windows are down, your dog
   (should, not)
   can get too hot and become sick very quickly.

4. You _____ your dog go outside without a leash. It's safer for your dog, other
   (had better, not)
   dogs, and other people if your dog is on a leash. In some places it's even illegal to take your
   dog in public without a leash.

5. You _____ your dog to the veterinarian, or animal doctor, for regular checkups
   (had better)
   at least once a year. It's important to keep your dog healthy.

6. You _____ your dog too much food. Dogs can get fat if they eat extra food.
   (should, not)

5 | EDITING: BACK IN SCHOOL

Ron started classes to become a teacher. Correct his conversation with his wife, Tanya. There are six mistakes. The first mistake is already corrected.

TANYA: What do you want to do tonight?

RON: I ought ˄to finish some homework. Then I better had study for a test.

TANYA: You're so busy with work and school. I want to help you. Should I to do something?

RON: I don't think you can really do anything. I should just organize my schedule better.

TANYA: Well, you shouldn't to work so much now that you're back in school. You ought to working only in the mornings. That way, you can study more.

RON: You're right. Besides, I've better not complain. Going back to school was my idea!

Name _____   Date _____

Unit 39 Achievement Test

30 Items
Score: _____

1 LISTENING: PLANS FOR THE DAY

🎧 **A.** *Listen to Keith's conversation with his roommate, Don. Complete their conversation by writing the words that you hear. You will hear the recording two times.*

DON: Hey, aren't your parents coming to visit tonight?

KEITH: Yes. They'll be here this evening, and I have so much to do! To start with, I ___have to clean___ the apartment, and I have to wash my clothes.
                                                                                 0.

DON: _____ for your history test, too?
              1.

KEITH: Yes. I have to take it this afternoon, and I have to prepare for it if I'm going to do well. I also have to wash the car.

DON: I remember you complaining about some English assignment. Do you still _____ that in?
                                                                                                    2.

KEITH: Yeah, I have to give that to my professor by 5:00.

DON: Well, you don't have to do everything by yourself. I can help.

KEITH: Oh, you don't have to help. I know you're busy.

DON: We're both busy, but I live here, too. I'll clean the apartment. Don't worry about it.

KEITH: Thanks, Don. I really appreciate it. I'm going to put some clothes in the washer, then I _____ study.
                                                                                                         3.

DON: OK. Since I have some free time, I'll get started on the cleaning right now.

B. *Reread the conversation. Then read each statement and circle **T** (true) or **F** (false).*

Ⓣ **F** 0. Keith needs to wash his clothes.

T **F** 1. Keith needs to take a test today.

T **F** 2. Keith doesn't need to prepare for his test.

T **F** 3. Keith needs to wash the car.

T **F** 4. Keith must give an assignment to his English professor.

T **F** 5. Don thinks Keith doesn't need to do everything by himself.

T **F** 6. Keith says Don doesn't need to help clean the apartment.

UNIT 39 ■ ACHIEVEMENT TEST   213

Name _____   Date _____

2 | FACTS AND CONCLUSIONS

Match the facts about Keith with the conclusions.

Facts

_f_ 0. Keith's car is very dirty.

____ 1. The floor is clean.

____ 2. Keith's clothes are dirty.

____ 3. Keith has a test today.

____ 4. Keith had a big project due today.

____ 5. Keith doesn't have any food for lunch.

____ 6. Keith is planning a surprise party for his mother.

____ 7. Keith is allergic to eggs and milk.

____ 8. Keith and his parents are going to a restaurant for dinner.

Conclusions

a. He had to work on it yesterday.

b. He must not eat those foods.

c. He must tell her about it.

d. He has to go to the grocery store.

e. Keith has to wash them.

~~f.~~ Keith has to take it to the car wash.

g. He has to clean it.

h. Keith doesn't have to cook dinner.

i. He must study soon.

j. Keith doesn't have to clean it.

k. Keith must not say anything to her about it.

3 AT DINNER

Complete Keith's conversation with his parents at a restaurant. Use the correct forms of the words in parentheses. Put the words in the correct order.

MOM: Oh, the food here is so good! But I'm eating too much. **I have to go** on a diet.
　　　　　　　　　　　　　　　　　　　　　　　　　　　　　0. (go / I / have to)

DAD: You know, Keith, she always says the same thing: _____ a little weight.
　　　　　　　　　　　　　　　　　　　　　　　　　1. (she / have to / lose)

KEITH: That's true. Mom, _____ everything on your plate if you're full.
　　　　　　　　　　　　2. (you / eat / not / have to)

MOM: I know. But enough about me. Let's talk about our plans for the weekend.

_____, Keith?
3. (have to / you / work)

KEITH: Tomorrow, yes. But _____ there on Sunday. Actually, I'm glad you didn't
　　　　　　　　　　　　　4. (be / have to / I / not)

get here earlier. _____ in yesterday, too.
　　　　　　　　5. (go / have to / I)

DAD: Well I'm glad we have a little time together tonight. I'd like to get back to the hotel

early, though. I'm tired, and _____ some things before bed.
　　　　　　　　　　　　　　　6. (your mom / have to / do)

MOM: Yes, _____ my suitcase. You know I like to be organized.
　　　　7. (I / unpack / have to)

KEITH: OK. _____ some homework anyway. What about Sunday?
　　　　8. (have to / I / finish)

_____ at a certain time?
9. (leave / have to / you)

DAD: No, we're flexible. We can stay most of the day.

4 EDITING: AT THE HOTEL

After dinner, Keith's parents, Debra and Collin, return to their hotel. Correct their conversation. There are five mistakes. The first mistake is already corrected.

　　buy
DEBRA: That was a nice dinner. But Keith looks too thin! We have to ~~buying~~ him some food!

COLLIN: Well, you mustn't to forget that he is an adult. He can take care of himself. And he has

plenty of food at his apartment.

DEBRA: Well, I want to take him some food, even if you think it's not necessary.

COLLIN: OK, but you not have to go to the store right now. Why don't you wait until tomorrow

morning? Let's go to bed. I'm so tired!

DEBRA: OK, but I am must brush my teeth, and I have take a shower first. But you don't have

to wait for me. You can go to bed now if you're tired.

Name _____   Date _____

Part XI Achievement Test

60 Items
Score: _____

1 | LISTENING: SHOPPING FOR A PET

🎧 **A.** Randall works at Tito's pet store. Listen to Randall's conversation with a customer. Complete the conversation by writing the words that you hear. You will hear the recording two times.

TITO: Randall, I __*have to finish*__ this paperwork. Can you help this customer, please?
                        0.

RANDALL: Sure! Good afternoon. Welcome to Tito's Pets.

CUSTOMER: Hi. I'd like a fish for my apartment. _____ me what you have?
                                                            1.

RANDALL: Of course. These fish right here make nice pets.

CUSTOMER: I was thinking about something smaller. May I see what other kinds you have?

RANDALL: Sure. These fish here are nice, too. They're small, and they're very easy to care for.

CUSTOMER: Yeah, that's more like what I was thinking about.

RANDALL: Would you like to take one of these?

CUSTOMER: Yes, I think so.

RANDALL: You can pick the one you like.

CUSTOMER: I'll take the striped one.

RANDALL: Of course. I'll put it in a bag for you. But you can't keep it in there too long. You'll need a fishbowl when you get home. Would you like to see some of our fishbowls? We have some right here.

CUSTOMER: Ummm . . . that one looks good. I'll take it and the fish, please.

RANDALL: _____ to buy some fish food, too?
              2.

CUSTOMER: Yeah. I'd like this food here.

RANDALL: Certainly. OK, your total is $34.99.

CUSTOMER: _____ you a check?
              3.

RANDALL: Only if you have identification. You may not write a check without a photo ID.

CUSTOMER: No problem. I have my driver's license right here.

Name _____ Date _____

B. Reread the conversation. Find three statements or questions with *can* or *may* for permission and two questions that are offers. Write them in the table below. (Note: Only use sentences that are given in the conversation. Do not use any sentences that you wrote.) An example is given.

CAN OR MAY FOR PERMISSION	OFFERS
0. *May I see what other kinds you have?*	1. _____
1. _____	2. _____
2. _____	
3. _____	

2 | PET INFORMATION

A. Match the facts about pets with the conclusions.

Facts

_g_ 0. Cats like to eat fish.

____ 1. Exercise keeps your dog healthy.

____ 2. Raw meat is bad for dogs.

____ 3. Cats enjoy being outdoors.

____ 4. Last month my neighbors went on vacation.

____ 5. Your pet needs fresh water any time it wants it.

____ 6. Fish are probably the easiest pets to take care of.

Conclusions

a. He had to work on it yesterday.

b. You should keep fresh water in your pet's bowl.

c. You don't have to do a lot for them.

d. Your dog should exercise every day.

e. You have to do a lot for them.

f. You shouldn't play with your dog.

~~g.~~ You shouldn't leave pet fish where a cat can get them.

h. But they don't have to go outdoors to be healthy.

i. I had to take care of their pets.

j. You shouldn't feed it to them.

Name _____ **Date** _____

B. *Match some additional facts about pets with the conclusions.*

Facts

_c_ 0. Dogs can develop dental problems.

____ 1. Snakes need to be warm.

____ 2. Chocolate is bad for dogs.

____ 3. Dogs like to be with people.

____ 4. Dogs can get into trouble if you walk them without a leash.

____ 5. Birds need vitamins to stay healthy.

____ 6. This fish is too fat.

Conclusions

a. You had better not walk your dog without a leash.

b. You ought to walk your dog without a leash.

c. You should brush their teeth.

d. You must let them get cold.

e. You'd better not leave them alone for a long time.

f. They must not get very cold.

g. You ought to give it less food.

h. You have to give your bird vitamins.

i. You must not let them eat it.

j. It should eat it more.

Name _____ Date _____

3 | CONVERSATIONS IN THE PET STORE

Complete Tito and Randall's short conversations. Circle the correct answers.

TITO: You can / (Can you) / Can move this box of dog toys?
                     0.

RANDALL: OK. I'd like / I'd would like / I like to move the dog food, too. People can't see it
                                             1.

here.

TITO: You could / Could you / You work on Sunday afternoon?
                      2.

RANDALL: That depends. Could you trade / You could trade / Could trade you shifts with me on
                                            3.

Monday?

TITO: You would like / I'd like you / Would you like this bone for your dog? It came
                                4.

out of its package.

RANDALL: No, thanks. I'd like / I like / I would to start giving him more nutritious foods.
                                   5.

RANDALL: I should / Should / Should I order more of this fish food?
                       6.

TITO: No. I'd like / I like / I to order a different brand next time.
                    7.

RANDALL: Can I where / Where can I / Can I put the cat calendars?
                       8.

TITO: I'd like / Would I like / I'd to like them near the front.
                 9.

RANDALL: I may feed / May I feed / I feed the cats now?
                  10.

TITO: Sure. Here's the food. Could you to feed / You could feed / Could you feed the dogs
                                            11.

too?

RANDALL: Should I clean / I should clean / Clean I should the floor before I leave?
                      12.

TITO: You don't have / don't have to / do haven't to clean the floor. I'll do it.
                         13.

Name _____   Date _____

4 | ANOTHER CUSTOMER

Complete Tito's conversation with a customer. Write the letter of the best answer on each line.

RANDALL: Tito, __c__ (a. may you help b. I'd help c. can you help d. I'd like to help) this customer?
　　　　　　　　0.

TITO: Sure. . . . _____ (a. May you help b. Can I help c. Would I help d. Can you help) you?
　　　　　　　　1.

CUSTOMER: Yes. I'm looking for a fish for a birthday gift, and _____ (a. would like b. would I
　　　　　　　　　　　　　　　　　　　　　　　　　　　　　　　　　　　2.
like c. I'd better like d. I'd like) some suggestions. I know _____ (a. I can b. I may c. I'd
　　　　　　　　　　　　　　　　　　　　　　　　　　　　　　　　　3.
better d. I'd like) something unusual. _____ (a. Would you like to b. I can see c. Ought I
　　　　　　　　　　　　　　　　　　　　4.
d. May I) see what you have?

TITO: Sure. And _____ (a. do you have to b. could you please c. would you like to d. may I)
　　　　　　　　5.
suggest this fish? The colors are very unusual.

CUSTOMER: Yeah, it's very pretty. _____ (a. Would you like to b. Could you tell me how to c. Could you
　　　　　　　　　　　　　　　　　　6.
d. Can I) care for it?

TITO: Of course. It's easy. _____ (a. You should b. You shouldn't to c. Should you d. You ought)
　　　　　　　　　　　　　7.
feed it just once a day.

CUSTOMER: And I heard that _____ (a. you can give b. may give you c. can give you d. can give) fish
　　　　　　　　　　　　　8.
extra food on one day and none on the next. Is that true?

TITO: No. You _____ (a. shouldn't b. oughtn't c. can't to d. mayn't) give them a lot of food
　　　　　　　　9.
at one time. A little each day is best. And these fish don't like changes in their water
temperature. So you _____ (a. may let b. had better let c. can't let d. would like to let) its
　　　　　　　　　　　10.
water get too cold.

CUSTOMER: OK, and how do I take the fish home? _____ (a. Would you please b. Can I c. Could
　　　　　　　　　　　　　　　　　　　　　　　11.
you d. Can you) take it in a bag, or do I need a special container?

TITO: I'll give you a container so the fish is safe. _____ (a. Would you like b. May you like
　　　　　　　　　　　　　　　　　　　　　　　　　　　　12.
c. Can you need d. May I need) anything else?

CUSTOMER: Just one thing. _____ (a. Could you please b. May you please c. Would you like d. May I
　　　　　　　　　　　13.
please) tell me what kind of food to get?

TITO: Sure. This brand is very good.

220 | PART XI ■ ACHIEVEMENT TEST

Name _____ Date _____

5 | PARROTS

Tito writes pet care tips for a newspaper. Complete each sentence with a word or phrase to indicate advice or necessity. The first letter of each word or phrase is provided. Some items may have more than one right answer.

If you are thinking about getting a pet, you s___*hould*___ think about getting a
                                                      0.
parrot. Parrots are beautiful tropical birds that can learn to copy human speech. They are

intelligent. They don't need a lot of exercise, and they usually live for a long time.

These birds like attention. So if you get a parrot, you s_____ give it a lot of
                                                              1.
attention. Also, parrots need fresh food and water every day. You h_____ feed
                                                                         2.
them and change their water daily. But extra food isn't good for them either. You'd

b_____ give a parrot more food than it needs. Parrots like to play with toys, so
   3.
you o_____ have some toys for him or her. The toys d_____ be
        4.   **5.**
expensive or complicated. Simple, homemade toys can entertain parrots for hours.

For more information on caring for parrots, visit www.titospets.com.

6 | EDITING: TITO'S WEBSITE

Correct this page from Tito's website about pets. There are 10 mistakes. The first mistake is already corrected.

If you have a child, you should ~~to~~ think carefully before adding a dog to your family. Some

dogs are great with children, but you have to being careful with others. You always have watch

your child when he or she is with a dog. A dog can be a wonderful addition to a family, but you

better had understand that it is a big responsibility as well.

Before you buy any dog, you'd better had see how it acts with the child. Don't take the dog

home if the dog and your child do not get along. You have not to take the dog home to know

that you're choosing the right dog.

You don't have buying a specific kind of dog to be sure that it is good with children. Training

your dog is more important than the kind of dog that it is.

Your dog shouldn't to conflict with your lifestyle. You have be sure you have the time and

energy to care for your child *and* a dog. Would like you to see tips on dog training? Click here.

Name _____ Date _____

PART XII Diagnostic Test

60 Items
Score: _____

1 | LISTENING: STOCKMANS

🎧 **A.** *Listen to this radio ad for a grocery store called Stockmans. Complete the ad by writing the words that you hear. You will hear the recording two times.*

___Which store___ offers you better prices than any other in town? Which store has
0.

_____ fruits than anyone else? _____ has more tender cuts of meat
1.   2.

than the store you shop at now? Stockmans! At Stockmans, we have _____
3.

produce. The fruits and vegetables in our store taste _____ they do on the local
4.

farms where they're grown. We also sell the finest baked goods available. We guarantee that our

products are the most excellent _____!
5.

Stockmans is _____ other stores. Other stores _____ listen to
6.   7.

their customers. Other stores are too expensive, and the quality of their products is too low! At

Stockmans, we really understand our customers' needs. That's the reason that our prices are less

expensive than those at other stores. And our employees are friendlier than anywhere else.

Stockmans: It's where you deserve to shop!

B. *Read each statement based on the radio ad. Write **C** if the underlined word or phrase is a comparative adjective, **S** if it is a superlative adjective, **ADJ** if it is an adjective, and **ADV** if it is an adverb.*

0. __C__ Stockmans has <u>better</u> prices than any other store in town.

1. _____ Stockmans sells the <u>finest</u> baked goods available.

2. _____ Other grocery stores are too <u>expensive</u>.

3. _____ The quality of products at other grocery stores is too <u>low</u>.

4. _____ Stockmans <u>really</u> understands its customers' needs.

5. _____ Stockmans's prices are <u>less expensive</u> than the prices at other stores.

6. _____ Stockmans's staff is <u>friendlier</u> than the staff at other grocery stores.

Name _____ Date _____

2 | MAKING A RADIO AD

Monique, an advertising specialist, and her client Reed are developing a radio ad for Computer One, Reed's computer store. Complete their conversation. Circle the correct phrases.

MONIQUE: How does the ad sound to you?

REED: The music is a little very slow / (too slow) / slow enough. I like that the music is
0.
the same from / different as / different from the music in our old ad. But the new
1.
music isn't too exciting / as exciting as / exciting enough the music from our old ad.
2.
The new music should be fast and exciting.

MONIQUE: Let me speed it up a bit. Now is it fast enough / as fast as / enough fast?
3.

REED: It still sounds boring enough / as boring as / too boring. The melody is
4.
very nice / too nice / as nice as, but the brass section isn't
5.
enough loud / much too loud / loud enough.
6.

MONIQUE: Let me adjust it. Now does the brass section sound better?

REED: Yes, but now the music might be as loud as / too loud / enough loud. I don't think
7.
the voice should be the same volume as / different volume as / too volume the music.
8.
The speaker's voice is enough soft / as soft as / too soft.
9.

MONIQUE: Really? Do you think she was too quiet / quiet enough / as quiet as? I thought she
10.
was enough loud / loud enough / as loud as.
11.

REED: Not really. Her voice isn't as loud as / loud enough / very loud it should be.
12.

MONIQUE: I think I can fix that on the computer. All right. Let's try it now. . . .

3 | AD FOR COMPUTER ONE

Read the radio advertisement. Find three comparative adjectives, three superlative adjectives, and four adverbs. Write them in the table on the next page. (Note: Be sure to write the entire word or phrase.) An example is given.

Name _____ Date _____

Computer One is more likely than any other store to have the computer parts you need. We have a larger selection of computer accessories than anyone else. Computer One also has the most helpful staff in the area! Our staff is more knowledgeable than staff you'll find anywhere else. And now is a great time to visit Computer One because we're having a special sale this week! Everything is 10 percent off! If your computer operates slowly, we can upgrade it to run fast. If you want a flatter screen for your computer, we have a great selection for you to choose from. If your speakers perform badly, you should come look at our selection of loud speakers. We're one of the most popular computer businesses in the state, so call us today! You can easily save lots of money when you shop at Computer One! We guarantee that Computer One has the cheapest prices.

COMPARATIVE ADJECTIVES	SUPERLATIVE ADJECTIVES	ADVERBS
0. more likely	1. _____	1. _____
1. _____	2. _____	2. _____
2. _____	3. _____	3. _____
3. _____		4. _____

4 | ADVERTISER OF THE YEAR

A. *A group of judges is choosing a winner for an advertising contest. They are comparing the top two candidates. Write their questions with comparative adjectives. Use the words in parentheses.*

0. (Which / advertiser / productive)

   Which advertiser is more productive?

1. (Which / advertiser / creative)

   _____

2. (Which / advertiser / successful at increasing sales)

   _____

3. (Which / advertiser's ads / funny)

   _____

4. (Which / advertiser / friendly to clients)

   _____

5. (Which / advertiser / hardworking)

   _____

B. Complete this magazine article about Monique, who won the advertising contest. Write the adverb form or the superlative form of each adjective.

This year's award for ___Best___ Advertiser of the Year goes to Monique Johnson.
0. (good)

She produced this year's _____ advertisements. One of her _____
1. (excellent)   2. (creative)

ads was for Fair Hair beauty studios. After the ad ran, Fair Hair's business _____
3. (quick)

doubled. Johnson's _____ television ad was for a furniture store. In this ad, she set
4. (colorful)

up a conversation between one of the biggest and _____ athletes in America and a
5. (popular)

cartoon image of a hummingbird, _____ bird. It was very interesting and very
6. (small)

effective!

Johnson _____ deserved to win. She works _____, and she
7. (definite)   8. (hard)

_____ helps her clients create _____ advertisements possible. Her
9. (patient)   10. (great)

fellow advertisers _____ congratulate Johnson for her wonderful accomplishments
11. (sincere)

in advertising. Great job, Monique!

5 | EDITING: THE CAR COMMERCIAL

Correct Monique's television ad for a new car called the Millennium Fantasy. There are 10 mistakes. The first mistake is already corrected.

                            perfect
Meet the world's most ~~perfectest~~ car. Forget about driving noisy along the road. We made quietest car possible. It has the most powerfulest engine. It's more comfortabler than any car ever made. We believe that your safety is more important your image. But you'll look good in our car, and you'll be in the most safe car ever built. Live good, and drive this car. Go the farest that you can go. The Millennium Fantasy. It's one step more close to perfection.

Name _____   Date _____

Unit 40 Achievement Test

30 Items Score: _____

1 | LISTENING: COMPARING SCHOOLS

🎧 **A.** *Listen to Andrea and Marta's conversation about two medical schools. Complete their conversation by writing the words that you hear. You will hear the recording two times.*

MARTA: Congratulations on being accepted to medical school! That's wonderful!

ANDREA: Thanks. Actually I was accepted to two schools, Cornwell University in Greenwood and Grant Medical College in Carberry. Which is ___*better*___ for me? That's
                                                                                                                        0.
the tough question I have to answer.

MARTA: _____ cheaper?
              1.

ANDREA: Cornwell has lower tuition.

MARTA: Yes, but you must also consider the cost of living. Which city is _____
                                                                                                                                                2.
to live in?

ANDREA: Carberry, I think.

MARTA: Which school has a _____ reputation?
                                                      3.

ANDREA: Probably Grant, but Cornwell is also very good.

MARTA: Which has _____ class sizes?
                                           4.

ANDREA: Grant does, but class sizes at Cornwell aren't _____. Also, I think the
                                                                                                       5.
people at Cornwell are probably friendlier.

MARTA: So, _____ you closer to choosing?
                        6.

ANDREA: I'm still not sure.

226 | UNIT 40 ■ ACHIEVEMENT TEST

Name _____ Date _____

B. *Reread the conversation between Marta and Andrea. Find two comparative adjectives that end in -er and one that ends in -ier. Write them in the table below. (Note: Only use words that are given in the conversation. Do not use any words that you wrote.) An example is given.*

COMPARATIVE ADJECTIVES ENDING IN -ER	COMPARATIVE ADJECTIVE ENDING IN -IER
0. *cheaper*	1. _____
1. _____	
2. _____	

2 | COMPARING WEATHER

Andrea's friend George lived in Greenwood and Carberry. Andrea asks him to compare the two cities to help her make her decision. Complete their conversation. Circle the correct words or phrases.

ANDREA: Which city is a <u>more good / (better) / gooder</u> place to live?
　　　　　　　　　　　　　　　　　　　　　0.

GEORGE: That depends. What concerns do you have?

ANDREA: Well, I don't like lots of wind. Which place is <u>windyer / more windy / windier</u>?
　　　　　　　　　　　　　　　　　　　　　　　　　　　　　　　1.

GEORGE: Definitely Carberry.

ANDREA: That's good to know. I've heard Greenwood is <u>warmer / more warm / warmier</u> than
　　　　　　　　　　　　　　　　　　　　　　　　　　　　　　　2.
　　　　　Carberry. Is that true?

GEORGE: Yes, Greenwood is pretty warm most of the year.

ANDREA: Which city is <u>humidier / humider / more humid</u>?
　　　　　　　　　　　　　　3.

MARY: Greenwood is not very humid. It's very comfortable there. The elevation of
　　　　　Greenwood is <u>more high / higher / hightier</u> than the elevation in Carberry.
　　　　　　　　　　　　　　　　4.

ANDREA: Is Greenwood <u>greener / more green / greenier</u> than Carberry?
　　　　　　　　　　　　　　　　5.

GEORGE: Yes, Greenwood is very green. Carberry isn't, because the area doesn't get much rain.

ANDREA: Thanks for the information, George! You gave me a lot to think about.

Name _____   Date _____

3 | COMPARING CITIES

Andrea is comparing Greenwood and Carberry. Change the comparative adjectives in parentheses to write statements with the **OPPOSITE** meaning. Use **less** for only two of your answers. Some items may have more than one right answer.

0. The people in Carberry are ____poorer____ than the people in Greenwood.
   (richer)

1. Parties are _____ in Greenwood than in Carberry.
   (louder)

2. The population of Carberry is _____ than the population of Greenwood.
   (lower)

3. Greenwood is _____ a major airport.
   (closer to)

4. Carberry is a _____ city than Greenwood.
   (much better)

5. It is _____ to find a job in Greenwood than in Carberry.
   (easier)

6. Greenwood's nightlife is _____ than the nightlife in Carberry.
   (more interesting)

7. Medical care in Carberry is _____ than it is in Greenwood.
   (cheaper)

8. Greenwood has _____ hospitals.
   (worse)

9. The air in Greenwood is _____ than it is in Carberry.
   (dirtier)

10. The scenery around Greenwood is _____ than it is around Carberry.
    (less beautiful)

11. Greenwood is _____ than Carberry.
    (busier)

12. The crime rate is _____ in Greenwood than it is in Carberry.
    (higher)

228 | Unit 40 ■ Achievement Test

4 | EDITING: THE DECISION

Correct Andrea's e-mail to her friend Marta. There are five mistakes. The first mistake is already corrected. (Note: There is often more than one way to correct a mistake.)

Hi Marta,

    I finally decided which school to go to. I'm going to go to Cornwell University in Greenwood—not Grant Medical College in Carberry. The main reason is that Cornwell University is ~~more cheap~~ *cheaper* than Carberry. I also like that Greenwood's neighborhoods are quieter than Carberry. Plus, Greenwood is less dangerous. Greenwood may be more boring than Carberry, but I'm sure I won't be boreder than I was growing up in Gronlid. I'll be too busy studying. Also, I think the Cornwell campus is nicer. But the best news is that I'll be closer to home, so it will be easier for you to visit me. By the way, which highway is more fast for driving to Greenwood, Route 10 or the Interstate?

See you soon,

Andrea

Name _____   Date _____

Unit 41 Achievement Test

30 Items
Score: _____

1 | LISTENING: *STORY OF LOVE:* ACT 1

🎧 **A.** *Listen to the first part of a story about Mario and Danielle. Complete the story by writing the words that you hear. You will hear the recording two times.*

Mario is poor, but he works ____hard____ . He really wants to leave the country and
                                  0.
go to the city. He's tired of getting up early, working all day, going to bed late, and always

feeling hungry. One day, he takes the small amount of money he has and jumps on a train as it

moves _____ through his town. He hides quietly so that no one will hear him.
            1.

When he arrives in the city, he finds an apartment and a job. One day, he goes to his landlord's

house to give him the rent. The house looks _____ . The landlord's beautiful
                                                  2.

daughter Danielle quickly opens the door. She is dressed _____ . Danielle and
                                                                 3.

Mario look at each other for a long time. They are clearly interested in each other, but Mario

can't stay long. He has to leave to go back to work.

B. *Reread the first part of the story. Find three adverbs of manner that are formed by adding -ly to an adjective and three adverbs of manner that have the same form as adjectives. Write them in the table below. (Note: Only use words that are given in the story. Do not use any words that you wrote.) An example is given.*

ADVERBS: ADJECTIVE + -LY	ADVERBS: SAME FORM AS ADJECTIVES
0. really	1. _____
1. _____	2. _____
2. _____	3. _____
3. _____	

230 | UNIT 41 ■ ACHIEVEMENT TEST

Name _____ Date _____

2 | STORY OF LOVE: ACT 2

Complete the second part of Mario and Danielle's story. Circle the correct words.

One day, when Mario isn't working, he waits cheerful / (cheerfully) outside Danielle's house to
try to see her again. It's Saturday, and she leaves her house to take her dog on a walk. Mario
approaches her <u>nervously / nervous</u> and says hello. She answers him <u>shy / shyly</u>. Their
conversation begins <u>slowly / slow</u>, but they soon become <u>comfortable / comfortably</u> with each
other. Mario tells her that he <u>real / really</u> wants to have a better life, to make a little money, and
to live <u>good / well</u>. Danielle tells him that she is tired of always watching her behavior
<u>careful / carefully</u> in her "polite society," and that she would <u>gladly / glad</u> begin another life as
an ordinary girl. As the days go by, Mario shows Danielle the joys of fishing <u>quietly / quiet</u> at the
river, waiting <u>patient / patiently</u> to catch his dinner. Danielle shows Mario how to eat
"<u>proper / properly</u>" in the finest restaurant in town. Both of them are <u>happily / happy</u> and very
much in love. It seems <u>impossibly / impossible</u> that their love could ever end.

3 | STORY OF LOVE: ACT 3

Read the third part of Mario and Danielle's story. Then read each numbered statement based on this part of the story. Rewrite each underlined adverb as an adjective.

Danielle's father worries constantly because Danielle is interested in Mario—a man with no money. One night, while it is raining hard outside, Danielle sees that her father doesn't look happy. He is frowning seriously. She asks him what is wrong. He angrily tells Danielle that she must not see Mario anymore. Danielle calmly tells her father that she loves Mario and that she wants to marry him.

0. Danielle's father worries <u>constantly</u> because Danielle is interested in Mario. His worry is *constant*.

1. It is raining <u>hard</u> outside. The rain is _____.

2. Danielle's father frowns <u>seriously</u>. His frown is _____.

3. Danielle's father speaks <u>angrily</u> to Danielle. His speech is _____.

4. Danielle responds to her father <u>calmly</u>. Her response is _____.

4 | EDITING: *STORY OF LOVE*: ACT 4

Correct the fourth part of Mario and Danielle's story. There are five mistakes. The first mistake is already corrected.

Danielle runs to Mario's home and ~~happy~~ *happily* tells him that she wants to marry him. The day of the wedding, Danielle's father suddenly arrives at the chapel. He looks sadly. He does not usually apologize good, but he decides to try. He says to Danielle softly, "I thought hardly about you and Mario, and I decided that you have my blessing to get married." Danielle smiles warm and says, "Thank you!" Mario and Danielle get married, and they live happily ever after.

Name _____   Date _____

Unit 42 Achievement Test

30 Items
Score: _____

1 | LISTENING: PHOENIX, ARIZONA

🎧 **A.** *Listen to this radio report from World Radio News about very high temperatures in Phoenix, Arizona. Complete the report by writing the words that you hear. You will hear the recording two times.*

DELGADO: You're listening to World Radio News. I'm Alisa Delgado. It was too uncomfortable for much of anything in Phoenix, Arizona, today, as temperatures reached 121 degrees Fahrenheit, or 49 degrees Celsius. The temperature of the ground was 180 degrees Fahrenheit, or 82 degrees Celsius, which is ___*hot enough*___ to cook an egg. Resident Alex Watson says it was too hot to even go outside.
0.

WATSON: It was just way too miserable for outdoor activities today. I mean, I went out to get the mail, and it was as hot as an oven outside. At least it's only 70 degrees indoors.

DELGADO: Yes, 70 degrees is _____ for us, too. That temperature is the same as
1.
we have in the radio studio. We're lucky we have air conditioning! Thanks, Alex. . . . Now, a lot of people have been reporting problems with water that is too warm, too. Hot water is coming out of the cold water faucets. Health officials were working hard to make sure people stayed cool enough _____ the heat. Let's hear from
2.
health official, Jay Shapiro.

SHAPIRO: Hi, Alisa. Yes, Arizona health officials are _____ about the heat and
3.
want everyone in Phoenix to stay cool. We're especially worried about older people, since they sometimes live alone and are not as strong as other people. They have a harder time with the heat.

DELGADO: Thanks, Jay. And that's all for now. Alisa Delgado, World Radio News, Phoenix.

Name _____ Date _____

B. Reread the radio report. Find three phrases with *too + adjective* and two phrases with *as + adjective + as*. Write them in the table below. (Note: Only use words that are given in the radio report. Do not use any words that you wrote.) An example is given.

TOO + ADJECTIVE	AS + ADJECTIVE + AS
0. too uncomfortable	1. _____
1. _____	2. _____
2. _____	
3. _____	

2 | ANTARCTICA

Complete Alisa Delgado's report on Chuck Malone, a scientist working in Antarctica. Circle the correct phrases.

We go now from hot to cold: all the way to Antarctica. Temperatures there were −120 degrees Fahrenheit, or −84 degrees Celsius today. But the weather doesn't stop scientist Chuck Malone from working there. During the winter, it's enough dark / (too dark) / as dark as
0.
to see your hand in front of your face. But, with the help of electricity, it's
enough light / too light / light enough for him to see. When it's very cold, like it was today, it's
1.
too cold / enough cold / as cold as for him to go outside to do any work, so he works inside.
2.
The heaters keep him enough warm / as warm as / warm enough. He needs a humidifier, too,
3.
since it's very dry / as dry as / enough dry there. Antarctica is enough dry / very dry / as dry as a
4.   5.
desert. In fact, it gets enough rainfall / the same amount of rainfall as / rainfall enough the
6.
Sahara Desert. If you're interested in traveling to the South Pole, it's possible, but it's
too expensive / expensive enough / as expensive as for most people. The trip costs around
7.
$40,000.

Name _____   Date _____

3 | ACROSS THE UNITED STATES

Read each numbered statement about cities and regions in the United States. Then circle the letter of the sentence that best describes each situation.

0. New York City is too expensive for me.
   a. I can buy some things in New York City.
   (b.) I can't buy a lot of things in New York City.
   c. I can buy a lot of things in New York City.

1. Yuma, Arizona is too dry for me to like it.
   a. Yuma is drier than places I like.
   b. Yuma is not very dry, so I like it.
   c. Yuma is as dry as some other cities I like.

2. There aren't enough things to do in Morrisonville, Illinois.
   a. There are many things to do in Morrisonville.
   b. There is a sufficient number of things to do in Morrisonville.
   c. There is not a sufficient number of things to do in Morrisonville.

3. Portland, Oregon is too cloudy to please me.
   a. Portland has as many clouds as necessary to please me.
   b. Portland has more clouds than necessary to please me.
   c. Portland does not have enough clouds to please me.

4. Chicago, Illinois is not as cloudy as Portland.
   a. Chicago has more clouds than Portland.
   b. Chicago has as many clouds as Portland.
   c. Chicago has fewer clouds than Portland.

5. Dodge City, Kansas is too windy to make me happy.
   a. Dodge City is not very windy, so it doesn't make me happy.
   b. Dodge City is windier than necessary to make me happy.
   c. Dodge City is not windy enough to make me happy.

6. International Falls, Minnesota is too cold. I don't like it.
   a. International Falls is colder than I like.
   b. International Falls is not cold enough for me to like it.
   c. International Falls is not very cold, so I don't like it.

7. The cold temperatures in Minnesota feel the same as those in Alaska.
   a. The temperatures in Minnesota feel warmer than the temperatures in Alaska.
   b. The temperatures in Minnesota feel cooler than the temperatures in Alaska.
   c. The temperatures in Minnesota feel very similar to the temperatures in Alaska.

8. The climate in California is very nice.
   a. The climate in California is nicer than necessary.
   b. The climate in California is more than just nice.
   c. The climate in California is too nice.

9. California is different enough from the east coast.
   a. California is sufficiently different from the east coast.
   b. California is too different from the east coast.
   c. California is not very different from the east coast.

4 | EDITING: TOO MUCH RAIN

Dylan is from Swansea, Wales, where it rains a lot. Correct his blog, or online journal, about the weather in Swansea. There are seven mistakes. The first mistake is already corrected.

                                                    way too

    In my opinion, Swansea is ~~too way~~ rainy. I like the sun, and it's too cloudy here for me. I enjoy being outside, but sometimes I get wet as a mop! Also, my clothes always get dirty from the muddy streets, and I'm to poor to spend all my money cleaning them. Sometimes the streets are wet enough ride a boat in. Unfortunately, the weatherpeople don't know enough soon if it's going to rain. Sometimes the day starts out beautiful and sunny, but then it gets wet very by lunchtime. The weather in Anglesey isn't the same from the weather here in Swansea. So I think I'll move to Anglesey, where it's much drier!

Name _____   Date _____

Unit 43 Achievement Test

30 Items
Score: _____

1 | LISTENING: OMAR

🎧 **A.** *Sadie, Nicole, and, Jessica are roommates. Listen to Sadie and Nicole's conversation. Complete the conversation by writing the words that you hear. You will hear the recording two times.*

SADIE: Hey, who was that on the phone?

NICOLE: It was that guy Omar calling for Jessica. You know, I think he has __*the deepest*__ voice I've ever heard.
                                                                                              0.

SADIE: I know. He sings in the university choir, and he always has the lowest parts.

NICOLE: He sings in the choir? I thought he was a football player.

SADIE: He is. He's in the choir and on the football team. In fact, he's one of the most talented players _____.
                                                                                                              1.

NICOLE: Really? I didn't know that.

SADIE: Yeah. He's not _____ guy, but he's fast. And do you know that the school
                          2.
newspaper just voted him _____ guy on campus? Jessica says he has the
                              3.
best smile in the world.

NICOLE: Wow. Is he smart, too?

SADIE: Very smart. Jessica says he's the smartest guy _____.
                                                            4.

NICOLE: So Jessica really likes him?

SADIE: Mmm-hmm. It's the coolest thing because they're both great people. Omar is probably the friendliest guy I know.

NICOLE: That's good. Jessica deserves a good guy. She's the nicest person ever.

SADIE: Yeah, they're perfect for each other.

UNIT 43 ■ ACHIEVEMENT TEST | 237

Name _____   Date _____

B. *Reread the conversation. Find three regular superlatives (adjective + -est), one superlative formed from a two-syllable adjective ending in y (adjective + -iest), and one irregular superlative. Write them in the table below. (Note: Only use words that are given in the conversation. Do not use any words that you wrote.) An example is given.*

SUPERLATIVES ENDING IN -EST	SUPERLATIVE ENDING IN -IEST	IRREGULAR SUPERLATIVE
0. *the lowest*	1. _____	1. _____
1. _____		
2. _____		
3. _____		

2 | JESSICA

Complete Omar's conversation with his friend Morgan. Circle the correct words or phrases.

MORGAN: Are you going to ask Jessica to the dance?

OMAR: Of course.

MORGAN: Perfect. I hear she's the goodest / most good /(best) dancer at the university.
⠀⠀⠀⠀⠀⠀⠀⠀⠀⠀⠀⠀⠀⠀⠀⠀⠀⠀⠀⠀⠀⠀⠀⠀⠀⠀⠀⠀⠀⠀⠀**0.**

OMAR: Really? I only know she's the prettiest / most pretty / prettyest girl around here. She's
⠀⠀⠀⠀⠀⠀⠀⠀⠀⠀⠀⠀⠀⠀⠀⠀⠀⠀⠀⠀⠀⠀⠀⠀⠀⠀⠀⠀⠀⠀⠀**1.**
the interestingest / most interesting / most interestingest girl, too. Before the dance I
⠀⠀⠀⠀⠀⠀⠀⠀⠀⠀⠀⠀⠀⠀⠀⠀⠀⠀⠀⠀⠀⠀⠀⠀⠀**2.**
want to take her to that restaurant Frango Mango.

MORGAN: I ate there once, and I think it's the most bad / baddest / worst restaurant in town!
⠀⠀⠀⠀⠀⠀⠀⠀⠀⠀⠀⠀⠀⠀⠀⠀⠀⠀⠀⠀⠀⠀⠀⠀⠀⠀⠀⠀⠀⠀⠀⠀⠀⠀**3.**

OMAR: Maybe you went on a bad night. I think they have the
most wonderful / wonderfulest / most wonderfulest food around!
⠀⠀⠀⠀⠀⠀⠀⠀⠀⠀⠀⠀⠀⠀⠀⠀**4.**

MORGAN: They also have the most expensivest / expensivest / most expensive food around. You
⠀⠀⠀⠀⠀⠀⠀⠀⠀⠀⠀⠀⠀⠀⠀⠀⠀⠀⠀⠀⠀⠀⠀⠀⠀⠀⠀**5.**
should go somewhere else.

Name _____ Date _____

3 | THE DANCE

A. Complete these sentences about the dance that Omar invited Jessica to. Use the superlative forms of the adjectives in the box.

| bad | fine | ~~good~~ | large | old | small | tall |
| beautiful | funny | green | new | rare | sweet | |

0. There was _____the best_____ of everything at the dance.

1. The dance was held in _____ building in the city. It was 50 stories high.

2. The building is also one of _____ places in the city. It was built in the 1700s.

3. The dance was in _____ room in the building. The room was big enough for 400 people.

4. The room was decorated with _____ plants the event planner could find. Their color was beautiful.

5. The room was decorated so well that it was _____ room in the building.

6. The chef served _____ grapes he could find. They were delicious.

7. Each table had _____ flowers available. These flowers only grow on one tiny island in the Pacific Ocean during the spring.

8. The band had _____ musicians in the city. They were all really talented.

9. They played their _____ music. They wrote it recently especially for the dance.

B. Complete these sentences about the dance. Use **one of the** and the superlative forms of the adjectives and plural forms of the nouns in parentheses.

0. __One of the most talented event planners__ in the area organized the dance.
   (talented / event planner)

1. _____ in town attended the event.
   (rich / businessman)

2. _____ in the city provided the food.
   (good / chef)

3. The music was provided by _____ in the area.
   (famous / band)

4. The dance was _____ ever.
   (great / party)

Name _____ **Date** _____

4 | EDITING: JESSICA'S DIARY

Correct Jessica's diary entry about the dance with Omar. There are four mistakes. The first mistake is already corrected.

          most
I had the ^ incredible evening last night. Omar took me to the most wonderfulest dance in the world. They had the nicest of everything. Omar is the most great guy I know. He's also the most popular guy on campus. It was the bestest date of my life.

Name _____ Date _____

Part XII Achievement Test

60 Items
Score: _____

1 | LISTENING: JED'S WEBSITE

🎧 **A.** *Jed owns a clock- and watch-repair business. Melissa, a web designer, is discussing with Jed plans for the business's website. Listen to their conversation. Complete the conversation by writing the words that you hear. You will hear the recording two times.*

MELISSA: I started building your website. I wanted to meet with you briefly and ask you some questions. That way I'll know ____better____ how to build it.
                                                                           0.

JED: OK.

MELISSA: Here's your homepage. _____ do you prefer for the words, blue or black?
                                       1.

JED: I think black is less interesting to look at, but it's easier to read.

MELISSA: True. Black is _____ color to read. And _____ of the
                              2.   **3.**
clock do you want, the big one, the medium-sized one, or the little one?

JED: I think the big one is _____, and it has the brightest colors. The small
                                  4.
one is too hard to see. But the big one is way too big. Can we make it

_____ this picture here?
      5.

MELISSA: Sure, let me change that quickly. There. Do you want the title to be

_____ the rest of the text?
      6.

JED: Let's use a different color so the title stands out _____ from the other
                                                                  7.
text.

B. *Read each statement based on the conversation. Write* **C** *if the underlined word or phrase is a comparative adjective,* **S** *if it is a superlative adjective,* **ADJ** *if it is an adjective, and* **ADV** *if it is an adverb.*

0. __ADV__ Melissa wanted to meet with her client Jed <u>briefly</u>.

1. _____ Jed thinks that black words are <u>less interesting</u> to look at than blue words.

2. _____ Jed thinks black words are <u>easier</u> to read than blue words.

3. _____ Jed thinks the big picture has <u>the brightest</u> colors.

4. _____ Jed thinks the small picture is too <u>hard</u> to see.

5. _____ Jed thinks the big picture is way too <u>big</u>.

6. _____ Melissa <u>quickly</u> changes the size of the big picture.

PART XII ■ ACHIEVEMENT TEST |241

Name _____ **Date** _____

2 | DEVELOPING JED'S WEBSITE

Melissa and Jed are still working on the website. Complete their conversation. Circle the correct phrases.

MELISSA: How do you think the website looks so far?

JED: The colors are a little (**too boring**) / boring enough / very boring. The words aren't
enough dark / **dark enough** / as dark as. Also, the background color is
difficult enough / as difficult as / **too difficult** to look at. It would be nice to have a
background color **different from** / different as / the same from green—maybe yellow?
That would be pretty.

MELISSA: OK, I can change that. Give me a second. . . . There. Is that yellow
enough good / **good enough** / too good?

JED: It's great, but I just realized that the picture in the corner of the screen is
low enough / enough low / **too low**. Can you raise it? I think it should be at
a different level as / a same level as / **the same level as** the other photograph.

MELISSA: Sure. It's **very easy** / too easy / enough easy to do that.

JED: Great. Since you're already adjusting that picture, can you change its size? It seems
large enough / **too large** / as large as, in my opinion.

MELISSA: Absolutely. Do you have any other suggestions?

JED: Well, do you think the page is **too busy** / enough busy / as busy as? I mean, there's a
lot of information.

MELISSA: No, I think it's enough plain / the same plain / **plain enough**. I think you made it
as simple as / the same simple as / a different simple as it can be. Plus, I like that the
design is **different from** / a same as / different as the design of your old website. This
new one is really more interesting.

Name _____ Date _____

3 | JED'S RADIO ADVERTISEMENT

Read the radio advertisement. Find three comparative adjectives, three superlative adjectives, and four adverbs. Write them in the table below. (Note: Be sure to write the entire word or phrase.) An example is given.

Good Time is the best clock and watch repair center in town! We are more experienced than anyone else at repairing clocks and watches. Our staff is the most knowledgeable of any watch repair staff for miles around. If your watch is running badly, we can fix it for you. We work hard to fix all watches and clocks on the same day that we receive them. We have a larger selection of batteries than any other shop. Of all of the repair shops in town, we have the cheapest prices. If you want your watch to keep time perfectly, you should come to our store for all of your repairs. Don't show up late for any more appointments because your watch or clock is broken. We're one of the most popular clock and watch repair businesses in the country. Our staff is friendlier than any other. So stop by today!

COMPARATIVE ADJECTIVES	SUPERLATIVE ADJECTIVES	ADVERBS
1. _____	0. *the best*	1. _____
2. _____	1. _____	2. _____
3. _____	2. _____	3. _____
	3. _____	4. _____

4 | TOP WEB DESIGNER

A. *A group of judges is choosing a winner for a web design contest. They are comparing the top two candidates. Write their questions with comparative adjectives. Use the words in parentheses.*

0. (Which / designer's websites / attractive)

   Which designer's websites are more attractive?

1. (Which / web designer / modern)

   _____

2. (Which / web designer / creative)

   _____

3. (Which / web designer / helpful to other designers)

   _____

4. (Which / web designer / nice to customers)

_____

5. (Which / web designer / artistic)

_____

B. Complete this magazine article about Melissa, who won the web design contest. Write the adverb form or the superlative form of each adjective.

This month's award for _____Best_____ Web Designer goes to Melissa Jackson. She
                         0. (Good)
created this month's _____ website for one of the _____ bands in
                      1. (interesting)   **2. (famous)**
New York. After creating the site, the band _____ received contract offers from
                                             3. (quick)
two record companies.

Jackson _____ deserves the award. Her websites are the _____
        4. (definite)   **5. (exciting)**
on the web, and they are some of the _____ to use. They set the
                                      6. (easy)
_____ standard in web design. But her recipe for success is no secret. She works
7. (high)
_____ and _____ designs websites that are _____
8. (hard)   **9. (careful)**   **10. (technological)**
advanced but easy to use. Here's what the lead singer of the band said: "We made the

_____ decision of our career when we decided to ask Melissa Jackson to create our
11. (great)
website." Way to go, Melissa!

5 | EDITING: THE HOTEL WEBSITE

Correct part of Melissa's website about a hotel. There are 10 mistakes. The first mistake is already corrected.

        most luxurious
 Stay in the world's ~~luxuriest~~ hotel. Stay in nicest hotel possible. You're guaranteed to real enjoy your stay with us. We have the most deliciousest meals. Our beds are more comfortable any others. Our prices are lower than our competitor. When you stay with us, you'll relax good. You'll feel gooder here than at home. Our hotel is the goodest that you can find. The Charles Hotel Suites. It's wonderfullest place on earth.

Audioscript

PART I Diagnostic Test

DAVE: I'm hungry. Are you hungry?

TAMMY: Yes, I am. I'm very hungry. Let's go to Caruso's Restaurant.

DAVE: My friend Nancy was there last week. She wasn't happy with the food. It wasn't very good.

TAMMY: Are you sure? I was there last week, too. The food wasn't bad at all!

DAVE: OK. Let's go to Caruso's.

Unit 1 Achievement Test

CAROLINE: Who's in this picture?

LYDIA: This is the Price family. They're my friends. They're from California. Mr. Price is a professor there. His first name is Ralph. He's married to Pat. Ralph and Pat have three children. This is Lynnette. She's 27. This is Michelle. She's 24. And this is Nate. He's 19.

CAROLINE: They're all very good-looking! They look rich and famous!

LYDIA: They aren't rich or famous, but they are wonderful!

Unit 2 Achievement Test

TIM: Excuse me. Is this Acting 101?

DALE: Yes, it is. Are you in the class?

TIM: Yes, I am. Are you?

DALE: Yes, I am.

TIM: You look familiar. . . . I know! Are you Molly's friend?

DALE: Molly? I don't think so.

TIM: Well. . . . Are you from Washington?

DALE: No, I'm not. I'm from Michigan.

TIM: Michigan? That's pretty far away from here!

DALE: You're right. It isn't close at all.

TIM: Is this a good class?

DALE: I think so. I'm the teacher!

TIM: Oh! You're Dale Shumway, the actor! I'm Tim.

Unit 3 Achievement Test

LINDA: Were you at your sister's play last night?

NANCY: Yes! It was great! All of her friends were there. They were in the play. It was really funny!

LINDA: Were your parents there to watch it?

NANCY: No, they weren't. They were out of town yesterday.

LINDA: Was your sister in the play?

NANCY: No. Julie wrote the play, but she's not an actor.

PART I Achievement Test

RYAN: It's hot, and I'm thirsty. Are you thirsty?

DENISE: Yes, I am. I'm very thirsty. Let's go to Tom's Diner.

RYAN: My friend Shinji was there yesterday. He wasn't happy. It was very dirty.

DENISE: Are you sure? I was there on Monday. The restaurant wasn't dirty!

RYAN: OK. Let's go.

PART II Diagnostic Test

PAUL: Where is the museum?

JUDY: Downtown. It's near the train station. There is a big sign in front of it. It's next to the park with the tall trees.

PAUL: Oh. Where's the park?

JUDY: It's on First Avenue. It's called Jefferson Park.

PAUL: OK. It looks like rain. Bring an umbrella.

Unit 4 Achievement Test

JEN: Hi, Holly! Wow! I like your earrings!

HOLLY: Thanks. And I really like your clothes.

JEN: Thank you! My pants and shirt are from France. I was in Europe last summer.

HOLLY: Really? Do you have photos?

JEN: Yes! In fact, I have an album. . . . Here it is. OK, here I am at the Eiffel Tower.

HOLLY: Very nice! Who's the woman with you?

JEN: Oh, she's a friend from class. Her name is Cheryl. She's a photographer.

Unit 5 Achievement Test

The Painted Desert is an unusual place in Arizona. It is very colorful. You can drive through it, or you can walk on easy trails. There are helpful signs with interesting information. It is hot in the summer but nice in the winter. It is almost always sunny and dry. If you walk, take a big bottle of water and a good hat. It is a beautiful place to visit.

Unit 6 Achievement Test

JAY: I need directions to your party. Do you live in the city?

MOLLY: Well, I live near the city. I'm at 301 Cherry Avenue. It's an apartment building next to the train station. It's on the corner of Cherry Avenue and Main Street.

JAY: So is the entrance on Cherry or Main?

MOLLY: It's on Cherry. There's a big sign in front of the building that says Mountain Plaza Apartments. The parking lot is in back of the building.

JAY: What's your apartment number?

MOLLY: My apartment number is 217, but the party is in the clubhouse. The clubhouse is behind the pool. It's easy to find.

JAY: Great! I'll see you tonight.

Unit 7 Achievement Test

TONY: Hey, Allan. I want to show you something.

ALLAN: OK. Where are you?

TONY: I'm at the computer.

ALLAN: I'm here. What is it?

TONY: Look at this picture. It's my family.

ALLAN: Oh, interesting. Who's that next to you?

TONY: That's my sister.

ALLAN: It's a beautiful photo. Where were you?

TONY: We were on vacation in Segovia.

ALLAN: Segovia? Where's that?

TONY: It's in Spain; it's near Madrid.

ALLAN: I like Spain. Why were you there?

TONY: My father is from Spain. My grandmother is still there.

ALLAN: So, your family is Spanish. What's your last name?

TONY: It's Domínguez.

PART II Achievement Test

PAULA: Where is the restaurant?

JAMES: On the corner of First Avenue and Main Street. It's near the art museum. There are flowers in front of it. The building is very modern.

PAULA: Oh, yes. It's behind the mall. What's the name of the mall?

JAMES: Mall of the World.

PAULA: That's right. OK. See you there in an hour.

PART III Diagnostic Test

SUSAN: Hi, I'm Pam's friend Susan. Are you a friend of Pam's, too?

FRANK: Yes, I am. I'm Frank. It's nice to meet you.

SUSAN: You, too. So, how do you know Pam?

FRANK: She and I take a Japanese cooking class together.

SUSAN: Oh, that's interesting. I love sushi. Do you know how to make it?

FRANK: Yeah, it's pretty easy.

SUSAN: Really? That's great. Who teaches the class?

FRANK: A Japanese professor from the community college. He's really good. Come to class with Pam sometime—it's a lot of fun!

SUSAN: Do I sign up somewhere?

FRANK: No, you don't. Just come by and visit. Actually, there is a little party in class next week. That's a good day to go.

SUSAN: That sounds great! When does the party start?

FRANK: Well, the class is at 7:45 on Tuesday.

SUSAN: Oh no. I don't know.

FRANK: Are you busy on Tuesday?

SUSAN: Yes, I am. I have dinner plans.

FRANK: Well, maybe another time.

SUSAN: Yes, I hope so. . . .

Unit 8 Achievement Test

MEGAN: I don't have a car, but I need to go to the store.

KEVIN: You don't need a car. I walk to the store. I go twice a week because I don't buy a lot. I take my backpack with me, and I carry my food home in it.

MEGAN: That is a good idea. I think you're right. I don't need a car.

Unit 9 Achievement Test

ANDRÉS: Excuse me, do you work here?

HARVEY: Yes, I do. Do you need some help?

ANDRÉS: Actually, I need a job.

HARVEY: Well, the owner isn't here right now. But you can leave your name and number for her. Do you have experience with music?

ANDRÉS: Yeah, I'm in a band.

HARVEY: That's cool. Is it popular?

ANDRÉS: Well, we play at Jake's Steaks every Tuesday, Wednesday, and Thursday night, so yes, it is.

HARVEY: Does your band play on weekends?

ANDRÉS: No, we don't. In fact, I want to work on weekends. Hey, let me ask you something about the owner. Does she take good care of the employees?

HARVEY: Yes, she does. She's great.

ANDRÉS: Excellent. Here's my name and phone number. She can call me anytime.

Unit 10 Achievement Test

GRETCHEN: Hello?

MRS. TOMKINS: Hi, Gretchen. It's your mother. How are you?

GRETCHEN: Terrible!

MRS. TOMKINS: Oh no! What do you need? Tell me everything.

GRETCHEN: Thanks. I'm fine, I'm just so tired. The kids are noisy, the house is messy, I have so much work. . . . How do people have kids *and* a life?!

MRS. TOMKINS: What do you mean?

GRETCHEN: I never finish my work. I'm always busy!

MRS. TOMKINS: Oh, that's simple! Let me ask you a question: How do you relax?

GRETCHEN: Relax?! When do I have time to relax?

MRS. TOMKINS: Well, if you don't have time, you need to make time to relax. Listen, what happens when you're tired and stressed?

GRETCHEN: I feel terrible. I get angry easily.

MRS. TOMKINS: Right. And who wants to feel like that? You need to take 15 minutes each day to rest, relax, or do something that you enjoy.

GRETCHEN: Where do the children go while I'm relaxing? What do they do?

MRS. TOMKINS: They can read or draw or relax in their rooms. Explain that it is a special time just for you. They can understand.

GRETCHEN: Thanks, Mom. Who told you all this?

MRS. TOMKINS: My mother, of course!

PART III Achievement Test

ALEX: Hey, Lisa, you carry that camera with you everywhere. Why do you do that? Are you a photographer?

LISA: No, I'm not. Not professionally, anyway. But I take pictures all the time.

ALEX: What do you take pictures of?

LISA: Oh, anything. People, nature . . . I love photography.

ALEX: Are you a good photographer?

LISA: I guess so. Yeah, I'm pretty good.

ALEX: I don't take pictures, but I love to look at them.

LISA: Oh. Do you want to see my photos?

ALEX: I'd love to. Do you have some with you?

LISA: No, I don't. But I'll bring some tomorrow. When do you have some time?

ALEX: Umm . . . let's have lunch again tomorrow. You can show them to me then.

LISA: OK, great.

PART IV Diagnostic Test

CHRIS: Hi! Sorry I'm late. I took the car to the shop. It will be ready tomorrow. What time does the concert start tonight?

STACIE: At 7:30. We need to get ready! They say this is going to be the best concert of the year. The orchestra and its conductor are from Italy.

CHRIS: Great! So, whose car can we take?

STACIE: I called our neighbors. . . . We can take Kim's car. It's in the driveway.

CHRIS: Do you have the key?

STACIE: Yes, I have her extra key. It's right here.

CHRIS: Great! By the way, those are nice earrings. Your dress is nice too.

STACIE: Thank you!

Unit 11 Achievement Test

Most people celebrate New Year's Day on January 1st. In some countries, New Year's Day is in the winter. In other countries, it is in the summer. On New Year's Eve, or December 31st, people stay up late at night. They watch fireworks that begin at 12:00 midnight. They go to bed early in the morning. Most people do not work on January 1st. People in Ethiopia celebrate the new year on September 11th. People in Thailand celebrate the new year from April 13th to April 15th.

Unit 12 Achievement Test

KATHY: Hi. My name is Kathy. What's your name?

GREG: My name is Greg. Nice to meet you.

KATHY: Nice to meet you, too. Do you like our professor?

GREG: Yes, I do. I like his way of teaching. . . . Hey, whose book is this?

KATHY: It's not my book. Maybe it's Asami's book.

GREG: Whose book?

KATHY: Asami's book. Asami is the girl from Japan. Maybe it's her book.

GREG: Oh. I'll ask her.

Unit 13 Achievement Test

MEGAN: This is a big museum. Let's start on this side. Oh, look at that! Are those dinosaur bones or elephant bones?

JOSH: These are bones of an old animal that was like an elephant. It's called a mammoth. Mammoths lived during the last Ice Age. In those days, early man ate them. But the mammoths all died about 10,000 years ago.

MEGAN: Did they all die because of humans or because of another reason?

JOSH: That's a good question. No one knows.

MEGAN: Interesting. Where do you want to go next, this way or that way?

Unit 14 Achievement Test

DAN: Look at these orange fish. Those are nice ones.

MARA: They're OK. Do you like this black fish?

DAN: That's a strange one. Here are some blue fish.

MARA: Those are interesting ones. But I like these red fish. They're better than the blue ones.

DAN: Here are some frogs. They're cute!

MARA: I don't think so. I don't want one. But look at that suckerfish. It helps keep the tank clean.

DAN: Let's get one. And we need a big fish tank. Here's one.

MARA: Let's put it in the shopping cart. Where is it?

DAN: It's right here.

MARA: Did you bring your wallet?

DAN: Yes, it's in my pocket.

PART IV Achievement Test

RICH: I'm home! I took your dress to the cleaners. It will be ready tomorrow. What time does the movie start tonight?

WENDY: At 6:45. Hey, did you read that review of the movie in the newspaper last night? They say it's wonderful! And its director is famous.

RICH: Good! Hey, whose pants are those?

WENDY: They're my sister's pants. All my pants are dirty.

RICH: Those are nice. Your sister has nice clothes.

WENDY: I know. I like them, too. So, do you have the key to the house?

RICH: Yes, I do. Do you have your purse?

WENDY: Yes. Let's go.

PART V Diagnostic Test

ALICE: Is this the only café around here? It seems so unfriendly. Where are the employees? Who is working? Let's go somewhere else.

JOANNE: Wait. I think that guy over there is a waiter. Is he coming this way?

ALICE: Yeah, he sees us.

WAITER: Welcome to the Cold Cut Café. Follow me. . . . Here are your menus. Let me know when you're ready.

JOANNE: OK. These chairs are so uncomfortable. And it's so cold in here. Look, you're shaking. Excuse me! Can you turn up the heat, please? We're really cold.

WAITER: Sorry, our heater isn't working.

ALICE: You know, this part of Vancouver needs a good café. Let's start our own café, where people can be comfortable! We can call it the Comfort Café!

JOANNE: That's a great idea!

Unit 15 Achievement Test

ANNOUNCER: You're listening to NRI, Network Radio International.

ERIC ENSLEY: Early this morning, there was a sudden, violent shaking across the city of Kobe, Japan. People soon realized that it was an earthquake. NRI's Yoko Arisaka is reporting live from Kobe. Yoko, tell us what you're seeing there at the moment.

YOKO ARISAKA: Well, right now, Eric, I'm standing in downtown Kobe. Many homes are badly damaged, so there are many people on the streets. Thousands of people are walking on the sidewalks. Many people want to leave the city. But taxis are full, and the subway is not working. Buses and trains are not on schedule. So people are looking for other ways to get around. Far away, smoke from a fire is rising in the sky. It is a difficult day for many people in Kobe.

ERIC ENSLEY: And I understand that people from all over the country are trying to help. Everyone wants to cooperate.

YOKO ARISAKA: That's true, Eric. The government is asking people to give food, water, and clothes, and people are giving as much as they can.

ERIC ENSLEY: Thank you, Yoko. That was NRI's Yoko Arisaka in Kobe, Japan.

Unit 16 Achievement Test

AMY: Hi, Gina. I need to borrow your cake pan, please. Are you using it?

GINA: No, I'm not. What are you making?

AMY: A cake—a chocolate one with vanilla frosting. Oh! Is your refrigerator working?

GINA: Of course it is! What's going on? Are you feeling OK?

AMY: Yes, I'm fine. I'm just busy. I'm cooking, and I need more room for the food.

GINA: Why are you making so much food? Are you having a party?

AMY: Yes! The birthday party!

GINA: Who is having a birthday?

AMY: David! Don't you know about the party?

GINA: No, I don't. Is David working today?

AMY: Yes. It's a surprise party. It's at 6:30. Can you come?

GINA: Of course! Do you need help? Where are the kids? Are they playing outside?

AMY: Yes, thank goodness! I have to run and get some eggs.

GINA: Wait! Where are you going? Use my eggs! And I'll get the cake pan.

AMY: Perfect! Thanks so much!

Unit 17 Achievement Test

OK, everyone . . . listen to this! Come to Gary's Downtown Auto Mall today. Bring your family and friends! Don't miss the biggest car sale of the year! Find the car of your dreams at a low, low price. Choose from our huge selection, and drive away in a new car or truck the same day! Get $1,000 cash back. Don't wait because these deals won't be around for long! Visit us today!

Unit 18 Achievement Test

Are you hungry, but you can't decide what to eat? Presto Pesto's can help! We offer a variety of traditional Italian dishes. And you can dine in, you can take out, or we can deliver. Also, you can enjoy your meal on our garden patio. And now, for a short time only, you can get two pizzas for the price of one! That's right: two for one! You can look, but you can't find better prices or better food anywhere in town! Next time you're hungry, remember Presto Pesto's. Presto Pesto's—when you just can't wait to eat!

Unit 19 Achievement Test

GREG: It's a beautiful day. Why don't we go to the beach today?

JEFF: Great idea. But let's not go to the same one we went to the other day. Let's go to Lantau Island and see the Giant Buddha statue near the beach.

SHARON: I don't know. I want to see the Dragon Boat Festival. Why don't we see that today?

STEPHANIE: That sounds good to me. I'm really interested in the festival. And I want to see the Dragon Boat races. Let's find out when they are.

SHARON: I'm sure there's information about them on the Internet. Why don't we check online?

JEFF: OK.

SHARON: Tonight I want to watch the Symphony of Lights. Let's go to the Tsim Sha Tsui waterfront. I hear that's the best place to see the lights.

GREG: Let's not sit on the waterfront. Let's take a harbor cruise tour. The view is even better from the water!

STEPHANIE: That's a good idea. Why don't you call and reserve our tickets?

GREG: OK.

PART V Achievement Test

ALFRED: I hope we can sit down and eat soon. I'm really hungry.

LUIS: Me, too. Where is the waitress going?

JAMIE: I don't think she sees us. Let's try to get her attention.

LUIS: Is she coming over here yet? . . . Finally! The service here is *so* slow!

WAITRESS: Welcome to Fiesta Taco. Come this way. . . . Our special today is the taco salad. Look at the menu, and I can come back to take your order.

JAMIE: Uh . . . It's so hot in here. Look, I'm sweating. Excuse me, can you turn on the air conditioning? We're really hot.

WAITRESS: I'm sorry, I know it's hot. But our air conditioning isn't working.

ALFRED: Hey, I have an idea. Let's open our own Mexican restaurant. I think we can make a lot of money. We can call it the Tres Amigos.

LUIS: That's a good idea!

JAMIE: Yeah, I like it.

ALFRED: I can start to check out how to do it.

PART VI Diagnostic Test

PAM: It feels so good to be home. I missed you.

MRS. UNVER: We missed you too! How was your flight?

PAM: Perfect. I slept the whole way. I only woke up when we landed. I think I needed the rest! Maybe I'm trying to do too much.

MRS. UNVER: You *are* busy with work and school. Did you do well on your English paper?

PAM: I don't know yet. We get them back next week.

MRS. UNVER: What did you write about?

PAM: It was about my trip to South Africa last year. The professor wanted us to write about a personal experience. At first, I didn't know what to write, but I wrote about the trip. I realized it was really important to me.

MRS. UNVER: Great! I hope you do well.

PAM: Me, too!

Unit 20 Achievement Test

RAÚL: How is your trip so far?

STAN: Good. I arrived two days ago. At the airport, a hotel shuttle picked me up. The driver dropped my suitcase. Now my suitcase is broken, and some of my clothes got dirty because it opened. But he was nice, and he was very sorry. He told me all about Caracas. At the hotel, I tried to give him a tip, but he didn't take it.

RAÚL: Do you need to wash any of your clothes? You can wash them at my place.

STAN: That's OK. I washed them last night at the hotel.

RAÚL: So, how do you like Caracas?

STAN: I walked around the city yesterday. The people are really nice. Yesterday afternoon it started to rain, so I returned to the hotel.

RAÚL: Well, I'm glad you're here!

Unit 21 Achievement Test

MR. COOPER: Welcome back, everyone. How was your vacation?

YOLANDA: I had a great time. I went to see my friend in Los Angeles. The weather was beautiful. My friend has a pool, so we swam every day.

MR. COOPER: That sounds wonderful. What about you, Maria? Did you have a nice vacation?

MARIA: Not really. I didn't go anywhere. I was sick, so I just stayed home. I read two good books.

MR. COOPER: In English?

MARIA: No, in Spanish. What did *you* do, Mr. Cooper?

MR. COOPER: I visited my sister. We talked a lot, and we went to the movies. It was fun!

Unit 22 Achievement Test

ALICE: What happened, Norma? You look upset.

NORMA: I lost my ring.

ALICE: Oh, that's terrible. Where did you lose it?

NORMA: I think I left it at school in the cafeteria. I reported it to the school office, but they didn't have it.

ALICE: Did it cost a lot?

NORMA: No, it didn't, but it was valuable to me. It belonged to my grandmother. My mother gave it to me a few days ago.

ALICE: When did you have the ring last?

NORMA: Well, I know I had it at lunch this afternoon.

[Norma's cell phone rings.]

NORMA: Hello?

MR. JACKSON: Hi. Is this Norma Damron?

NORMA: Yes.

MR. JACKSON: This is Principal Jackson from the high school. I heard that you lost a ring. I found one in the cafeteria. Did you lose your ring there?

NORMA: Oh, yes, I think I did! Was it on the floor?

MR. JACKSON: Yes, it was.

NORMA: Thank you very much for calling!

MR. JACKSON: You're welcome. You can pick it up at the front office.

NORMA: Thank you!

PART VI Achievement Test

JULIE: Hello?

LINDA: Hi, Julie! Finally, you're home! I tried to call you all day yesterday, but no one answered. Where were you?

JULIE: I just got home. I was in the hospital.

LINDA: Oh no! Why were you in the hospital?

JULIE: I fell and broke my leg on Sunday. I guess I picked the wrong day to go ice skating.

LINDA: Oh, wow, did you hurt anything else?

JULIE: No, but my leg is bad enough. I have to stay home this week. You know, I missed my math test yesterday morning. I'm really worried about it. I wanted to call my professor, but I didn't have his phone number with me. I hope I don't fail the class. He even told me last week that I need to do better in his class.

LINDA: Oh, I'm sure you can take the test later. Just tell him what happened. I'm glad you're OK. I was really worried!

PART VII Diagnostic Test

SANDRA: You aren't eating very much of your lunch. Don't you like your chicken?

HEATHER: Yes, it's delicious.

SANDRA: Then why do you look so sad? Do you still miss your home in Canada?

HEATHER: Yeah. This town is very different from my home. There's a lake near the town I'm from in Alberta. It's called Cameron Lake.

SANDRA: Oh, I've been there. It's gorgeous!

HEATHER: When did you go to Alberta?

SANDRA: Chad and I went there last year. He took me for our anniversary. We had a picnic at the lake. In fact, Chad gave me this watch there. The lake was beautiful. I liked it a lot.

HEATHER: Yeah, it's wonderful. There aren't many places like it in the world. I miss swimming there. The water is so beautiful. Are there any places like that around here?

SANDRA: No, not like that.

Unit 23 Achievement Test

ROBERT: Here's your key. Rent is due by the first of the month. If it's late, there's a $20 fee. There's a laundry room by the office. There are mailboxes by the parking lot. There isn't anyone in the office on Sundays. Do you have any questions for me?

PATRICK: Yeah, are there any bank machines nearby?

ROBERT: There aren't any very close, but there's one on Fourth Avenue. It's in the grocery store.

PATRICK: OK, I went there yesterday, so I know where it is.

Unit 24 Achievement Test

REIKO: Hello?

MR. ITO: Hi, Reiko! How are you?

REIKO: Oh hi, Dad. I'm great! Beth and I have a new roommate named Federica. She's from Italy, and she knows how to cook.

MR. ITO: Oh, terrific!

REIKO: I know. She made spaghetti last night, and she gave us a lot. She gave me three servings. I loved it.

MR. ITO: That sounds great. Is she teaching you any Italian?

REIKO: Yes, and she wants to learn some Japanese, so I'm teaching her. Oh, and this morning Federica and I went shopping. We bought Beth a few small things. We'll give them to her tomorrow. It's her birthday, and we want to celebrate it.

MR. ITO: Well, it sounds like you're all getting along well.

REIKO: We are. I have to go to class now, but I'll talk to you later.

MR. ITO: OK, bye.

REIKO: Bye.

Unit 25 Achievement Test

NICOLE: I love street fairs. There are always interesting things for sale.

TIM: Yes, there are. Hey, I'm hungry. I want to get a sandwich and some soda at the restaurant over there.

NICOLE: Wait a minute, I want to buy some soap here.

TIM: Why do you want to buy that? It smells strange.

NICOLE: No, it doesn't. I think it smells good. Besides, it's pretty, and it doesn't cost much money. There's a lot of nice clothing here, too. I bought a few shirts here once.

TIM: Well, I'm going over there to try some cheese. I need a little food!

PART VII Achievement Test

HEIDI: Do you miss Ireland?

AMY: I miss swimming. I love to swim, but there isn't any place to go swimming in this town. In Leitrim, the town I grew up in, there's a huge lake called Lough Melvin.

HEIDI: Really? What's it like there?

AMY: It's beautiful. Billy and I were engaged on Lough Melvin. Early in the morning, he took me out on a boat and asked me to marry him.

HEIDI: Wow! That sounds romantic.

AMY: It was. Billy caught a big fish that day, and we ate it for lunch. I really like to be on a boat, and I love to go fishing. Are there any places to fish around here?

HEIDI: No. There aren't many lakes, but the grocery store in the center of town sells fresh fish.

AMY: Really? I'll have to check it out.

PART VIII Diagnostic Test

Welcome to *Entertainment Nightly*. The romance between pop stars Liza Russet and Jeremy Whithers seems to be heating up. The two are spending lots of time together, and they are seldom apart. They avoid talking to the press about their relationship, but they often appear in public hand in hand.

In fact, they are appearing in public a lot these days. Fans were surprised that they didn't appear at last night's awards ceremony.

And the singers sound as good as they look together. They just released a new album, called *Dream World*, and their fans love it. How did it do in its first few weeks on the charts? Well, it started out at number one, and after three weeks, it is still the best-selling album in the country. Do you like to listen to Liza and Jeremy? Tell us what you think of their new album on our website, www.enshow.com.

Unit 26 Achievement Test

DR. RICE: You're listening to *Love Matters*. I'm your host, Dr. Naomi Rice. We have 24-year-old Cara in Manhattan on the line with us. What's your question, Cara?

CARA: Hi, Dr. Rice. My question is, how do I tell my dentist that I love him?

DR. RICE: Your dentist?

CARA: Yes! Every time I visit his office, I just believe that he is the right man for me.

DR. RICE: Every time you visit his office? Most people go the dentist about once a year. But it sounds like you see your dentist more frequently. How often do you visit him?

CARA: Every month.

DR. RICE: Wow! I imagine your teeth look great!

CARA: Yeah, they're pretty healthy.

DR. RICE: And what is this incredible dentist's name, just in case there are any listeners who need a dentist?

CARA: Dr. Adam West.

DR. RICE: OK, Cara, stay on the line. Let's talk some more after the break. We're talking with Cara in Manhattan who's in love with her dentist. You're listening to *Love Matters* with me, Dr. Naomi Rice. Don't go away.

Unit 27 Achievement Test

PAUL: We need to buy fruit for tonight's dessert with Aaron and Brenda. Do you want to buy some apples?

RACHEL: Apples? Apples are boring. Let's get a pineapple instead.

PAUL: Oh, I love pineapples, but they're usually expensive. How much do they cost here?

RACHEL: Only $2 each, and they look really good.

PAUL: Hey, do you remember the pineapple we ate in Hawaii?

RACHEL: Yeah. I want to go back there. I can almost smell the tropical air.

PAUL: You know, Connie at work has a son who lives in Hawaii. He owns an apartment on the beach. Maybe we can use his apartment sometime.

RACHEL: Hmm . . . that sounds a little strange. I don't want to bother him. I don't even know him! I think I prefer to stay in a hotel.

Unit 28 Achievement Test

Good afternoon. Today I want to show you the results of my study on students and procrastination. Procrastination means avoiding doing something, usually because it is boring or unpleasant. I decided to conduct this study because I'm interested in students' motivations. All students need to do homework and study. But many of them dislike doing schoolwork, and as a result, they procrastinate.

In my study, I compared students who procrastinate with students who prefer to do their schoolwork as early as possible. I found that students felt less stress when they finished doing their homework in the afternoon or early in the evening. Students who procrastinated felt much more stress about their assignments.

Also, when students tried to do their homework as soon as possible, they generally expected to receive higher grades, and they liked going to school more. But students who refused to do their homework early generally didn't hope to get good grades. Now, in the next part of my study . . .

Unit 29 Achievement Test

SILVIA: I looked for your name on the school website, and I found your student profile. I didn't know you played hockey when you were younger. That's really neat.

CARMEN: Oh, yeah! I was on a team in my hometown. It was a lot of fun.

SILVIA: Did you play for a long time?

CARMEN: Six years.

SILVIA: Wow.

CARMEN: Yeah. I loved playing. Our team won lots of awards. I got the Most Valuable Player award my last two years.

SILVIA: Why did you stop playing?

CARMEN: Well, there are a few reasons. But mostly I'm too busy to play since I came to college.

PART VIII Achievement Test

You're listening to NGN, Network Global News. Author Lenore Penner and illustrator Justin Cohen seem to be changing the world of children's books. They are famous for their wonderful stories and illustrations. The two are working together a lot nowadays, and you rarely see their names separately anymore. Their series of children's books about Marty the Monster is very popular. Even adults love the Marty books. Penner and Cohen avoid talking to the press, but their names are often in the news. They didn't go to the annual Convention of Children's Books last week, which surprised many people. After 12 weeks, their newest book, *Marty Finds a Friend*, is still number one on the bestseller list for children's books. Cohen's beautiful illustrations look amazing, as always, and Penner's writing is inspired. Do you like the Marty books? Tell us what you think at our website, www.networkglobalnews.org.

PART IX Diagnostic Test

RAQUEL: Now that you sold your business, you won't need to worry about money. What will you do with all your money?

LOIS: I'm not sure. I may give it all away.

RAQUEL: Really?

LOIS: No. I might give some of it away, but not all of it. I'm probably going to buy a new house.

RAQUEL: Will you move away from Springfield?

LOIS: Maybe I will, but I probably won't. I like it here. I'm going to talk about it more with my husband.

RAQUEL: Do you think you're going to like staying at home instead of working?

LOIS: Well, I won't be so stressed, that's for sure. I may not see my friends from work as often, but I sure will enjoy my time at home.

RAQUEL: That sounds very nice. I might sell my business soon so that I can join you.

Unit 30 Achievement Test

DAN: Hello?

JEFF: Hi, Dan. It's Jeff. Listen, are you going to be around tomorrow?

DAN: Yeah, I think so. Why? What's going on?

JEFF: Well, a group of us are going to go to the lake tomorrow. Do you want to come?

DAN: Sure! Who's going?

JEFF: Well, it's going to be Rebecca, my wife Angie, and me. Lloyd and Sharon aren't going because Lloyd's going to be working this weekend.

DAN: Yeah, I think I can go. When are you leaving?

JEFF: We're going to leave around 9:00 tomorrow morning. Rebecca is going to bring lunch.

DAN: Do you know what the weather's going to be like?

JEFF: Yeah, it's going to be sunny and warm. Bring your swimsuit. We're probably going to go swimming.

DAN: That sounds great! See you tomorrow at 9:00!

Unit 31 Achievement Test

LISA: When will you go to Korea? Will it be in June?

PETE: Yes, we'll be in Seoul for part of June, and we're also thinking about spending a week on Jeju Island.

LISA: I have a vacation package in Jeju that you'll love! You'll stay in a great resort hotel in Jeju.

TANYA: Will we be able to go swimming?

LISA: Sure, you'll be able to swim on Hyeopjae Beach.

PETE: Will we have time to see Manjanggul Cave?

LISA: Yes. The cave is near Hyeopjae Beach.

TANYA: Will the First Full Moon Field Fire Festival take place while we're there?

LISA: No, it won't. That will be in February. Will you be there again next February?

TANYA: No, I don't think so. Will we be able to climb Hallasan Mountain this summer?

LISA: No, you won't. The trails are closed in the summer because they're dangerous. But you'll be able to ride in a helicopter over the mountain and see the crater lake.

TANYA: How much will the helicopter ride cost?

LISA: I don't know the exact price, but it probably won't cost a lot of money. I'll find out the price and let you know by tomorrow.

PETE: That sounds good. We'll probably go to Jeju, then. How much is the hotel? . . .

Unit 32 Achievement Test

JULIE: I'm worried about Chris. Where is he?

NORM: He might be at a friend's house. He'll probably be home soon.

JULIE: But he's never this late! He might be in trouble. He might be hurt.

NORM: He'll probably call. He may be in the library studying, or he may be doing homework with a friend.

JULIE: Oh, Norm! Will you go look for him, please?

NORM: Maybe I will a little later. It's still early. He might come home after I leave.

JULIE: I'm not going to wait for him to come home. I'll call the police.

NORM: It might be a good idea to wait just a little longer. Don't panic.

PART IX Achievement Test

RICK: I heard that you got a new job. Congratulations! Will you have a long commute?

LYLE: No, I won't. I got a job at Wilson's Furniture Factory on Highway 1. I'm going to start tomorrow.

RICK: Interesting. Will you make me a table?

LYLE: Sorry, I'm not going to make the furniture. I'm going to be an advertising specialist. I might get to buy the furniture more cheaply, though. Come take a look at it sometime.

RICK: Maybe I'll go look at it, but I might not buy anything. I don't have much money right now. I'm going to save money for a while.

LYLE: That's fine. When can you come?

RICK: I might not be able to go this week. I'll probably be able to stop by next week on Tuesday. But if I can't go on Tuesday, then I might go on Thursday during my lunch break.

LYLE: OK. Any day is fine with me.

PART X Diagnostic Test

WENDY: I'm going to have some juice. Would you like a glass?

LISA: Sure. That sounds great. Do you have any ice?

WENDY: Of course.

LISA: So, I had to buy five books for my classes, and they were really expensive. How many books did you buy?

WENDY: I bought five, too.

LISA: Oh, really? How much money did you spend?

WENDY: Let me think . . . about $180, I guess.

LISA: Wow, yours were much cheaper than mine.

WENDY: Well, I bought them online from bookdeals.com. Their prices aren't as bad as the prices at our campus bookstore.

LISA: Maybe I need to check that out. I won't have enough money for the rest of the semester if I shop at the campus bookstore again. Its prices are really high.

WENDY: I know. My friend Jeremy bought his books online, too, and he saved about $50. But he used cheapcheapbooks.com. He says their discounts are really good.

LISA: Were his cheaper than yours?

WENDY: I think ours were about the same price.

LISA: Wow, I'll have to check out both websites.

Unit 33 Achievement Test

LORI: Where are you from, Tom?

TOM: I'm from a city in Texas called Arlington.

LORI: Oh, interesting. How many people live there?

TOM: About 400,000.

STAN: Hmm. I didn't realize Arlington was that big. So, with a population of that size, does the city have an airport?

TOM: No. Arlington isn't far from Dallas and Fort Worth, which have a few airports—three actually. And there aren't enough people in Arlington for it to have its own airport.

STAN: I see. And how far is it from downtown Arlington to downtown Dallas?

TOM: About 20 miles. But Arlington is actually considered part of the Dallas–Fort Worth metropolitan area. The whole area is growing a lot.

LORI: So is crime a problem since the city is part of a big metropolitan area?

TOM: There are a few crimes every year, but it's pretty safe. A big part of the growing population is older people who retire there because they like the climate.

LORI: Yeah, I bet it doesn't get cold there like it does here. Do you ever get snow?

TOM: We usually don't get any snow. I remember that it snowed once when I was a kid, but not a lot. There wasn't even enough snow to make a snowball.

STAN: Well, that's a big difference from here. Arlington sounds like a nice place.

TOM: It is. I'm glad to call it home.

Unit 34 Achievement Test

Hello, I'm Avery Hudson from the food critic's corner. This week I'm reviewing Simply Spaghetti, a new Italian restaurant on the east side of town.

The first thing you notice when you enter the restaurant is that everything is crowded. There are too many tables, and there's too little space between them. The restaurant was also uncomfortable because it was too hot. There are too few windows to let cool air in. They play lively Italian music, which is nice, but sometimes it's too loud. So, in general, the restaurant doesn't have a very good atmosphere.

The service is pretty good. The waiters are friendly, but they come to the table too many times during the meal. And I suggest making a reservation. I waited too long to get a table.

And, unfortunately, the food wasn't worth the wait. I tried the vegetable soup, but it was too salty. I can't recommend the spaghetti and meatballs, either. The dish had too much sauce and too few meatballs.

The prices are too expensive for the experience that you get. Overall, Simply Spaghetti was simply awful, and I do not recommend it.

Unit 35 Achievement Test

KEN: I noticed the pictures on your desk. Are they pictures of your family?

JULIE: Yeah, that's my husband in the picture on the left. And those are our children in the other one. Emma is 10, Kristen is 8, and Mark is 5.

KEN: They're very good-looking kids.

JULIE: Thanks. And you can see they don't look anything alike! Well, Emma and Kristen both have blond hair, and their eyes are blue. But Mark's hair is brown, and his eyes are green.

KEN: And none of them have the same kind of hair, either.

JULIE: Yeah, Emma's hair is straight. But Kristen and Mark have totally different hair. Theirs is so curly.

KEN: Mark looks a lot like you.

JULIE: True. His body is tall and thin like mine.

KEN: You know, my wife and I have three children, too. But ours are much older than yours.

JULIE: Really? Do you have a picture?

PART X Achievement Test

WINONA: I'm going to make some lunch. Would you like some salad?

LESLIE: That sounds great. I'm really hungry. But do we have any dressing?

WINONA: My dressing is gone, but we still have some of yours.

LESLIE: What kind is mine? I always forget what I buy.

WINONA: Let me look. . . . It's a bottle of ranch dressing.

LESLIE: Oh, good, I like that kind. Its flavor is delicious. Hey, by the way, do you want to go shopping with me later today?

WINONA: I can't. You know I have to work on a paper.

LESLIE: Yes, I know. And how many times do I have to tell you: You can work on your paper later! Come with me!

WINONA: What are you shopping for?

LESLIE: Shoes. I want to buy some sandals like the black pair Ericka has. Hers are so pretty.

WINONA: Where are you going?

LESLIE: To City Savers. It's the best shoe store in the world. A friend's brother first told me about it, believe it or not. He buys all his shoes there. Anyway, City Savers is great because their prices are very reasonable. I think maybe Ericka got her black sandals there.

WINONA: I really like those sandals, too. How much money do you think she paid for them?

LESLIE: Not a lot at City Savers. Their discounts are really good. Nobody has prices like theirs.

WINONA: Well, if the prices can fit budgets like ours, then I'll go, but not for too long.

PART XI Diagnostic Test

TINA: Robin, here comes a customer. Can you help him, please?

ROBIN: Sure! Good morning. Would you like any help this morning?

CUSTOMER: Yes. Can you show me some indoor plants? I like that one in the window. May I see it?

ROBIN: Of course. . . . Here you go.

CUSTOMER: Yeah, I like it. But I don't like the pot it's in.

ROBIN: You can change it for another one. Would you like to see one of these?

CUSTOMER: Maybe. . . . This pot looks nice.

ROBIN: Here. You can take a closer look at it.

CUSTOMER: Hmmm. OK, I'll take it.

ROBIN: Great. Would you like anything else today? You may take a look around the store if you like.

CUSTOMER: Actually, can you help me choose some flowers for my girlfriend?

ROBIN: Sure. . . . How about these yellow roses?

CUSTOMER: Um . . . can I take the red ones instead?

ROBIN: No problem. They're a good choice, too.

CUSTOMER: Great. I think that's everything. Do you take checks?

ROBIN: Sure.

Unit 36 Achievement Test

MARTY: Excuse me. Can I ask you a question?

SALESPERSON: Sure you can.

MARTY: May I look at those digital cameras behind the glass?

SALESPERSON: Certainly. Which one do you want to look at first?

MARTY: Can I see the small black one? Oh, and may I see the one next to it, too?

SALESPERSON: Sure. Here you are. Can I help you decide between them?

MARTY: I'm not sure. Can I take a picture with this one?

SALESPERSON: That's fine, but you may not take more than a few.

MARTY: Where can I take the pictures?

SALESPERSON: Anywhere in the store.

MARTY: I want to try photographing people. Can I take your picture?

SALESPERSON: Sure.

MARTY: Thanks. May I take the camera outside to try it there?

SALESPERSON: I'm sorry, but you can't take anything out of the store without buying it. But you can try it outside if you buy it.

MARTY: If I'm not happy with the camera, may I return it?

SALESPERSON: Yes. You may return it within 30 days. Just keep your receipt.

MARTY: OK. May I see the instructions for this camera?

SALESPERSON: Of course.

Unit 37 Achievement Test

DUSTIN: Hey, Carla. Would you like to go to lunch with me?

CARLA: Sorry, I can't. I have a lot of work right now, but I'd like to go another time.

DUSTIN: OK. Well, I don't have any plans for this evening. Would you like to go to dinner tonight?

CARLA: Yes. That's perfect. Could you pick me up at 6:00?

DUSTIN: Sure. Where do you want to go?

CARLA: I'd like to try that new sushi restaurant downtown. How does that sound?

DUSTIN: Well, I'd like to eat sushi, but I'm allergic to seafood. Can you think of another place?

CARLA: Let me see. . . . Oh, I know! How about the Mexican restaurant on Broadway? I'd like that a lot.

DUSTIN: Yeah, that sounds great. So, I'll see you at 6:00.

CARLA: Actually, would you like to make it 6:30 instead? That way you won't have to hurry to get there.

DUSTIN: All right. I'll see you at 6:30.

CARLA: And would you please do me a favor and call me a few minutes before you get to my apartment?

DUSTIN: No problem, but could you remind me where you live?

CARLA: 301 Chestnut Street. It's the red building on the corner.

Unit 38 Achievement Test

EDDIE: Welcome back to the show. I'm Employment Eddie. Our next caller is in Santa Fe, New Mexico. Hi, Ron. What's up?

RON: Hi, Eddie. Here's my question: What should I do about my career? Right now, I'm the manager of a pet store. I make good money, but I think I ought to do something different with my life. I think I ought to become a teacher. My wife says I ought to try it, but I'm afraid. I don't know what to do. Should I keep my present job? Or should I follow my dream and become a teacher? It's something I've been thinking about for a long time.

EDDIE: Well, Ron, you shouldn't stay in a job just because you're afraid to change. But you shouldn't be irresponsible, either. Do you know much about teaching?

RON: No, not a lot.

EDDIE: Well, you'd better not make a decision without all the facts. Talk to some teachers. And you shouldn't talk to just one or two. Talk to as many different teachers as you can. Find out what their jobs are really like. And you'd better make sure your wife supports you.

RON: Oh, she does.

EDDIE: Great. But you'd better not quit your job yet. Take a couple of night classes while you work, and see how you feel about teaching. Then you can make an educated decision.

RON: OK, Eddie. Thanks for the advice.

Unit 39 Achievement Test

DON: Hey, aren't your parents coming to visit tonight?

KEITH: Yes. They'll be here this evening, and I have so much to do! To start with, I have to clean the apartment, and I have to wash my clothes.

DON: Do you have to study for your history test, too?

KEITH: Yes. I have to take it this afternoon, and I have to prepare for it if I'm going to do well. I also have to wash the car.

DON: I remember you complaining about some English assignment. Do you still have to turn that in?

KEITH: Yeah, I have to give that to my professor by 5:00.

DON: Well, you don't have to do everything by yourself. I can help.

KEITH: Oh, you don't have to help. I know you're busy.

DON: We're both busy, but I live here, too. I'll clean the apartment. Don't worry about it.

KEITH: Thanks, Don. I really appreciate it. I'm going to put some clothes in the washer, then I have to go study.

DON: OK. Since I have some free time, I'll get started on the cleaning right now.

PART XI Achievement Test

TITO: Randall, I have to finish this paperwork. Can you help this customer, please?

RANDALL: Sure! Good afternoon. Welcome to Tito's Pets.

CUSTOMER: Hi. I'd like a fish for my apartment. Can you show me what you have?

RANDALL: Of course. These fish right here make nice pets.

CUSTOMER: I was thinking about something smaller. May I see what other kinds you have?

RANDALL: Sure. These fish here are nice, too. They're small, and they're very easy to care for.

CUSTOMER: Yeah, that's more like what I was thinking about.

RANDALL: Would you like to take one of these?

CUSTOMER: Yes, I think so.

RANDALL: You can pick the one you like.

CUSTOMER: I'll take the striped one.

RANDALL: Of course. I'll put it in a bag for you. But you can't keep it in there too long. You'll need a fishbowl when you get home. Would you like to see some of our fishbowls? We have some right here.

CUSTOMER: Ummm . . . that one looks good. I'll take it and the fish, please.

RANDALL: Would you like to buy some fish food, too?

CUSTOMER: Yeah. I'd like this food here.

RANDALL: Certainly. OK, your total is $34.99.

CUSTOMER: Can I give you a check?

RANDALL: Only if you have identification. You may not write a check without a photo ID.

CUSTOMER: No problem. I have my driver's license right here.

PART XII Diagnostic Test

Which store offers you better prices than any other in town? Which store has sweeter fruits than anyone else? Which store has more tender cuts of meat than the store you shop at now? Stockmans! At Stockmans, we have the freshest produce. The fruits and vegetables in our store taste the same as they do on the local farms where they're grown. We also sell the finest baked goods available. We guarantee that our products are the most excellent in town!

Stockmans is different from other stores. Other stores rarely listen to their customers. Other stores are too expensive, and the quality of their products is too low! At Stockmans, we really understand our customers' needs. That's the reason that our prices are less expensive than those at other stores. And our employees are friendlier than anywhere else.

Stockmans: It's where you deserve to shop!

Unit 40 Achievement Test

MARTA: Congratulations on being accepted to medical school! That's wonderful!

ANDREA: Thanks. Actually I was accepted to two schools, Cornwell University in Greenwood and Grant Medical College in Carberry. Which is better for me? That's the tough question I have to answer.

MARTA: Which is cheaper?

ANDREA: Cornwell has lower tuition.

MARTA: Yes, but you must also consider the cost of living. Which city is more expensive to live in?

ANDREA: Carberry, I think.

MARTA: Which school has a stronger reputation?

ANDREA: Probably Grant, but Cornwell is also very good.

MARTA: Which has smaller class sizes?

ANDREA: Grant does, but class sizes at Cornwell aren't much bigger. Also, I think the people at Cornwell are probably friendlier.

MARTA: So, which are you closer to choosing?

ANDREA: I'm still not sure.

Unit 41 Achievement Test

Mario is poor, but he works hard. He really wants to leave the country and go to the city. He's tired of getting up early, working all day, going to bed late, and always feeling hungry. One day, he takes the small amount of money he has and jumps on a train as it moves slowly through his town. He hides quietly so that no one will hear him. When he arrives in the city, he finds an apartment and a job. One day, he goes to his landlord's house to give him the rent. The house looks expensive. The landlord's beautiful daughter Danielle quickly opens the door. She is dressed well. Danielle and Mario look at each other for a long time. They are clearly interested in each other, but Mario can't stay long. He has to leave to go back to work.

Unit 42 Achievement Test

DELGADO: You're listening to World Radio News. I'm Alisa Delgado. It was too uncomfortable for much of anything in Phoenix, Arizona, today, as temperatures reached 121 degrees Fahrenheit, or 49 degrees Celsius. The temperature of the ground was 180 degrees Fahrenheit, or 82 degrees Celsius, which is hot enough to cook an egg. Resident Alex Watson says it was too hot to even go outside.

WATSON: It was just way too miserable for outdoor activities today. I mean, I went out to get the mail, and it was as hot as an oven outside. At least it's only 70 degrees indoors.

DELGADO: Yes, 70 degrees is cool enough for us, too. That temperature is the same as we have in the radio studio. We're lucky we have air conditioning!

Thanks, Alex. . . . Now, a lot of people have been reporting problems with water that is too warm, too. Hot water is coming out of the cold water faucets. Health officials are working hard to make sure people stay cool enough to survive the heat. Let's hear from health official, Jay Shapiro.

SHAPIRO: Hi, Alisa. Yes, Arizona health officials are very concerned about the heat and want everyone in Phoenix to stay cool. We're especially worried about older people, since they sometimes live alone and are not as strong as other people. They have a harder time with the heat.

DELGADO: Thanks, Jay. And that's all for now. I'm Alisa Delgado, World Radio News, Phoenix.

Unit 43 Achievement Test

SADIE: Hey, who was that on the phone?

NICOLE: It was that guy Omar calling for Jessica. You know, I think he has the deepest voice I've ever heard.

SADIE: I know. He sings in the university choir, and he always has the lowest parts.

NICOLE: He sings in the choir? I thought he was a football player.

SADIE: He is. He's in the choir and on the football team. In fact, he's one of the most talented players on the team.

NICOLE: Really? I didn't know that.

SADIE: Yeah. He's not the biggest guy, but he's fast. And do you know that the school newspaper just voted him the most handsome guy on campus? Jessica says he has the best smile in the world.

NICOLE: Wow. Is he smart, too?

SADIE: Very smart. Jessica says he's the smartest guy at this school.

NICOLE: So Jessica really likes him?

SADIE: Mmm-hmm. It's the coolest thing because they're both great people. Omar is probably the friendliest guy I know.

NICOLE: That's good. Jessica deserves a good guy. She's the nicest person ever.

SADIE: Yeah, they're perfect for each other.

PART XII Achievement Test

MELISSA: I started building your website. I wanted to meet with you briefly and ask you some questions. That way I'll know better how to build it.

JED: OK.

MELISSA: Here's the homepage. Which color do you prefer for the words, blue or black?

JED: I think black is less interesting to look at, but it's easier to read.

MELISSA: True. Black is the simplest color to read. And which picture of the clock do you want, the big one, the medium-sized one, or the little one?

JED: I think the big one is the nicest, and it has the brightest colors. The small one is too hard to see. But the big one is way too big. Can we make it the same size as this picture here?

MELISSA: Sure, let me change that quickly. There. Do you want the title to be the same color as the rest of the text?

JED: Let's use a different color so the title stands out clearly from the other text.

Answer Key

PART I Diagnostic Test

1 | LISTENING: DINNER PLANS

A.
1. Are you U2
2. Yes, I am U2
3. last week U3
4. Are you U2
5. wasn't U3

B.
1. Yes, she is U1, U2
2. she U1, U3
3. was U3
4. it wasn't U3
5. No, they aren't. U2

2 | AT THE RESTAURANT

1. Yes, it is U2
2. is U1
3. Is U2
4. it's U1
5. Was U3
6. I don't know U2
7. I'm U1
8. was U3
9. wasn't U3
10. am U1
11. was U3

3 | TALKING WITH THE SERVER

Note: Both contracted and noncontracted forms are acceptable.

1. the food was delicious U2, U3
2. Is there U2
3. there isn't U2
4. was here U3
5. wasn't U3
6. it's possible U1
7. isn't bad U1
8. 's wonderful U1
9. Was she U3
10. Is there U2
11. was there U3

4 | NEW ACQUAINTANCES

Note: Both contracted and noncontracted forms are acceptable.

1. am U1
2. Are U2
3. am U2
4. Are U2
5. am U1
6. is U1
7. is U1
8. is U1
9. is U2
10. was U3
11. was U3
12. were U3
13. were U3
14. was U3
15. Were U3
16. was U3
17. was U3
18. were U3
19. Were U3
20. was U3
21. was U3
22. was U3

5 | EDITING: GOOD FOOD

DAVE: My pizza ~~are~~ *is* very good. ~~Are~~ *Is* U2 your salad good?

NANCY: Yes, ~~they are~~ *it is* U2! ~~They are~~ *It's / It is* U1 delicious.

TAMMY: Are you happy we're not at Colucci's?

NANCY: Yes! The food at Colucci's ~~were~~ *was* U3 bad. Also, the restaurant ~~were~~ *was* U3 dirty and the prices ~~was~~ *were* U3 high.

Unit 1 Achievement Test

1 | LISTENING: THE PRICE FAMILY, PART I

A.
1. They're N5
2. He's N5
3. She's N5
4. She's N5
5. He's N5
6. They're N5
7. aren't N4, N5

B.
1. are N2, N3
2. are N2, N3
3. is not N4

2 | THE PRICE FAMILY, PART II

1. (He's) a professor. N5
2. ✓ They are not rich. N4
3. ✓ They are not famous. N4
4. (They're) very good-looking. N5
5. (They're) friends of Lydia's. N5

3 | THE PRICE FAMILY, PART III

Note: Both contracted and noncontracted forms are acceptable.

1. are N2, N3
2. is N2, N3
3. isn't N4, N5
4. are N2, N3
5. They N1
6. is N2, N3
7. She N1
8. isn't N4, N5
9. is N2, N3
10. He N1

4 | EDITING: LYDIA'S FAMILY

My family *is* in Mexico. My mother *is* N2, N3 a teacher, and my father *is* N2, N3 an engineer. They

ANSWER KEY | 263

are (N2, N3) in Mexico City. They ^*are* sad because I am far away from them. I ^*are* here because I *am* (N2, N3) ^a student of English.

Unit 2 Achievement Test

1 | LISTENING: FIRST DAY OF CLASS

1. Yes, it is (N2)
2. Are you (N1)
3. Yes, I am (N2)
4. Yes, I am (N2)
5. don't think so (N4)
6. Are you (N1)
7. No, I'm not (N2)
8. It isn't (N3)
9. Is (N1)
10. I think so (N4)

2 | ASKING QUESTIONS

1. g (N2)
2. f (N3)
3. b (N3)
4. a (N3)
5. c (N2)
6. e (N2)

3 | WAITING FOR CLASS

1. Am I early? (N1)
2. Is this the right room? (N1)
3. Are you a new student? (N1)
4. Are you from Ireland? (N1)
5. Is this your bag? (N1)
6. Is this my pen? (N1)
7. Is this your first class? (N1)
8. Are they in this class? (N1)
9. Is she the teacher? (N1)
10. Is the teacher late? (N1)
11. Is Dale Shumway our teacher? / Is our teacher Dale Shumway? (N1)

4 | EDITING: LUNCHTIME

TIM: I'm hungry. ~~Hungry you are~~? *Are you hungry*
GINA: Yes, ~~am I~~. *I am* (N4)
TIM: ~~The cafeteria is~~ close? *Is the cafeteria* (N1)
GINA: I think ^. *so* (N4)

Unit 3 Achievement Test

1 | LISTENING: LAST NIGHT'S PLAY

A.
1. last night (N5)
2. was (N1)
3. were (N1)
4. were (N1)
5. No, they weren't (N2, N3)
6. yesterday (N5)
7. Was your sister (N4)

B.
1. Were (N4)
2. were (N1)
3. was (N1)

2 | SENTENCE ORDER

A: Were Nate and Gina in class on Monday? (N4)
B: Yes, they were. Why? (N1)
A: I was in the cafeteria. They weren't there. (N1, N2, N3)
B: They were at a restaurant during lunch. (N1)

3 | AFTER A TRIP

1. was (N1)
2. was (N1)
3. was (N1)
4. Were (N4)
5. was (N1)
6. were (N1)
7. weren't (N2, N3)
8. Were (N4)
9. were (N1)
10. were (N1)
11. were (N1)
12. were (N1)

4 | EDITING: JULIE'S PLAY

NANCY: Julie, your play ^ great. ~~Your friends were~~ *was* *Were your friends* (N4) happy with the play?
JULIE: Yes, they ~~was~~. But I ~~was no~~. It was bad! *were* (N1) *wasn't / was not* (N2, N3)
NANCY: No, it wasn't!

PART I Achievement Test

1 | LISTENING: THIRSTY

A.
1. Are you (U2)
2. Yes, I am (U2)
3. yesterday (U3)
4. Are you (U2)
5. wasn't (U3)

B.
1. Yes, she is (U2)
2. he (U1, U3)
3. was (U3)
4. was (U3)
5. No, they aren't. (U2)

2 | AT TOM'S DINER

1. Yes, it is (U2)
2. is (U1)
3. Is (U2)
4. it's (U1)
5. Was (U3)
6. I don't know (U2)
7. I'm (U1)
8. was (U3)
9. were (U3)
10. am / was (U1)
11. was (U3)

3 | TALKING WITH THE SERVER

Note: Both contracted and noncontracted forms are acceptable.

1. the drinks were fine (U3)
2. Is there (U2)
3. there isn't (U2)
4. was here (U3)
5. wasn't clean (U3)
6. it's possible (U1)
7. is very clean (U1)

8. aren't dirty [U1]
9. was here [U3]
10. Was he [U3]
11. Is there [U2]

4 | AN OLD FRIEND

1. 'm / am [U1]
2. Are [U2]
3. am [U2]
4. Are [U2]
5. 'm / am [U2]
6. is [U1]
7. is [U1]
8. 's / is [U1]
9. is [U2]
10. was [U3]
11. was [U3]
12. were [U3]
13. was [U3]
14. was [U3]
15. Were [U3]
16. was [U3]
17. was [U3]
18. were [U3]
19. Were [U3]
20. was [U3]
21. was [U3]
22. was [U3]

5 | EDITING: GOOD FOOD

RYAN: These fries ~~is~~ *are* very good. ~~Are~~ *Is* [U2] your hamburger good?

SHINJI: Yes, ~~they are~~ *it is* [U2]! ~~They are~~ *It's / It is* [U1] delicious.

DENISE: I'm happy we're here and not at the other diner.

SHINJI: Yes. The food at Joe's Diner ~~weren't~~ *wasn't / was not* [U3] good. The diner ~~were~~ *was* [U3] dirty and the prices ~~was~~ *were* [U3] high.

PART II Diagnostic Test

1 | LISTENING: DIRECTIONS TO THE MUSEUM

A.
1. big [U5]
2. trees [U4]
3. Park [U4]
4. an [U4]

B.
Contraction of a wh- question
1. Where's the park? [U7]

Short answer to a wh-question
1. Downtown. [U7]

Prepositions of place
1. in front of [U6]
2. next to [U6]
3. on [U6]

2 | E-MAIL FROM LONDON

1. a [U4]
2. in / near [U6]
3. England [U4]
4. Birmingham Prep [U4]
5. school [U4]
6. people [U4]
7. picture [U4]
8. in front of / near [U4]
9. Who [U7]
10. why [U7]

3 | EUGENE'S ANSWER

Prepositions of place
1. in [U6]
2. near [U6]
3. in [U6]

Singular noun
1. an artist [U4]

Plural noun
1. friends [U4]

Proper nouns
1. Sudbury [U4]
2. England [U4]

Adjectives
1. lonely [U5]
2. good [U5]

***wh*-words**
1. What [U7]

4 | EUGENE'S PICTURES

1. a picture [U4]
2. my grandparents [U4]
3. my brothers [U4]
4. in [U6]
5. between [U6]
6. Where [U7]
7. in [U6]
8. Japan [U4]
9. an international bank [U4]
10. smart [U5]

5 | DAVID'S PICTURES

1. We were at home. [U6]
2. I like the picture. [U4]
3. Who is it? [U7]
4. She was in Frankfurt, Germany. [U6, U4]
5. It's a famous hotel in Frankfurt. [U4, U5, U6]
6. The hotel was beautiful. [U4]
7. We were on the 20th floor. [U6]

6 | EDITING: THINGS TO SEE IN LONDON

EUGENE: ~~Who are your favorite place~~ *What are your favorite places / is your favorite place* [U7] in London?

DAVID: There are some ~~wonderfuls~~ *wonderful* [U5] museums. The British Museum is ~~interest~~ *interesting* [U5]. And the Tower of London is ˄*a* [U4] famous building. Also, the Royal ~~botanic~~ *Botanic* [U4] Gardens are ~~beautifuls~~ *beautiful* [U5] now. Where is your hotel?

EUGENE: My hotel is ˄*on* [U6] the corner of Knightsbridge and Wilshire. The name is ~~king~~ *King* [U4] ~~george~~ *George* [U4] Hotel. I have ˄*a* [U4] room on ˄*the* [U6] fourth floor.

Unit 4 Achievement Test

1 | LISTENING: PICTURES OF PARIS

A.
1. clothes N4
2. France N5
3. photos N4
4. a friend N2
5. a photographer N2

B.

Proper nouns	Singular nouns	Plural nouns
1. Europe N5	1. an album N3	1. pants N4
2. the Eiffel Tower N5	2. the woman N2	
	3. shirt N2	

2 | FRIENDS IN ITALY

1. a picture N2
2. Antonio N5
3. an actor N3
4. Rome N5
5. an apartment N3
6. friends N4
7. Italy N5
8. a restaurant N2
9. men N4
10. friends N4
11. a teacher N2

3 | EDITING: POSTCARD

Hello, ~~erin~~! *Erin*

I am in ~~rome, italy~~. The ~~peoples~~ are very nice.
Rome N5 Italy N5 people N4

This postcard is ∧picture of downtown. The
a N2

~~building are~~ beautiful. Last week, I was in ~~paris,~~
buildings are / building is N4   Paris N5

~~france~~.
France N5

I will show you ~~picture~~ when I return.
pictures / a picture N4

Love,
Jen

Unit 5 Achievement Test

1 | LISTENING: THE PAINTED DESERT

A.
1. easy N2
2. hot N2
3. big N4

B.
1. helpful N2
2. interesting N5
3. nice N2
4. sunny N2
5. dry N2
6. good N4
7. beautiful N4

2 | A SPECIAL PLACE

I'm in a motel in Oregon. The motel is in a (little) town by the ocean. The motel is (old), but it is (comfortable). The rates are not (expensive). The ocean is (blue), and the air is (fresh) and (salty). The beach is (clean). This place is (fun), and I am (relaxed). It's (easy) to forget about time here.

N2 throughout; "salty" N5

3 | SYDNEY, AUSTRALIA

1. The lights are bright. N2
2. The seafood is fresh. N2
3. The people are friendly. N5
4. The Sydney Opera House is big. N2
5. We are happy to be here. N2

4 | EDITING: PICTURES

TIM: This is a ∧picture ~~good~~ of you. The colors
good
are ~~beautifuls~~.
beautiful N3

PETRA: Thank you. The picture is from the Painted Desert. It was a few years ago. The weather ∧perfect.
was N2

TIM: I was there last year, but the weather ~~unusual was~~. There were very ~~strongs~~ winds, and it was cold.
was unusual N2   strong N3

PETRA: That ∧interesting.
is N2, N5

Unit 6 Achievement Test

1 | LISTENING: DIRECTIONS TO MOLLY'S PARTY

A.
1. near N1
2. next to N1
3. on the corner of N2
4. in front of N1
5. behind N1

B.
1. near N1
2. on N2
3. in front of N1
4. on the N2
5. at N2

2 | NUMBERS GAME

1. under / near N1
2. between / near / next to N1
3. near N1
4. next to / near N1
5. between / near / next to N1
6. under / near N1

3 | DIRECTIONS

1. of N1
2. near N2
3. at N1
4. in front of / near N2
5. next to / near N1
6. on the N2
7. in / at N3

4 | EDITING: PEOPLE AND PLACES

1. __X__ He lives ^(on / near) Main Street. **N2**
2. __✓__ We live near a river. **N1**
3. __X__ They live on ^(the) first floor. **N2**
4. __X__ He's ^(in) Canada now. **N1**
5. __✓__ She's at home. **N3**
6. __X__ We are in back ^(of) the house. **N1**
7. __✓__ They are on the corner of Broadway and Main Street. **N2**

Unit 7 Achievement Test

1 | LISTENING: NEW ROOMMATES

1. What **N3**
2. Who's **N6**
3. Where **N4**
4. Where's **N6**
5. Why **N5**
6. What's **N6**

2 | THE PHOTOGRAPH

Contractions of *wh-* questions
1. Why's it orange? **N6**
2. Who's the photographer? **N6**

Short answers
1. Me. **N7**
2. My sister, Jana. **N7**

3 | QUESTIONS FOR A NEW ROOMMATE

1. What **N3**
2. Why **N5**
3. Who **N2**
4. Who **N2**
5. What **N3**
6. Where **N4**
7. What's **N6**
8. Where **N4**

4 | GEOGRAPHY QUIZ

1. What **N3**
2. Who **N2**
3. Where **N4**
4. What **N3**
5. Where **N4**
6. Who **N2**
7. Why **N5**
8. What **N3**

5 | EDITING: MORE GEOGRAPHY QUESTIONS

1. Q: ~~Where~~ ^(What) is the name of a big city in Hungary? **N3**
   A: Budapest.
2. Q: What ~~is~~ ^(are) the names of the Great Lakes? **N1**
   A: Huron, Ontario, Michigan, Erie, and Superior.
3. Q: ~~What~~ ^(Where) is the country of Namibia? **N4**
   A: Namibia is in Southern Africa.
4. Q: Who ^(was) Winston Churchill ~~was~~? **N1**
   A: He was a very famous prime minister of England.

PART II Achievement Test

1 | LISTENING: DIRECTIONS TO THE RESTAURANT

A.
1. flowers **U4**
2. modern **U5**
3. World **U4**
4. an **U4**

B.
Contraction of a *wh-* question
1. What's the name of the mall? **U7**

Short answer to a *wh-* question
1. On the corner of First Avenue and Main Street. **U7**

Prepositions of place
1. on the corner of **U6**
2. in front of **U6**
3. behind **U6**

2 | E-MAIL FROM MELBOURNE

1. in **U6**
2. Australia **U4**
3. an **U4**
4. Australian Art **U4**
5. in **U6**
6. store **U4**
7. photograph **U4**
8. Albert Namatjira **U4**
9. Who **U7**
10. why **U7**

3 | LORI'S ANSWER

Prepositions of place	Singular nouns	Plural nouns
1. in **U6**	1. an artist **U4**	1. parents **U4**
2. near **U6**		
3. in **U6**		

Proper nouns	Adjectives	*wh-* words
1. Canberra **U4**	1. bored **U5**	1. What **U7**
2. Australia **U4**	2. great **U5**	

4 | NANCY'S PICTURES

1. a photo **U4**
2. my parents **U4**
3. my sisters **U4**
4. in **U6**
5. between **U6**
6. Where **U7**

7. in U6
8. Korea U4
9. a computer company U4
10. intelligent U5

5 | AMY'S PICTURES

1. I have photos. U4
2. They're in an album. U6
3. Where were you? U7
4. I was in Puerto Rico. U6, U4
5. They're good friends. U5, U4
6. I was in front of a famous building. U6, U4
7. It's in San Juan. U6

6 | EDITING: THINGS TO SEE IN MELBOURNE

What are your favorite things / is your favorite thing U7
NANCY: ~~Who are your favorite thing~~ in Melbourne?

AMY: The National ~~gallery~~ Gallery U4 of Victoria is ~~interest~~ interesting U5.
It is a U4 museum. Most ~~person~~ people U4 like to see the beach. There are some ~~greats~~ great U5 restaurants.
Also, the ~~melbourne~~ Melbourne U4 Aquarium is ~~funs~~ fun U5. Where is your hotel?

NANCY: My hotel is on the corner of U6 Queen and Lonsdale. I have a U4 room on the U6 seventh floor.

PART III Diagnostic Test

1 | LISTENING: DINNER PLANS

A.
1. Do you know U9
2. Who teaches U10
3. No, you don't U9
4. sounds U8
5. don't know U8
6. I am U9

B.
Wh- questions
1. (So) how do you know Pam? U10
2. When does the party start? U10

Yes / no questions
1. Do I sign up somewhere? U9
2. Are you busy on Tuesday? U9

2 | DINNER CONVERSATION

1. do U9
2. is U8
3. does U9
4. doesn't U8
5. am U8
6. how U10
7. cook U8
8. Do U9
9. don't U8
10. Who U10
11. what U10
12. has U8
13. Who U10

3 | AN ARTIST

1. Do you paint U9
2. make U8
3. do you get U10
4. give U8
5. Who is U10
6. don't know U8
7. don't need U8
8. Do you sell U9
9. I do U9
10. who buys U10
11. come U8
12. do you want U9
13. When is U10

4 | COMPUTER BUSINESS

1. have a computer business U8
2. sell new computers U8
3. repair old computers U8
4. Do you like your work U9
5. Yes, I love it U9
6. Who(m) do you sell your services to U10
7. Do you have a computer U9
8. No, I don't U9
9. Are your computers inexpensive U9
10. Yes, they are U9
11. how do I know U10
12. do you have U9
13. Yes, I do U9
14. how do people find U10
15. Who(m) do I learn U10
16. Do you have U9

5 | EDITING: WORKING FROM HOME

TINA: Your business ~~seem~~ seems great. ~~Do is~~ Is U9 it easy to have a business in your home?

GEORGE: It's not always easy, but I like it. I don't drive or ~~don't~~ U8 sit in traffic to get to work, and that's nice. Some of my neighbors ~~thinks~~ think U8 that I ~~not~~ don't U8 work because they don't see me leave the house every day. But I'm very busy at home.

TINA: Who ~~does~~ U10 helps you?

GEORGE: What do you mean?

TINA: Well, for example, who ~~does~~ U10 brings you the computers?

GEORGE: The mail carrier.

TINA: Oh, that makes sense. And ~~whom~~ who U10 helps you do the repairs?

GEORGE: A friend works with me two days a week. On the other days, it's just me.
TINA: Wow, it sounds like a lot of work.
GEORGE: It is, but I love it.
TINA: Well, I need to go now. But ~~do~~ are you busy tomorrow? I want to look at your computers. [U9]

Unit 8 Achievement Test

1 | LISTENING: SHOPPING

A.
1. walk [N4]
2. go [N4]
3. take [N4]
4. carry [N4]
5. is [N8]
6. think [N4]

B.
1. You don't need a car. [N6]
2. I don't buy a lot. [N6]
3. I don't need a car. [N6]

2 | MY FAMILY

1. studies [N4]
2. doesn't [N6]
3. works [N4]
4. don't [N6]
5. come [N4]
6. eat [N4]
7. drink [N4]

3 | AFFIRMATIVE AND NEGATIVE STATEMENTS

1. a. drives [N4]
   b. doesn't drive [N6]
2. a. go [N4]
   b. don't go [N6]
3. a. want [N4]
   b. doesn't want [N6]
4. a. wear [N4]
   b. don't wear [N6]
5. a. practice [N4]
   b. doesn't practice [N6]

4 | EDITING: WITHOUT A CAR

Megan ~~shop~~ *shops* at the store twice a week. She usually ~~walk~~ *walks* [N4] with her friend Kevin. They ~~doesn't~~ *don't* [N6] have cars, but that ~~be~~ *is* [N8] fine with them. They don't work or ~~don't~~ [N6] study far from home.

Unit 9 Achievement Test

1 | LISTENING: LOOKING FOR A JOB

A.
1. Yes, I do [N2]
2. Do you have [N1]
3. yes, it is [N2]
4. No, we don't [N1]
5. Does she take [N2]
6. Yes, she does [N3]

B.
1. Do you need some help? [N1]
2. Is it popular? [N3]
3. Does your band play on weekends? [N1]

2 | TALKING ABOUT FRIENDS

1. visit [N1]
2. don't [N2]
3. have [N1]
4. do [N2]
5. live [N1]
6. doesn't [N2]
7. Do [N1]
8. do [N2]

3 | QUESTIONS AND ANSWERS

1. a. Do . . . have [N1]
   b. I do [N2]
2. a. Does . . . live [N1]
   b. he doesn't [N2]
3. a. Do . . . visit [N1]
   b. they don't [N2]
4. a. Do . . . walk [N1]
   b. they do [N2]
5. a. Does . . . go [N1]
   b. she doesn't [N2]

4 | EDITING: WHERE ARE YOU FROM?

SHANNON: You have an accent. ~~Is~~ *Are* you from Mexico?
GABRIEL: No, I'm not. Guess again.
SHANNON: ~~Do are~~ *Are* [N3] you from Spain?
GABRIEL: No. Try again.
SHANNON: Do ~~live you~~ *you live* [N1] in Brazil?
GABRIEL: No.
SHANNON: I give up. ~~Does~~ *Do* [N1] you come from Argentina?
GABRIEL: Yes! I'm from Argentina.

Unit 10 Achievement Test

1 | LISTENING: HELP FROM MOTHER

A.
1. How do [N1]
2. When do I [N1]

3. what happens N2
4. who wants N2
5. Where do N1
6. Who N2

B.
1. What do you mean? N1
2. How do you relax? N1
3. What do they do? N1

2 | MUSIC QUESTIONS AND ANSWERS

1. f N3
2. b N2, N3
3. h N1
4. a N1
5. d N3
6. j N1
7. e N2, N3

3 | QUESTIONS

1. Who calls his friend every week N2, N3
2. Who / Whom does the student call every week N1, N3
3. What stays on the desk N1
4. Where does the computer stay N1
5. Who has a cell phone N2, N3
6. What does Jack have N1
7. Who sees their dad every day N2, N3
8. Who / Whom do Tom and Linda see every day N2, N3
9. What feels hot N1, N2
10. Why does the apartment feel hot N1

4 | EDITING: A NEW DOG

SHERRY: Hey, Barbara. I hear you have a new dog.
How ~~it feels~~ *does it feel* to have an addition to your family?
BARBARA: Great! The dog is wonderful. Hey, I have a question. Where does your dog ~~sleeps~~ *sleep*? N1
SHERRY: In my bed, with me. Why ~~you do~~ *do you* ask? N1
BARBARA: Well, I don't want my dog to sleep in the bed. How *do* I teach him to sleep on the floor? N1
SHERRY: I don't know the answer to that. Let me think. . . . Who ~~know~~ *knows* a lot about dogs? Oh, Mike knows a lot about dogs. Ask him. N3
BARBARA: OK, thanks. I will.

PART III Achievement Test

1 | LISTENING: LISA AND ALEX

A.
1. Are you U9
2. No, I'm not U9
3. take U8
4. love U8
5. don't take U8
6. Do you have U9
7. No, I don't U9

B.
1. What do you take pictures of? U10
2. When do you have some time? U10
3. Are you a good photographer? U9
4. Do you want to see my photos? U9

2 | LOOKING AT PICTURES

1. like U9
2. do U9
3. are U8
4. Where U10
5. Who U10
6. does U10
7. need U8
8. How U10
9. use / like U8
10. why U10
11. know U8
12. don't U8
13. teaches U10
14. who U10

3 | CLASSICAL MUSIC

1. like music U8
2. Do you play U9
3. I play U8
4. write U8
5. Do you have U9
6. is U8
7. Who do you listen to U10
8. Do you know U9
9. I don't U9
10. Who do you like U10
11. starts U8
12. Who do I buy tickets U10

4 | A SMALL BUSINESS

1. have a small school U8
2. What do you teach U10
3. teach English U8
4. give Spanish and French classes U8
5. Do you like your work U9
6. Yes, I love it U9
7. Do you want language classes U9
8. No, I don't U9
9. Who studies with you U10
10. What do you mean U10
11. do you work with children U9
12. Who does my friend call U10
13. someone answers the phone U8
14. Yes, I do U9

5 | EDITING: OWNING A BUSINESS

NEIL: Your job ~~sound~~ *sounds* fun. ~~Do~~ *Is* it nice to have your own business? U9
MEGAN: I like it. I ~~doesn't~~ *don't* want to work for someone else. U8 Some people think teachers ~~not~~ *don't* work much, but we do! U8

270 | ANSWER KEY

NEIL: ~~Does the work is~~ *Is the work* [U9] hard?
MEGAN: Yes, it is, but I enjoy it. And I have help.
NEIL: Oh, who ~~does~~ helps you? [U10]
MEGAN: I have a secretary, and there are two other teachers.
NEIL: Do the teachers work every day?
MEGAN: Yes, they do ~~work~~. [U9]
NEIL: Who find⌃s the students? [U10]
MEGAN: We advertise online. Students come to us.
NEIL: ~~You~~ *Do you* [U9] have a lot of students?
MEGAN: Yes, business is very good right now. In fact, we ~~doesn't~~ *don't* [U8] have enough classes for all our students. We plan to offer more classes soon.

PART IV Diagnostic Test

1 | LISTENING: GOING TO THE CONCERT

A.
1. What time [U11]
2. At [U11]
3. this [U13]
4. those [U13]

B.
1. its [U12]
2. whose [U12]
3. our [U12]
4. Kim's [U12]
5. her [U12]
6. Your [U12]

2 | AN EVENING WITH FRIENDS

1. your [U12]
2. this [U13]
3. It [U14]
4. one [U14]
5. whose [U12]
6. or [U13]
7. second [U11]
8. her [U12]
9. Jamie's [U12]
10. my [U12]
11. on [U11]

3 | AT THE STORE

1. When [U11]
2. in [U11]
3. your / his [U12]
4. my [U12]
5. my / those [U12]
6. boss's [U12]
7. boss's [U12]
8. These [U13]
9. this [U13]
10. these [U13]
11. or [U13]
12. ones [U14]

4 | AT THE MEETING

Pronouns
1. ones [U14]
2. one [U14]
3. That [U13]
4. It [U14]
5. one [U14]

Possessive adjectives
1. our [U12]
2. Whose [U12]
3. my [U12]
4. her [U12]

Possessive noun
1. Kim's [U12]

Cardinal numbers
1. ten [U11]
2. four [U11]

5 | SLEEP WELL

1. his / her / my doctor's [U12]
2. in / during [U11]
3. your / a person's [U12]
4. Second [U11]
5. your / a person's [U12]
6. one [U14]
7. one [U14]
8. it [U14]

6 | EDITING: THE NEW PILLOW

STACIE: ~~Who's~~ *Whose* pillow is this? [U12]
CHRIS: It's ~~Jamies~~ *Jamie's* pillow. [U12]
STACIE: Which Jamie? ~~Ours~~ *Our* [U12] neighbor Jamie, ~~and~~ *or* [U13] our friend Jamie?
CHRIS: The ~~two~~ *second* [U11] Jamie, our friend. I don't sleep well ~~in~~ *at* [U11] night, so he thinks I should try ~~pillow his~~ *his pillow* [U12]. I like⌃ *it* [U14].

Unit 11 Achievement Test

1 | LISTENING: NEW YEAR'S DAY

1. 1st [N3]
2. in [N2]
3. in [N2]
4. at [N2]
5. at [N2]
6. in [N2]
7. on [N2]
8. 11th [N3]
9. 13th [N3]
10. 15th [N3]

2 | GRANDPARENTS DAY

1. on [N2]
2. first [N3]
3. in [N2]
4. on [N2]
5. second [N3]
6. in [N2]
7. on [N2]
8. first [N3]
9. seven [N3]
10. on [N2]
11. in [N2]
12. first [N3]

3 | GRADUATION

1. When [N1]
2. on [N2]
3. What [N1]
4. at [N2]

4 EDITING: AFTER GRADUATION PLANS

LOUIS: ~~When~~ *What* are your plans after you graduate?

SARA: My ~~one~~ *first* [N3] plan is to visit my parents in Ohio.

My ~~two~~ *second* [N3] plan is to visit my ~~third~~ *three* [N3] brothers. They live in California.

LOUIS: ~~When~~ *What* [N1] day do you start work?

SARA: Work? Umm . . .

Unit 12 Achievement Test

1 LISTENING: BEFORE CLASS

A.
1. My name [N3]
2. whose book [N5]
3. Asami's book [N1, N2]

B.
1. our [N3]
2. his [N3]
3. my [N3]
4. Asami's [N1, N2]
5. Whose [N5]
6. her [N3]

2 ASAMI'S FAMILY

1. Whose [N5]
2. your [N3]
3. My [N3]
4. brother's [N4]
5. His [N3]
6. Her [N3]
7. sister [N4]
8. her [N3]
9. their [N3]
10. Her [N3]
11. Your [N3]
12. your [N3]

3 BOOKS

1. my [N3]
2. my [N3]
3. mother's [N1, N2]
4. my brother Jack's [N1, N2]
5. Whose [N5]
6. my [N3]

4 EDITING: THE ART BOOK

ASAMI: This is a beautiful art book. ~~Who~~ *Whose* is it? Is it ~~you're~~ *your* [N3] book?

KATHY: No, it's my ~~dads~~ *dad's* [N2] book.

Unit 13 Achievement Test

1 LISTENING: AT THE MUSEUM

A.
1. or [N7]
2. those [N4]
3. That's [N6]

B.
1. A [N5]
2. P [N5]
3. A [N5]
4. P [N5]
5. A [N5]

C.
1. Did they all die because of humans or because of another reason? [N6]
2. Where do you want to go next, this way or that way? [N6]

2 THE BLUE WHALE

1. or [N7]
2. that [N2]
3. that [N2]
4. this / that [N2]
5. or [N7]
6. That [N6]
7. these [N4]
8. That [N6]
9. these / those [N3]
10. or [N7]
11. These / Those [N3]

3 BUTTERFLIES

1. or [N7]
2. this / that [N2]
3. these / those [N3]
4. or [N7]
5. This [N2]
6. These / Those [N3]

4 EDITING: AFTER THE MUSEUM

JOSH: I think ~~these~~ *this* is the exit.

MEGAN: That movie was really good. And ~~that~~ *those* [N3] butterflies were beautiful. Thank you for bringing me to ~~those~~ *this / that* [N2] museum.

JOSH: You're welcome. Now, do you want to see the gift shop, ~~and~~ *or* [N7] do you want to eat lunch?

Unit 14 Achievement Test

1 LISTENING: BUYING PET FISH

1. one [N3]
2. ones [N3]
3. ones [N3]
4. one [N1]
5. It [N7]
6. one [N2]
7. it [N5]
8. It [N5]
9. it [N6]

2 LUNCH

1. one [N1]
2. that one [N4]
3. one [N2]
4. ones [N3]
5. ones [N3]
6. It [N5]
7. it [N5]
8. It [N6]

3 | LOOKING AT CARS

1. ones [N3]
2. one [N3]
3. one [N4]
4. one [N3]
5. one [N2]
6. it [N5]
7. It [N5]
8. one [N4]
9. one [N4]

4 | EDITING: NO NEW CAR

DAN: Mike and I looked at cars, but I didn't buy ~~it~~ *one*.

MARA: Really? Why not?

DAN: Well, I liked one a lot, but ~~one~~ *it* [N5] was yellow. Mike thinks it looks like a taxi. I like the model of the car. Sometimes they have white ~~one~~ *ones* [N3] and silver ~~one~~ *ones* [N3], but not right now.

MARA: That's OK. Our car is old, but we don't need a new ~~ones~~ *one* [N1] right now.

PART IV Achievement Test

1 | LISTENING: GOING TO THE MOVIES

A.
1. What time [U11]
2. At [U11]
3. that [U13]
4. Those [U13]

B.
1. whose [U12]
2. my [U12]
3. sister's [U12]
4. my [U12]
5. Your [U12]
6. your [U12]

2 | THE NEW APARTMENT

1. This [U13]
2. your [U12]
3. It [U14]
4. one [U14]
5. whose [U12]
6. or [U13]
7. second [U11]
8. our [U12]
9. Wendy's [U12]
10. her [U12]
11. on [U11]

3 | AT THE MALL

1. When [U11]
2. on [U11]
3. your [U12]
4. My [U12]
5. my [U12]
6. mom's [U12]
7. mom's [U12]
8. These [U13]
9. this [U13]
10. that [U13]
11. or [U13]
12. ones [U14]

4 | AT THE BIRTHDAY PARTY

Pronouns
1. ones [U14]
2. one [U14]
3. this [U13]
4. That [U13]
   It [U14]

Possessive adjectives
1. your [U12]
2. Whose [U12]
3. my [U12]
4. Her [U12]
   our [U12]

Cardinal numbers
1. two [U11]
2. one [U11]

5 | HELEN'S SECRET

1. on [U11]
2. her / that [U12, U13]
3. her / Helen's / their / her family's [U12]
4. first [U11]
5. my [U12]
6. Helen's / her [U12]
7. one [U14]
8. one [U14]

6 | EDITING: THE JACKET

HELEN: ~~Who's~~ *Whose* jacket is this? I like ~~.~~ *it* [U14].

WILL: It's ~~Richs~~ *Rich's* [U12] jacket.

HELEN: ~~Ours~~ *Our* [U12] friend Rich, ~~and~~ *or* [U13] our neighbor Rich?

WILL: Our friend Rich. He was here this morning, but he forgot his jacket.

HELEN: This is the ~~two~~ *second* [U11] time that he forgot ~~jacket his~~ *his jacket* [U12] at our house!

WILL: I'll give it to him ~~in~~ *on* [U11] Monday.

PART V Diagnostic Test

1 | LISTENING: AT THE COLD CUT CAFÉ

A.
1. Follow [U17]
2. Let [U17]
3. Can you turn [U18]
4. isn't working [U15]
5. can call [U18]

B.

Present continuous verbs
Is he coming [U16]
you're shaking [U15]

Suggestion
Let's start [U19]

Response to suggestion
That's a great idea! [U19]

ANSWER KEY | 273

2 PLANNING THE COMFORT CAFÉ

1. a (U16)
2. c (U15)
3. d (U16)
4. b (U15)
5. d (U18)
6. c (U19)
7. d (U19)
8. a (U18)
9. b (U17)
10. b (U18)
11. a (U15)

3 A COOK FOR THE COMFORT CAFÉ

1. can (U18)
2. Don't (U17)
3. is working (U15)
4. can't (U18)
5. Why don't we (U19)
6. is he looking (U16)
7. is thinking (U15)
8. Let's (U19)
9. Is he working (U16)
10. is visiting (U15)
11. can't (U18)

4 CLOSING TIME

1. Why are they closing (U16)
2. couldn't get / could not get (U18)
3. Is business going (U16)
4. 're doing / are doing (U15)
5. are coming in and buying (U15)
6. 're finishing / are finishing (U15)
7. 're not stopping / aren't stopping / are not stopping (U15)
8. could do (U18)
9. Let's go (U19)
10. Please help (U17)

5 OLD FRIENDS

1. are . . . doing (U16)
2. are . . . working (U16)
3. 're enjoying / are enjoying (U15)
4. 'm going / am going (U15)
5. Come (U17)
6. can't (U18)
7. Don't worry (U17)
8. don't say (U17)
9. can (U18)
10. Sit (U17)

6 EDITING: ANOTHER COMFORT CAFÉ

ALICE: We *are* having a busy week! Business *is* not (U15) slowing down at all! *Can you* ~~You can~~ (U18) check how much money we have in the bank?

JOANNE: Sure. I can check it online. OK, here is our bank information.

ALICE: Are we ~~do~~ *doing* (U16) well this week?

JOANNE: We are ~~make~~ *making* (U15) a lot of money right now. People are coming and ~~are~~ bringing their friends. (U15)

ALICE: ~~Print please~~ *Please print* (U17) our bank statement. . . . This is great. Why ~~we don't~~ *don't we* (U19) open another Comfort Café?

JOANNE: That *'s* (U19) a good idea.

ALICE: ~~You call~~ *Call / You can call* (U17, U18) tomorrow and see if there are any good places for a second café.

JOANNE: OK!

Unit 15 Achievement Test

1 LISTENING: AFTER THE EARTHQUAKE

1. 're seeing (N2)
2. 'm standing (N2)
3. are walking (N1)
4. is not working (N1)
5. are looking (N1)
6. is rising (N1)
7. are trying (N1)
8. is asking (N1)

2 SATURDAY MORNING

1. is standing (N1)
2. is making (N1)
3. is frying (N1)
4. is not working (N4)
5. is sitting (N1)
6. is running (N1)
7. is exercising (N4)

3 SCENES FROM A STORE

Note: Both contracted and noncontracted forms are acceptable.

1. are looking (N1)
2. is sitting (N1)
3. is giving (N1)
4. is leaving (N1)
5. is playing (N4)
6. is asking (N1)
7. are talking (N1)
8. is eating (N1)
9. is helping (N1)

4 EDITING: AT THE PARTY

SHELLY: Great party, Dean. Everything is ~~being~~ wonderful!

RHONDA: Yeah, everything is very good. People are eating and ~~are~~ drinking a lot. (N3)

DEAN: Well, I'm glad they are ~~enjoy~~ *enjoying* (N1) everything.

SHELLY: Everyone is ~~has~~ *having* (N1) a great time, too. This party was a great idea. A lot of us ~~don't~~ *aren't* (N2) going out much nowadays. . . . Hey, where are Kevin and Heather?

RHONDA: They're walking around and ~~are~~ talking outside. (N3)

DEAN: They are not ~~spend~~ *spending* (N4) enough time together these days.

RHONDA: I know. I think that's why they want to be alone now.

Unit 16 Achievement Test

1 LISTENING: GOOD NEIGHBORS

A.
1. What are you making N2
2. Of course it is N1
3. Are you having N1
4. Who is having N3
5. are you going N2

B.
1. Are you feeling OK? N1
2. Is David working today? N1
3. Are they playing outside? N1

2 QUESTIONS

1. Are you sitting N1
2. are you talking N2
3. are they laughing N2
4. are you eating N2
5. are you talking N2
6. Is your wife feeling N1
7. Are they playing N1
8. are you working N2
9. Are you looking N1
10. traveling N1

3 BUSINESS TRIP

1. It is / It's going OK N1
2. Where are you calling N2
3. Why are you staying N2
4. Are you getting N1
5. What are you reading N2
6. What is happening N3
7. What are they working N2
8. Are they behaving N1

4 EDITING: AT THE DOCTOR'S OFFICE

DR. MONTOYA: How are you ~~feel~~ *feeling*?
AMY: I am not ~~cough~~ *coughing* N2. But I'm sneezing all the time.
DR. MONTOYA: Are you taking any medication?
AMY: Yes, I am.
DR. MONTOYA: Is it working?
AMY: Yes, it ~~does~~ *is* N1, but only for a few hours. I'm also taking some vitamins now.
DR. MONTOYA: What kind of vitamins ~~you use~~ *are you using* N2?
AMY: Vitamin C and a multivitamin.
DR. MONTOYA: How ~~is~~ *are* N2 you sleeping?
AMY: Just fine.
DR. MONTOYA: Good. Let me check your throat. Say "Ah"!

Unit 17 Achievement Test

1 LISTENING: CAR SALE

A.
1. Don't miss N3
2. drive N1
3. Visit N1

B.
1. Bring N1
2. Find N1
3. Choose N1
4. Get N1
5. Don't wait N3

2 CLASS RULES

1. Arrive N1
2. Don't N3
3. Be N1
4. Don't N3
5. Don't N3
6. Clean N1
7. Put N1
8. Turn N1
9. Please don't N3, N5
10. Pay N1
11. Please speak N5
12. Please don't N3, N5
13. Please don't N3, N5
14. Please don't N3, N5
15. Stay N1

3 EDITING: WIN A TRIP!

~~Winning~~ *Win* a trip for two to Hawaii!
Thank you for buying your car or truck from Gary's Downtown Auto Mall. Now try to win a trip to Hawaii! ~~Completes~~ *Complete* N1 this form. ~~Write please~~ *Please write* N5 your name and address. ~~Use blue please~~ *Please use blue* N5 or black ink. ~~Send not~~ *Don't send* N3 money. ~~Mailing~~ *Mail* N1 your entry before December 31. ~~You visit~~ *Visit* N4 our website for more contest information at www.garyauto.com. ~~You enjoy~~ *Enjoy* N4 your new car or truck!

Unit 18 Achievement Test

1 LISTENING: PRESTO PESTO'S

A.
1. can help N1
2. can take N1
3. can get N1
4. can't find N2
5. can't wait N2

B.
1. can deliver N1
2. can enjoy N1
3. can look N1

2 TANYA IS HUNGRY!

1. e N2
2. g N2
3. a N4
4. h N4
5. b N4
6. f N1

3 JOB HUNTING

1. Can she sing **N3**
2. can (sing) **N1**
3. Can she dance **N3**
4. couldn't dance **N4**
5. Can she play the drums **N3**
6. could (play the drums) **N4**
7. Could Mark drive **N5**
8. couldn't drive **N4**
9. Can he cut grass **N3**
10. can (cut grass) **N1**
11. Can he lift heavy boxes **N3**
12. Can he paint **N3**
13. couldn't paint **N4**

4 EDITING: A RIDE TO THE STORE

TANYA: ~~You can~~ *Can you* take me to the grocery store? I ~~could find not~~ *could not / couldn't find* **N4** anything to eat today.
RON: No problem. When do you want to go? I can ✗ take you now or later. **N1**
TANYA: Can you ✗ be ready in 15 minutes? **N3**
RON: Sure.

Unit 19 Achievement Test

1 LISTENING: PLANS FOR THE DAY

A.
1. Let's go **N1**
2. sounds good **N3**
3. Let's find **N1**
4. Why don't we **N2**
5. Let's not sit **N1**
6. That's a good idea **N3**

B.
1. Why don't we see **N2**
2. Let's go **N1**
3. Let's take **N1**
4. Why don't you call **N2**

2 LUNCHTIME

1. Let's get **N1**
2. don't we have **N2**
3. don't we try **N2**
4. That sounds good **N3**
5. Let's not go **N1**
6. Let's look for **N1**
7. let's not eat **N1**
8. Let's try **N1**

3 PLANS FOR THE EVENING

1. let's not **N1**
2. Let's **N1**
3. why don't we **N2**
4. let's **N1**
5. let's **N1**
6. why don't you **N2**
7. That sounds like a plan / That's a good idea **N3**
8. Why don't you **N2**
9. That's a good idea / That sounds like a plan **N3**

4 EDITING: THE NEXT TRIP

JEFF: This trip was so great, ~~let us~~ *let's* plan another one for next year.
GREG: Sounds good to me. Where do you want to go?
JEFF: Let's go to Tahiti.
GREG: That's ᵃ good idea. **N3** Why ~~you don't~~ *don't you* talk to your friend the travel agent? **N2**
JEFF: OK. Let's ✗ plan to go in June next year. **N1**
GREG: Perfect!

PART V Achievement Test

1 LISTENING: AT THE FIESTA TACO RESTAURANT

A.
1. Come **U17**
2. Look **U17**
3. can you turn **U18**
4. isn't working **U15**
5. can call **U18**

B.

<u>Present continuous verbs</u>
1. Is she coming **U16**
2. I'm sweating **U15**

<u>Suggestion</u>
1. Let's open **U19**

<u>Response to suggestion</u>
1. That's a good idea! **U19**

2 PLANNING THE TRES AMIGOS RESTAURANT

1. a **U16**
2. c **U15**
3. b **U16**
4. c **U15**
5. d **U18**
6. c **U19**
7. d **U19**
8. a **U18**
9. b **U17**
10. b **U18**
11. a **U15**

3 | A CHEF FOR THE TRES AMIGOS

1. Can we find (U18)
2. Don't (U17)
3. is she doing (U16)
4. is working (U15)
5. is thinking (U15)
6. Let's (U19)
7. Is she working (U16)
8. is staying (U15)
9. Why don't you (U19)
10. can tell (U18)
11. tell (U17)

4 | AFTER WORK

1. Why are they closing (U16)
2. couldn't make (U18)
3. Are a lot of customers coming (U16)
4. is growing (U15)
5. are coming in and eating (U15)
6. is finishing (U15)
7. are not / 're not / aren't making (U15)
8. could do (U18)
9. Let's go (U19)
10. Help (U17)

5 | DINNER

1. are . . . doing (U16)
2. am / 'm working (U15)
3. am / 'm having (U15)
4. is / 's making (U15)
5. Put (U17)
6. Can (U18)
7. don't worry (U17)
8. Can (U18)
9. Give (U17)
10. Don't forget (U17)

6 | EDITING: ANOTHER TRES AMIGOS RESTAURANT

ALFRED: I ^am thinking about our bank account.
~~You can~~ *Can you* (U18) look at it to see how much money we have? Check it on the Internet.
LUIS: OK.
ALFRED: How ^*is / 's* (U16) business going this month? Are we ~~make~~ *making* (U16) more than last month?
JAIME: Yes, Tres Amigos ~~is make~~ *is making* (U15) more these days! We ~~do~~ *are doing / 're doing* (U15) very well right now.
ALFRED: ~~You let~~ *Let* (U17) me see our bank statement. . . . This is excellent. Why ~~we don't~~ *don't we* (U19) open another Tres Amigos?
LUIS: That ^'s (U19) a good idea.

ALFRED: Jaime, ~~make please~~ *please make* some calls. Let's find out if there are any good places for a second restaurant.
JAIME: OK!

PART VI Diagnostic Test

1 | LISTENING: HOME FOR THE WEEKEND

A.
1. How was (U22)
2. landed (U20)
3. Did you do (U22)
4. did you write (U22)
5. last year (U20)
6. didn't know (U21)

B.
Simple past regular verbs
1. needed (U20)
2. wanted (U20)
3. realized (U20)

Simple past irregular verbs
1. slept (U21)
2. woke (U21)
3. wrote (U21)

2 | A BABY

1. was (U21)
2. Did you see (U22)
3. didn't (U22)
4. called (U20)
5. didn't have (U21)

3 | THE SPACE MUSEUM

1. went (U21)
2. did . . . go (U22)
3. visited (U20)
4. Did . . . have (U22)
5. thought (U21)
6. waited (U20)
7. didn't come (U21)
8. walked (U20)
9. was (U21)

4 | AT AUNT HELEN'S

1. ate too much (U21)
2. prepared it (U20)
3. didn't have any food (U21)
4. went to the store (U21)
5. bought some chicken (U21)
6. Did you know (U22)
7. went to the space museum (U21)
8. didn't know (U21)
9. was great (U22)

5 | LAST NIGHT

1. visited /ɪd/
2. cooked /t/
3. watched /t/
4. hugged /d/
5. arrived /d/

6 | EDITING: AUNT HARRIETT

JASON: Who's in this picture, Dad?

MR. UNVER: You never ~~did knew~~ *knew* her, but this is your Great Aunt Harriett.

PAM: ~~She was~~ *Was she* your dad's sister?

MR. UNVER: No, she ~~not~~ *wasn't / was not*. She was my Uncle Hubert's wife. She ^*was* born in Chicago in 1935.

JASON: Why ^*did* she wear that funny uniform?

MR. UNVER: She ~~work~~ *worked* as a nurse.

PAM: It's a great picture of her. Who ~~did take~~ *took* it?

MR. UNVER: Your Great Uncle Hubert ~~taked~~ *took* it. He ~~did~~ had a very nice camera, and he ~~know~~ *knew* how to use it.

PAM: Do you still have the camera?

MR. UNVER: No. Your Aunt Helen ~~borrow~~ *borrowed* it two years ^*ago* but she never ~~return~~ *returned* it. I ~~did~~ asked her about it last month, but she ~~not~~ *didn't / did not* know where it was.

PAM: Oh no! I hope she didn't ~~lost~~ *lose* it.

Unit 20 Achievement Test

1 | LISTENING: CARACAS

A.
1. dropped
2. opened
3. tried
4. washed
5. walked
6. started

B.
1. last night
2. yesterday
3. Yesterday afternoon

2 | ROOMMATES

1. talked
2. didn't listen
3. joked
4. didn't laugh
5. baked
6. didn't like
7. rented
8. didn't watch
9. borrowed
10. didn't return

3 | NEGATIVES IN THE PAST

Note: Both contracted and noncontracted forms are acceptable.
1. didn't walk
2. didn't shop
3. didn't stay
4. didn't work
5. didn't play

4 | EDITING: E-MAIL FROM STAN

Hi, Jen,

~~I three days ago~~ *Three days ago* arrived in Caracas, Venezuela. The plane ~~lands~~ *landed*, and I was happy to be here. ^I walked ~~Monday~~ around the city. *Monday I walked around the city. / I walked around the city Monday.* Then it ~~rains~~ *rained* a little bit, so I returned to my hotel. My friend Raúl ~~invites~~ *invited* me to dinner yesterday evening. The food ~~tastes~~ *tasted* delicious. ~~Today morning~~ *This morning* I toured downtown. I just want you to know that I am here and OK.

Take care,
Stan

Unit 21 Achievement Test

1 | LISTENING: OVER THE VACATION

1. went
2. swam
3. didn't go
4. read
5. visited

2 | MARIA'S SICKNESS

1. didn't go
2. called
3. told
4. cooked
5. listened

278 | ANSWER KEY

3 | YOLANDA'S TRIP

1. didn't fly N2
2. rented U20
3. drove N1
4. came N1
5. wanted U20
6. had N1
7. was N4
8. took N1
9. bought N1
10. wasn't N3
11. met N1
12. went N1

4 | EDITING: MR. COOPER'S VACATION

I ~~visit~~ *visited* my sister in Idaho during the vacation.
We ~~go~~ *went* N1 shopping, but I didn't ~~spent~~ *spend* N2 a lot of money.
I ~~finded~~ *found* N1 a nice pair of pants. They ~~are~~ *were* N3 on sale.
They ~~costed~~ *cost* N1 only $5. We also ~~cook~~ *cooked* U20 a lot together, and we ~~make~~ *made* N1 ice cream. Oh, my sister has a new little cat. She ~~is~~ *was* N4 born last month. The cat loved the ice cream!

Unit 22 Achievement Test

1 | LISTENING: NORMA'S RING

A.
1. did you lose N2
2. No, it didn't N4
3. did you have N2
4. Yes, it was N4

B.
1. Did it cost a lot? N1
2. Did you lose your ring there? N1
3. Was it on the floor? N1

C.
1. c N2, N4
2. b N2, N4
3. a N3, N4
4. a N1, N4

2 | BEKIR'S GRANDPARENTS

A.
1. Where did your grandparents live N2
2. What did your grandfather do N2
3. Did he work long hours N1
4. Did he have a large farm N1
5. Did your grandmother work, too N1
6. Did she have many children N1
7. Did your grandparents meet a long time ago N1

3 | THE REST OF THE CONVERSATION

1. Yes, they had a very happy marriage N4
2. No, they didn't N4
3. No, they didn't have a car N4
4. No, they didn't N4
5. Yes, I visited many times N4

4 | EDITING: NORMA'S GRANDMOTHER

ALICE: ~~You did~~ *Did you* get your ring?
NORMA: Yes, I did. I'm so glad I didn't lose it forever.
ALICE: ~~Your~~ *Did your* N1 grandmother wear it a lot?
NORMA: Yes, she ~~was~~ *did* N4.
ALICE: What ~~she was~~ *was she* N2 like? ~~You were~~ *Were you* N1 close to her?
NORMA: Yes. She was a very sweet woman. I loved her very much.
ALICE: Did she ever ~~lived~~ *live* N1 with you?
NORMA: No, she ~~not~~ *didn't / did not* N4, but she came to visit often.
ALICE: When ~~she died~~ *did she die* N2?
NORMA: She died when I was 13.

PART VI Achievement Test

1 | LISTENING: BROKEN LEG

A.
1. got home U21, U22
2. Why were you U22
3. did you hurt U21
4. missed U20
5. didn't have U21
6. last week U20

B.
1. picked U20
   wanted U20
   happened U20
2. fell U21
   broke U21
   told U21

2 | HOME FOR THE WEEKEND

1. was born U21
2. lived U20
3. Did you have U22
4. didn't U22
5. didn't even see U21

3 | THE WEEKEND

1. saw U21
2. did . . . see U22
3. didn't know U21
4. took U21
5. became U21
6. was U21

7. played U20
8. stayed U20
9. did U21

4 | THE LOST BASKETBALL

1. Did you lose it U22
2. didn't leave it U21, U22
3. took it to the car U21
4. had it with me U21
5. got home U21
6. didn't see it U21
7. what happened U22
8. Did you look for it U22
9. didn't U22

5 | WEEKEND BARBECUE

1. wanted U20
   /ɪd/ U20
2. rained U20
   /d/ U20
3. cooked U20
   /t/ U20
4. played U20
   /d/ U20
5. talked U20
   /t/ U20

6 | EDITING: SUMMER BREAK

LINDA: Did you ~~went~~ *go* anywhere over the summer?
MARTIN: No, I ~~not~~ *didn't / did not* U22. I ~~work~~ *worked* U20 all summer.
LINDA: Where ~~you worked~~ *did you work* U22?
MARTIN: I ~~selled~~ *sold* U21 cell phones for Whitting Wireless. I ~~leaved~~ *left* U21 the company a week ‸*ago* U20 to come back to school. I ~~maked~~ *made* U21 pretty good money. ~~You worked~~ *Did you work* U22 during the summer?
LINDA: No, I ~~not~~ *didn't / did not* U22. I ~~did took~~ *took* U21 summer classes. I also ~~visit~~ *visited* U20 my parents in Kansas City for a week. I just got back from there yesterday.
MARTIN: Are you from there?
LINDA: I ~~did~~ *was* U21 born in Chicago, but I ~~grow~~ *grew* U21 up in Kansas City.
MARTIN: Who ~~watch~~ *watched* U22 your cat when you were away?
LINDA: My roommate. She ~~not~~ *didn't / did not* U21 go anywhere.

PART VII Diagnostic Test

1 | LISTENING: CAMERON LAKE

A.
1. There's U23
2. there U23
3. I U24
4. me U24
5. me U24
6. it U24
7. many U25
8. any U23

B.
1. a U25
2. The U25
3. The U25

2 | HEATHER'S COOKIES

1. a U25
2. c U25
3. b U23
4. b U23
5. b U23
6. c U23
7. a U24
8. c U25
9. b U25
10. d U25
11. a U25
12. d U24
13. d U24
14. c U25

3 | A NEW TABLE

1. chicken U25
2. them U24
3. furniture U25
4. it U24
5. some U25
6. any U23
7. me U24
8. are U23
9. They U23
10. a U25
11. the U25
12. much U25
13. him U24

4 | FOOD AT SCHOOL

1. there's U23
2. the U25
3. It U24
4. Some U25
5. many U25
6. the U25
7. ø U25
8. any U25
9. I U24
10. the U25
11. her U24
12. any U25
13. me U24
14. aren't U23

5 | EDITING: WORRIED MOM

SANDRA: Hello, Heather. How's your ~~the~~ day going?
HEATHER: Good, thanks. How's yours?
SANDRA: OK, but I'm worried. ~~Me and Chad~~ *Chad and I* U24 talked about ‸*an* U25 article in ~~a~~ *the* U25 paper today. There ‸*'s* U23 ~~are~~ a problem at Josh's school. It has ‸*a* U25 lot of overweight students. Some parents say it's because ~~they~~ *there* U23 aren't any healthy food machines in the school.

HEATHER: Does Joshua buy a lot of junk food from the machines?

SANDRA: No, and we always give ~~them~~ *him* [U24] healthy food.

HEATHER: Then don't worry about ~~his~~ *him* [U24]. He's still young, and he's pretty thin.

Unit 23 Achievement Test

1 LISTENING: MOVING IN

A.
1. there's [N1]
2. There are [N2]
3. are there any [N4]
4. there [N5]

B.

Affirmative contractions	Negative contractions
1. There's	1. isn't
2. there's	2. aren't
3. It's	

2 PATRICK'S NEW APARTMENT

1. g [N2]
2. i [N3]
3. a [N1]
4. f [N3]
5. j [N1]
6. h [N6]
7. b [N3]
8. d [N2]

3 MORE QUESTIONS

1. are [N2]
2. aren't [N3]
3. any [N4]
4. there's [N1]
5. It's [N6]
6. any [N4]
7. there's [N1]
8. It's [N6]

4 EDITING: MOVIE NIGHT

PATRICK: You know, there ^'s nothing to do around here.

ALLEN: ~~Is~~ *There's / There is* [N1] a movie tonight at 9:00. Do you want to go? ~~Is~~ *It's / is* [N6] a good movie.

PATRICK: Sure, but is there a movie theater near here?

ALLEN: Yeah, there ~~is~~ *are* [N2] two theaters close by. The one on Sixth Street is nice, but it's small. There ^*'s / is* [N1] a candy counter, but there ~~aren't~~ *isn't / 's not / is not* [N3] any popcorn.

PATRICK: That's OK. I don't like popcorn anyway.

Unit 24 Achievement Test

1 LISTENING: NEW ROOMMATE

A.
1. She [N1]
2. me [N2]
3. you [N5]
4. she [N1]
5. her [N2]
6. I [N3]
7. it [N2]

B.

Singular object pronouns	Plural object pronouns
1. it [N2]	3. them [N2]
2. her [N2]	

2 FEDERICA'S PHOTOS

1. Liliana [N2]
2. Liliana [N1]
3. Federica's parents / my parents [N2]
4. other pictures [N2]
5. Tito / Federica's brother / my brother [N2]
6. the car [N2]
7. the car [N2]

3 REIKO'S PARENTS

1. Reiko's parents gave (it) to me. [N4, N5]
2. They write me (e-mails) regularly. [N4, N5]
3. They tell me (stories). [N4, N5]
4. I e-mail (pictures) to them once in a while. [N4, N5]
5. I teach them (words) in Italian. [N4, N5]

4 EDITING: TOASTER

REIKO: Where's our toaster?

FEDERICA: Our neighbor Julie has ~~him~~ *it*.

REIKO: Why does she have ^*it* [N2]?

FEDERICA: ~~Me and her~~ *She and I* [N3] were talking yesterday, and she wanted to borrow it. So I loaned ~~her~~ it ^*to her* [N5].

Unit 25 Achievement Test

1 LISTENING: STREET FAIR

A.
1. soap [N2]
2. clothing [N2]
3. cheese [N2]

B.

Indefinite article + a singular count noun
1. a minute N1

Definite article + a singular count noun
1. the restaurant N4

Quantifier + a plural count noun
1. a few shirts N6

Quantifiers + non-count nouns
1. some soda N6
2. much money N6
3. a little food N6

2 | LUNCH INVITATION

1. c N6
2. a N6, N7
3. a N5
4. b N6
5. c N5
6. c N6
7. b N7
8. a N7

3 | JOB DESCRIPTIONS

1. a N1
2. a N1
3. the N3
4. the N3
5. the N3
6. an N3
7. the N3
8. a N3
9. a N3
10. the N3

4 | EDITING: AT LUNCH THE NEXT DAY

TIM: Did you finish grading ~~much~~ *many* essays yesterday?

NICOLE: Yes. I don't have ~~some~~ *any* N5 more essays to read until next week.

TIM: Good. What do you want to order?

NICOLE: I want ∧ hamburger and fries, *a / one* N3 with ∧ ketchup ~~a lot~~. *a lot of* N6

TIM: That sounds good.

PART VII Achievement Test

1 | LISTENING: LOUGH MELVIN

A.
1. there's U23
2. there U23
3. I U24
4. me U24
5. it U24
6. any U23
7. many U25
8. the U25

B.
1. a U25
2. a U25
3. the U25

2 | MUFFINS

1. a U25
2. b U25
3. d U23
4. c U23
5. a U23
6. a U23
7. b U24
8. d U25
9. c U25
10. a U25
11. c U25
12. d U24
13. b U24
14. b U25

3 | LAMPS

1. cheese U25
2. the / a U25
3. it U24
4. a few / some U25
5. any U23
6. you U24
7. some / a few U25
8. are U23
9. me U24
10. they U24
11. a U25
12. me U24
13. a few / some U25

4 | CHEATING AT SCHOOL

1. There's U23
2. He U24
3. it U24
4. many U25
5. any U25
6. the U25
7. some U25
8. is U23
9. I U24
10. the U25
11. him U24
12. me U24
13. aren't U23
14. ø U25

5 | EDITING: WORRIED MOM

AMY: Hello, Heidi. How is your ~~X~~ day going?
HEIDI: OK, thanks. How are you?
AMY: Fine, but I'm a little worried.
HEIDI: Why?
AMY: Well, ~~me and Billy~~ *Billy and I* U24 talked about ∧ *a* U25 story on ~~a~~ *the* U25 radio yesterday. ~~Lot~~ *A lot* U25 of students at Jack's school copy their essays from the Internet.
HEIDI: Do you think Jack is copying his essays?
AMY: Jack's teacher said ~~they~~ *there* U23 aren't any websites that Jack can copy from. They write their essays in class. But I want to teach ∧ *him* U24 to do his own work.
HEIDI: You're right. ~~They~~ *There* U23 are many children who copy from the Internet. It's a good idea to teach ~~his~~ *him* U24 not to do it.

PART VIII Diagnostic Test

1 | LISTENING: *ENTERTAINMENT NIGHTLY*

A
1. are seldom U26
2. avoid talking U28
3. sound U27
4. did it do U29
5. is U26
6. Do you like to U27

B
1. b U26
2. a U27
3. c U26
4. e U29

2 | LIZA AND JEREMY

1. took U29
2. looked / look U29
3. worry U26
4. knows / sees U26
5. Did . . . hear / Didn't . . . hear U29
6. are U27
7. to get / to eat U28
8. to eat / to get U28
9. see U29
10. sounds U27

3 | REPORTER'S QUESTIONS

1. admired U29
2. do you see U26
3. see U26
4. do you talk U26
5. meet U29
6. met U29
7. go U29
8. decided U29
9. eat U29
10. went U29
11. watch U29
12. didn't see U29
13. recorded U29
14. getting U28
15. don't have U26
16. to have U28
17. to get U28

4 | MAGAZINE ARTICLE

1. costs U27
2. own U27
3. continue / are continuing U26
4. are spending U26
5. refuse U26
6. appeared U29
7. agreed U29
8. talked U29
9. are thinking about / think about U27
10. isn't looking U27
11. don't have U26
12. to have U28
13. prefer U27

5 | EDITING: FAN MAIL FOR LIZA AND JEREMY

Dear Liza and Jeremy,

My name ~~be~~ *is* Michelle, and I ^*am / 'm*^ probably your biggest fan! I ~~write never~~ *never write* to famous artists. But I ~~bought~~ *wanted* buy your album last week, and I ~~am wanting~~ *want / wanted* to tell you how much I love it! ~~I listen every day to it~~. *Every day I listen to it. / I listen to it every day.* I don't ~~thinking~~ *think* there is very much really good music nowadays. But you ~~are always making~~ *always make* wonderful, creative music. Your album ~~were~~ *was / is* the best thing to happen to music today. I ~~am loving~~ *love* it. Please, keep ~~make~~ *making* music together!

Sincerely,
Michelle Sutter

Unit 26 Achievement Test

1 | LISTENING: *LOVE MATTERS*

A.
1. do I tell N1
2. believe N1
3. once a year N6
4. How often do you N3
5. We're talking N2

B.
1. T N1
2. F N2
3. T N1
4. F N1
5. F N4

2 | DURING THE BREAK

1. b N2
2. a N2
3. d N1
4. d N2
5. c N4, N5
6. c N1, N4
7. a N1
8. a N1, N4
9. c N4, N5

3 | DR. RICE'S SUGGESTIONS

1. do . . . fall N1
2. feel N1, N4
3. think N6, N1
4. don't know N1
5. is . . . seeing N2
6. give N1
7. are . . . listening N2

4 | EDITING: A NOTE TO DR. WEST

Dear Dr. West,

I ~~write~~ *am writing* to you today because I need to tell you something. You are the most intelligent, thoughtful, and handsome man I know. I almost never ~~don't~~ have feelings like this. In fact, I

rarely do things N5 *don't expect / am not expecting* N1
~~do things rarely~~ like this. I ~~don't expecting~~ a
                                   want N1
relationship with you, but I ~~wanting~~ to get to
know you better.

Sincerely,
Cara Jenkins

Unit 27 Achievement Test

1 LISTENING: GROCERY SHOPPING

A.
1. are N2
2. love N2
3. cost N2
4. look N4
5. smell N2
6. owns N2
7. sounds N2

B.
1. need N2
2. remember N2
3. want N2

2 IN THE KITCHEN

1. taste N2
2. do . . . think N3
3. Does . . . need N2
4. is N2
5. like N2

3 GUESTS

1. understand N2
2. has N2
3. isn't feeling / doesn't feel N4
4. have N2
5. smells N2
6. loves N2
7. Do . . . need N2
8. is N2
9. sounds N2

4 EDITING: ASK AARON

Dear Aaron,
                 have N2   *owes* N2
 I ~~am having~~ a big problem. My friend ~~owe~~ me
a lot of money. I want to ask her for the money,
but now she isn't returning my phone calls. I don't
understand N2
~~understanding~~ why she's acting this way, and now
          hate N2
I'm angry. I ~~hates~~ feeling this way! Please help!
Angry and helpless

Dear Angry and helpless,
                                            dislike N2
 I understand your problem. I ~~am disliking~~
giving people money for that reason. The money
belongs N2
~~belong~~ to you, and your friend needs to pay you

back. Go to her house to discuss the problem
directly. Perhaps she can pay you some of the
                           have N2
money each month. I ~~having~~ a rule to help avoid
problems like this in the future: Don't give
something that you're not ready to lose.

Aaron

Unit 28 Achievement Test

1 LISTENING: A PRESENTATION

A.
1. avoiding doing N1
2. need to do N2
3. prefer to do N3
4. finished doing N1
5. tried to do N2
6. liked going N3
7. refused to do N2

B.
Verb + gerund
1. dislike doing N2

Verb + infinitive
1. expected to receive N1
2. (didn't) hope to get N1

2 DOING HOMEWORK

1. leaving N1
2. to finish N2
3. to get N2
4. getting N1
5. waiting N1
6. to do N2
7. writing N2

3 JAKE'S ADMIRER

1. calling N1
2. to talk N2
3. talking N1
4. to hear N2
5. spending N1
6. to marry N2
7. to speak N2

4 EDITING: MOVIE TIME

                              writing
LUIS: Did you finish ~~to write~~ your paper?
JAKE: Yes, I just need to print it out.
LUIS: Great. I'm done with my homework, too.
                                    to N2
 Adam and I are planning ^ go see a movie. Do
           to come N2
you want ~~coming~~ with us?
                                            to see N2
JAKE: Sure, what did you decide ~~seeing~~?
LUIS: *Procrastination.*
                                              telling N1
JAKE: Oh, my friend keeps ~~to tell~~ me that it's good.
             to N2
 I was hoping ^ see it this weekend, and I don't
        to N2
want ^ procrastinate. Let's go!

Unit 29 Achievement Test

1 | LISTENING: HOCKEY PLAYER

A.
1. didn't know (N3)
2. was (N1)
3. Did you play (N4)
4. loved (N1)
5. got (N2)
6. did you stop (N5)
7. came (N2)

B.
1. b (N5)
2. a (N5)
3. c (N5)

2 | FAMILY HISTORY

<u>Affirmative regular simple past verb</u>
learned (N1)

<u>Affirmative irregular simple past verbs</u>
went (N2)
had (N2)

<u>Negative simple past verb</u>
didn't care (N1, N3)

<u>Simple past yes / no question</u>
Did you always want (N4)

<u>Simple past wh- question</u>
Why did you decide (N5)

3 | FREDRICK CLARK

1. died (N1)
2. was (N7)
3. married (N1)
4. opened (N1)
5. became (N2)
6. Did . . . have (N4)
7. didn't have (N3)
8. happened (N6)
9. came (N2)
10. went (N2)

4 | EDITING: QUESTIONS TO ASK YOUR RELATIVES

            want
Did you ever ~~wanted~~ to know more about your family history? A good way to learn about your family's past is to talk to your relatives. Here are some questions you can ask:

 were (N7)
Who ~~did be~~ your parents?

          meet (N5)
How did your parents ~~met~~?

  did (N5)
Where ^ they come from?

          do (N5)
What did ~~do~~ your father for a living?
What did you like to do ^ as a child?
What were the best moments of your childhood?

PART VIII Achievement Test

1 | LISTENING: NETWORK GLOBAL NEWS

A.
1. seem (U27)
2. rarely see (U26)
3. love (U27)
4. avoid talking (U28)
5. surprised (U29)
6. is (U26)

B.
1. b (U26)
2. c (U26)
3. e (U29)
4. a (U27)

2 | LENORE AND JUSTIN

1. read (U29)
2. look / looked (U26)
3. loves / likes (U26)
4. are (U27)
5. met (U29)
6. 'm leaving / am leaving (U26)
7. to go / to eat (U28)
8. had / ate (U29)
9. love / like (U27)
10. eat / go (U26)

3 | INTERVIEW WITH NGN

1. admired (U29)
2. do you get (U26)
3. get (U26)
4. do you tell (U26)
5. frequently tell her (U26)
6. meet (U29)
7. met (U29)
8. didn't you go (U29)
9. to finish (U28)
10. did you learn (U29)
11. had (U29)
12. begin (U29)
13. painted (U29)
14. think (U29)
15. don't have (U26)
16. was (U29)
17. loved (U29)

4 | NGN'S ARTICLE

1. costs (U27)
2. own (U27)
3. continues / is continuing (U26)
4. are (U26)
5. to talk (U28)
6. allowed (U29)
7. agreed (U27)
8. to write (U28)
9. don't know (U27)
10. making (U28)
11. aren't looking (U26)
12. didn't confirm (U29)
13. to keep (U28)

ANSWER KEY | 285

5 | EDITING: FAN MAIL FOR LENORE AND JUSTIN

Dear Lenore and Justin,

  My name ~~be~~ *is* Michael, and you ^ my favorite author-and-illustrator team. How do you get such wonderful ideas? ~~You~~ *Did you* read a lot of children's books when you were young? Or did you ~~learned~~ *learn* from working together? I ~~buy~~ *bought* your first book six years ago, and now I buy every new book that you publish. I ~~am wanting~~ *want* to tell you that I love them! ~~My kids and I every day read them.~~ *Every day my kids and I read them. / My kids and I read them every day* I don't ~~thinking~~ *think* there are a lot of good children's books, but Marty is an exception. In fact, because of you, now I am ~~get~~ *getting* inspired to write a book myself. Oh, and I ~~am loving~~ *love* the art! Please keep ~~work~~ *working* together!

Sincerely,
Michael Farber

PART IX   Diagnostic Test

1 | LISTENING: RICH LOIS

A.
1. might give   U32
2. Will you move   U31
3. probably won't   U32
4. may not see   U32
5. might sell   U32

B.
1. a   U32
2. b   U30
3. a   U32
4. c   U30
5. c   U30

2 | MORE TIME AT HOME

LOIS: What (are we going to do) with all our
         0.
 money? (Are you going to quit) working?
      1. U30

CARLOS: I (may not quit) right away. Maybe
     2. U32
 (I'm not going to quit) until next year. I enjoy
  3. U30
 my job. Besides, it('ll be) good to get out of
       4. U31
 the house. But I (might work) fewer hours.
      5. U32

LOIS: I think working fewer hours is a good idea.
 Phillip (is going to like) having you home more.
    6. U30

(Will you spend) more time with him?
7. U31

CARLOS: Of course! I'm going to love that! His
       8. U30
 birthday (will be) this Friday. Do you know
   9. U31
 what he wants?

LOIS: No, he (won't tell) me. He says he doesn't
   10. U31
 need anything. (Will you ask) him? He
      11. U32
 (might tell) you.
  12. U32

CARLOS: I (may get) him a gift certificate. Then he
    13. U32
 can choose what he wants.

LOIS: That's a good idea.

3 | 16TH BIRTHDAY

Note: Both contracted and noncontracted forms are acceptable.

1. are . . . going to be   U30
2. are . . . going to get   U30
3. 'm probably not going to have   U30
4. Are . . . going to give   U30
5. 're probably going to get   U30
6. 're not going to buy / aren't going to buy   U30
7. 're going to turn   U30
8. 're going to be   U30
9. 're not going to get / aren't going to get   U30
10. Are . . . going to buy   U30
11. 'm not going to have   U30
12. 'm going to ride   U30

4 | PLANS FOR THE DAY

Note: Both contracted and noncontracted forms are acceptable.

1. Will . . . buy   U31
2. Will . . . drive   U31
3. 'll take   U31
4. will . . . pick out   U31
5. 'll choose   U31
6. 'll make   U31
7. won't eat   U31
8. won't start   U31

5 | WEEKEND PLANS

Note: Both contracted and noncontracted forms are acceptable.

1. are . . . going to do   U30
2. 'm going to finish   U30
3. 'll study   U31
4. 'll fail   U31
5. Will . . . help   U31
6. Are . . . going to be / stay   U30
7. won't be / won't stay   U31
8. 'll start   U31
9. 'll return / go / be   U31
10. Are . . . going to go / return / be   U30
11. 'll meet   U31

6 | EDITING: USED CAR

PHILLIP: The next time I see you, I ~~am~~ *will* probably have a car.

JULIAN: Really? When are you ~~get~~ *getting / going to get* [U30] a car?

PHILLIP: I ~~thinking~~ *think* [U32] I might get one soon. My dad and I will ~~looking~~ *look* [U31] at cars tomorrow.

JULIAN: What kind of car are you going ˄*to* [U30] get?

PHILLIP: I'm not sure yet. But I know that it'll ˄*be* [U31] a used car, and it won't be expensive. It ~~maybe~~ *may be / might be* [U32] ugly, though. Have you seen Bill's used car? It runs well, but it looks terrible!

Unit 30 Achievement Test

1 | LISTENING: GOING TO THE LAKE

A.
1. going to be [N2]
2. this weekend [N5]
3. are you leaving [N6]
4. is going to bring [N3]
5. it's going to [N2]
6. probably going to [N4]
7. tomorrow [N5]

B.
1. F [N2]
2. F [N3]
3. T [N2]
4. F [N3]

2 | BARBECUE

1. to find [N3]
2. 're going to tell [N2]
3. 're going to have [N2]
4. are probably going to swim [N4]
5. 're going to go [N2]

3 | AFTER GRADUATION

Note: Both contracted and noncontracted forms are acceptable.
1. 'm going to take / 'm taking [N2, N6]
2. 's going to be [N2]
3. are . . . going to do / are . . . doing [N3, N6]
4. 'm going to need [N2]
5. Are . . . going to stay / Are . . . staying [N3, N6]
6. 're not going to stay / aren't going to stay / 're not staying / aren't staying [N2, N6]
7. 're probably going to move / 're probably moving [N2, N6]
8. are . . . going to move / are . . . moving [N3, N6]
9. 're going to go / 're going [N2, N6]
10. Are . . . going to leave / Are . . . leaving [N3, N6]
11. 're going to stay / 're staying [N2, N6]
12. 'm going to fly / 'm flying [N2, N6]

4 | EDITING: BEFORE THE INTERVIEW

JEFF: Are you going ˄*to* ask about the salary for the job during your interview?

ANGIE: I don't think so. I ˄*'m / am* [N1, N2] going to wait for them to talk about it. I'm kind of nervous.

JEFF: You're going ˄*to* [N2, N3] do great!

Unit 31 Achievement Test

1 | LISTENING: JEJU ISLAND, KOREA

A.
1. June [N8]
2. You'll stay [N4]
3. Will we be able [N5]
4. Will we have [N5]
5. next [N8]
6. No, you won't [N6]

B.
1. a [N3]
2. b [N3]
3. a [N5]
4. c [N6]
5. b [N3]
6. c [N4]
7. c [N7]

2 | TANYA'S SUMMER PLANS

1. 'll / will be [N3]
2. will . . . do [N1, N5]
3. will work [N3]
4. 'll / will spend [N1, N3]
5. Will . . . bring [N5]
6. 'll / will bring [N4]
7. won't let [N6]

3 | JENNY'S SUMMER PLANS

Note: Both contracted and noncontracted forms are acceptable.
1. won't go [N6]
2. 'll be [N3]
3. 'll open [N3]
4. 'll probably ask [N7]
5. Will you have [N1, N5]
6. 'll contact [N4]
7. 'll try [N1, N4]

4 | EDITING: ON JEJU ISLAND

PETE: It'll ˄*be* hard to leave here.

TANYA: I know! It's so beautiful that I ~~willn't~~ *won't* [N6] want to go home.

PETE: Yeah, I'll ~~being~~ *be* [N4] sad to leave, but it'll ~~is~~ *be* [N3] nice to get home, too.

Unit 32 Achievement Test

1 LISTENING: WORRIED MOM

A.
1. might be N1
2. Will you go N3
3. might come N1
4. might be N1

B.
1. a N1
2. b N1
3. a N1
4. a N1
5. a N5
6. c N1

2 AT THE LIBRARY

1. may not be / might not be N1, N2
2. might write / may write N1
3. might need / may need N1
4. might research / may research N1
5. might talk / may talk N1
6. might ask / may ask N1
7. might tell / may tell / might ask / may ask N1

3 CONVERSATION WITH THE HISTORY TEACHER

1. might like N1
2. will be N4, N1
3. might tell N4
4. may not N1
5. might not N1
6. may not have N1
7. might not N1
8. Will N3

4 EDITING: PLANS FOR THE EVENING

CHRIS: Bye, Mom. ~~May be~~ *Maybe* I'll see you tonight.
JULIE: Maybe? Will you be going to your friend Rob's house again?
CHRIS: I ~~maght~~ *may / might* N1 go there, or I ~~maybe~~ *might / may* N5 go to the library.
JULIE: Well, we like to know where you are. I was worried about you the other day. Your father *may / might / doesn't* N1 not worry very much, but I do. Do you think you'll be home for dinner?
might not / may not / will probably not / probably won't N2
CHRIS: I ~~not might~~ make it in time for dinner. I'll be working on my paper, and I think it might *take* N2 ~~takes~~ a long time.

PART IX Achievement Test

1 LISTENING: NEW JOB

A.
1. Will you make U31
2. might get U32
3. Maybe I'll U32
4. might not buy U32
5. might not be able U32

B.
1. c U30
2. c U30
3. c U30
4. b U32
5. a U32

2 MORE MONEY

CATHY: I'm so excited about your new job! But it *will be* different from your old one.
0. *Are you going to like* the new company?
1. U30
LYLE: I don't know. I *might miss* my old job, but I
2. U32
   hope I'*m going to like* my new one. I
3. U30
   may not like it at first. I *won't know* until
4. U32   5. U31
   tomorrow when I start. It *might be* a nice
6. U32
   change from what I was doing. At least
   I'*ll make* more money.
7. U31
CATHY: And we'*re going to be* able to save
8. U30
   money for a new house. *Will you work* longer
9. U31
   hours though?
LYLE: No. I'*m going to be* home at 6:00, just like
10. U30
   with my old job.
CATHY: That's great. *Will you have* weekends off?
11. U31
LYLE: *I might work* some weekends. I'*ll ask* my
12. U32   13. U31
   boss about it tomorrow.

3 MOVING

Note: Both contracted and noncontracted forms are acceptable.

1. 'm / am not going to know U30
2. Are . . . going to stay U30
3. 're / are going to stay U30
4. 'm / am not going to change U30
5. are going to give U30
6. 're not / aren't / are not going to do U30
7. Are . . . going to be U30
8. 'm / am going to miss U30
9. 'm / am probably going to get U30
10. are . . . going to move U30
11. are . . . going to transport U30
12. are going to rent U30

4 EVENING PLANS

Note: Both contracted and noncontracted forms are acceptable.

1. Will . . . be U31
2. 'll take U31
3. will . . . get U31
4. Will . . . buy U31
5. 'll get U31
6. 'll take U31
7. won't be U31
8. won't come U31

5 | WEEKEND PLANS

1. will be [U31]
2. are . . . going to do [U30]
3. 'm / am going to study [U30]
4. 'll / will probably watch [U31]
5. Will . . . have [U31]
6. Are . . . going to stay / Are . . . going to be [U30]
7. will drive [U31]
8. Are . . . going to shop [U30]
9. won't give [U31]
10. 'll / will finish [U31]
11. 'll / will see [U31]

6 | EDITING: NEW HOUSE

PENNY: I think I'll ~~starting~~ *start* to pack tomorrow.

JANE: Really? When are you ~~move~~ *moving / going to move* [U30] into your new house?

PENNY: I ~~thinking~~ *think* [U32] we might move this week. My parents ~~will signing~~ *will sign / are going to sign / are signing* [U31] the papers tomorrow.

JANE: Where are you going ^*to* [U30] move to?

PENNY: It'll ^*be* [U31] pretty close to our old house, and I won't change schools! My parents might ~~lets~~ *let* [U32] me have a pet, too!

JANE: Great!

PART X Diagnostic Test

1 | LISTENING: SCHOOL BOOKS

A.
1. a glass [U33]
2. any ice [U33]
3. How many books [U33]
4. How much money [U33]
5. yours [U35]
6. enough money [U33]
7. their [U35]

B.

Possessive adjectives
1. Their [U35]
2. our [U35]
3. Its [U35]
4. My [U35]
5. his [U35]

Possessive pronouns
1. mine [U35]
2. his [U35]
3. yours [U35]
4. ours [U35]

2 | COMPLAINTS

A.
1. F [U34]
2. F [U34]
3. F [U34]
4. T [U34]
5. T [U34]
6. T [U34]

B.
1. g [U35]
2. e [U35]
3. a [U35]
4. f [U35]

3 | BAD FOOD

A.
1. N [U34]
2. C [U34]
3. A [U34]
4. A [U34]
5. C [U34]
6. N [U34]

B.
1. too little [U34]
2. too many [U34]
3. too much [U34]
4. too few [U34]
5. too much [U34]
6. too much [U34]

4 | APPLE PIE

1. some [U33]
2. an [U33]
3. an [U33]
4. a [U33]
5. How many [U33]
6. any [U33]
7. any [U33]
8. a little [U33]
9. a little [U33]
10. any [U33]
11. Half a teaspoon of [U33]
12. some [U33]
13. How much [U33]
14. any [U33]
15. a few [U33]

5 | EDITING: PHONE CONVERSATION

MOM: Hi, it's Mom. How are ~~yours~~ *your* first few weeks at college?

LISA: Things are going well.

MOM: What are you doing right now?

LISA: Not much. Just drinking a bottle ^*of* [U33] soda and studying.

MOM: So, how do you like college so far?

LISA: I'm very happy with ~~mine~~ *my* [U35] choice of schools. The college is great. Its campus is really beautiful.

MOM: How are your classes?

LISA: Well, I like them all, except for chemistry. My friend Wendy is taking chemistry too, and ~~hers~~ *her* [U35] professor is really easy. But ~~my~~ *mine / my professor* [U35] is so difficult! He gives us too much homework, and the book is ~~to~~ *too* [U34] hard.

MOM: Do you have ~~time enough~~ *enough time* [U33] to study?

LISA: Actually, I'm ~~too very~~ *too / very* [U34] busy with chemistry. I hardly have time for my other classes.

MOM: OK, I'll let you get back to studying. I just wanted to say hi.
LISA: All right. Thanks for calling. Bye.

Unit 33 Achievement Test

1 | LISTENING: ARLINGTON, TEXAS

A.
1. How many people [N3]
2. an airport [N1]
3. a few [N3]
4. enough people [N6]
5. a few crimes [N3]
6. any snow [N2]
7. enough snow [N6]

B.
1. snow [N3]
2. miles [N3]
3. crime [N3]

2 | DINNER

1. N [N3]
2. S [N1]
3. N [N2]
4. P [N3]
5. N [N2]
6. N [N2]
7. P [N3]
8. N [N2]
9. N [N2]

3 | GOING TO THE STORE

1. one [N1]
2. any [N2]
3. an [N1]
4. a few [N3]
5. a quart of [N5]
6. a package of [N5]
7. a few [N3]
8. a few [N3]

4 | EDITING: THIRSTY

CHRISTIE: Can I have ~~any~~ *some* water?
TOM: Sure. I have ˄*a* little juice, also, or do you prefer water? [N3]
CHRISTIE: Water, please.
TOM: Do you want any ice?
CHRISTIE: No, thanks. I didn't drink ~~water enough~~ *enough water* [N6] today. I think I only had one ~~glasses~~ *glass* [N1] of water all day. I really need to drink more.

Unit 34 Achievement Test

1 | LISTENING: FOOD CRITIC

A.
1. too hot [N2]
2. too many times [N1]
3. too much sauce [N1]

B.
1. a [N1]
2. b [N1]
3. c [N1]
4. a [N1]

C.
1. F [N2]
2. T [N2]
3. F [N2]

2 | MOVIE REVIEW

A.
1. N [N1]
2. C [N1]
3. C [N1]
4. C [N1]
5. C [N1]
6. N [N1]
7. N [N1]

B.
1. very slow [N2]
2. not the right age [N2]
3. difficult [N2]
4. were [N2]

3 | ADVERTISEMENT

1. too [N2]
2. too many [N1]
3. too little [N1]
4. too much [N1]
5. too [N2]

4 | EDITING: WEDDING

LARISSA: How was the wedding?
BARBARA: It was nice, but the party afterward wasn't great. It lasted too ~~much~~ *many* hours, and there were too ˄*many* [N1] speeches.
LARISSA: Oh, that's too bad.
BARBARA: Also, the bride and groom invited too ~~little~~ *few* [N1] friends and family members for the size of the hall. So it felt really empty. The lights were too bright, and the music was too old-fashioned.
LARISSA: Oh, no!
BARBARA: But it wasn't all bad. The food was delicious. And since there was too ~~many~~ *much* [N1] food and too ~~little~~ *few* [N1] guests to eat it all, I ate a lot!

Unit 35 Achievement Test

1 | LISTENING: FAMILY PHOTO

A.
1. my [N1]
2. our [N1]
3. their [N1]
4. his [N1]

B.

Possessive adjectives
1. His [N1]
2. my [N1]

Possessive pronouns
1. Theirs [N2]
2. mine [N2]
3. ours [N2]
4. yours [N2]

2 | WHOSE IS IT?

1. our N1
2. ours N2
3. Their N1
4. theirs N2
5. mine N2
6. my N1
7. yours N2
8. your N1

3 | BOOK COLLECTION

1. A N1
2. P N2
3. A N1
4. P N2
5. P N2
6. P N2
7. P N2

4 | EDITING: FAMILY PICTURES

JULIE: Are these ~~yours~~ *your* pictures? I'd like to see them.

KEN: Yes, they're ~~our~~. *ours / our pictures* N2 This is a picture of my daughter and her husband. They're standing in front of ~~theirs~~ *their* N1 house. This dog is ~~their~~ *theirs / their dog* N2 *mine / my dog* N2, but this one is ~~my~~.

JULIE: That dog is ~~your~~? *yours / your dog* N2 But you don't have a dog.

KEN: Well, he lives with my daughter now, but I still think he belongs to me.

PART X   Achievement Test

1 | LISTENING: NEW SHOES

A.
1. some salad U33
2. any dressing U33
3. mine U35
4. a bottle of U33
5. how many times U33
6. their U35
7. How much money U33

B.

<u>Possessive adjectives</u>
1. Its U35
2. your U35
3. his U35
4. her U35
5. Their U35

<u>Possessive pronouns</u>
1. yours U35
2. Hers U35
3. theirs U35
4. ours U35

2 | COMPLAINTS ABOUT THE CAFETERIA

1. T U34
2. F U34
3. F U34
4. F U34
5. T U34
6. T U34

3 | BAD FOOD

A.
1. N U34
2. A U34
3. C U34
4. A U34
5. N U34
6. C U34

B.
1. too few U34
2. too much U34
3. too little U34
4. too many U34
5. too little U34
6. too much U34

4 | ORANGE CAKE

1. some U33
2. an U33
3. any U33
4. a glass of U33
5. hers U34
6. his U34
7. my U34
8. yours U34

5 | ORANGE CAKE INGREDIENTS

1. a few U33
2. How many U33
3. one U33
4. a quart of U33
5. any U33
6. a little U33
7. one U33
8. How much U33
9. any U33
10. a teaspoon of U33
11. any U33

6 | EDITING: CALL FROM MOM

WINONA: Hello?

MOM: Hi, it's your mom. I wanted to see how ~~yours~~ *your* week is going. Am I interrupting you?

WINONA: No, I'm just eating a piece ^*of* U33 pizza for dinner.

MOM: That doesn't sound too good for you.

WINONA: Well, my roommate Leslie bought the pizza, and she gave some of it to ~~my~~ *me* U35. She's really nice about sharing ~~hers~~ *her* U35 things.

MOM: I'm glad. So, how are your classes? Are they ~~too very~~ *too / very* U34 difficult?

WINONA: Not really. I think ~~mine~~ *my* U35 Spanish level is ~~to~~ *too* U34 low for the class I'm in. But I like the language department and its teachers.

MOM: Are you learning ~~vocabulary enough~~ *enough vocabulary* U33?

WINONA: Actually, I have a vocabulary quiz tomorrow. I need to study for it.

MOM: OK. I'll let you go study. I just wanted to say hi.

WINONA: All right. Thanks for calling. Bye.

PART XI Diagnostic Test

1 | LISTENING: TINA'S PLANT STORE

A.
1. Would you like U37
2. can you help U37
3. can I take U36

B.
Can or *may* for permission
1. You can change it for another one. U36
2. You can take a closer look at it. U36
3. You may take a look around the store if you like. U36

Offers
1. Would you like to see one of these? U37
2. Would you like anything else today? U37

2 | PLANT INFORMATION

A.
1. g U38
2. j U38
3. h U39
4. d U39
5. c U39
6. f U38

B.
1. f U39
2. g U39
3. j U39
4. d U38
5. a U38
6. b U38, U39

3 | CONVERSATIONS IN THE STORE

1. I'd like U37
2. May I have U36
3. Could you U37
4. Would you like U37
5. I'd like U37
6. Should I U38
7. I'd like U37
8. Where can I U36
9. I'd like U37
10. Should I U38
11. don't have to U39
12. Can I U36
13. Of course. U37

4 | ANOTHER CUSTOMER

1. b U36
2. b U37
3. d U37
4. d U36
5. b U36
6. a U38
7. c U36
8. b U37
9. c U36
10. a U38
11. d U37
12. a U36
13. c U37

5 | CACTUS GARDEN

1. don't have to U39
2. should U38
3. have to / had better U39, U38
4. better not U38
5. ought to U38

6 | EDITING: TINA'S WEBSITE

Note: Both contracted and noncontracted forms are acceptable.

If you have a pond, you should ~~X~~ think about adding water plants. These are plants that live on or in the water. Many water plants have ~~X~~ beautiful flowers. U39

But before you start your water garden, you ~~better had~~ 'd better plan your planting schedule. U38 Usually, you have ˄to start water gardens in the spring. U39

Once you have water plants, you ˄'d better not change the water in your pond often because it's not good for the plants. U38 Instead, you have to ~~finding~~ find a way to clean the water. U39 You ~~haven't~~ don't have to have fish, but they can help keep your pond clean. U39 The fish eat tiny insects in the water, and you don't have ˄to feed them anything else. U39

Water plants should not ~~X~~ cover more than half of your pond. U38 If your plants cover more than half the water, you have ˄to remove some of them. U39 Click here to see photos of water plants.

Unit 36 Achievement Test

1 | LISTENING: SHOPPING FOR A DIGITAL CAMERA

A.
1. Can I help N2, N3
2. Where can I N2
3. May I see N2

B.
1. has permission to N2
2. gives N2
3. Marty can't N1
4. has permission to N2
5. not OK N1
6. can N2

2 | AT THE ART MUSEUM

1. Can I have one, please? N2
2. Can I leave it somewhere? N2
3. You can leave your bag in the lockers downstairs. N1
4. Can I take my camera in with me? N2
5. But you may not take any photos with a flash. N1
6. May we go into the modern art section? N2

292 | ANSWER KEY

7. You can visit any section of the museum that you like. **N1**
8. Can I have a map, please? **N2**
9. Can I take my bottle of water with me? **N2**

3 | THE MUSEUM CAFÉ

1. T **N3, N2**
2. F **N1**
3. T **N1**
4. F **N1**
5. F **N1**
6. T **N2**
7. T **N2**
8. T **N1**

4 | EDITING: CALLING THE DOCTOR

DIRECTORY ASSISTANCE: Directory Assistance, what city and listing please?

MARTY: Seattle. Can you ~~gives~~ *give* me the number for Dr. Jacob Stephen?

DIRECTORY ASSISTANCE: Sure. The number is 555-3094. Hold on, I'll connect you. . . .

SECRETARY: Dr. Stephen's office. May I ~~helping~~ *help* **N3** you?

MARTY: Yes, may I ~~to~~ speak with Dr. Stephen, please? **N2**

SECRETARY: I'm sorry, he's not available now. Can I help you?

MARTY: No, thanks. I really need to talk to the doctor. ~~I can~~ *Can I* **N2** have his cell phone number?

SECRETARY: I'm sorry, you ~~mayn't~~ *may not / can't* **N1** have his cell phone number. But if you give me your name and number, Dr. Stephen can call you back.

Unit 37 Achievement Test

1 | LISTENING: DINNER PLANS

1. I'd like to **N2**
2. Would you like to **N3**
3. Could you **N1**
4. I'd like **N2**
5. I'd like to eat **N2**
6. I'd like **N2**
7. would you like to **N3**
8. would you **N1**
9. could you **N1**

2 | AT THE RESTAURANT

1. Sure **N1**
2. I'd like **N2**
3. Can you **N1**
4. Would you like **N3**
5. we'd like **N2**

6. Would you please **N1**
7. Would you like **N3**
8. I'd like **N2**
9. would you like **N3**

3 | DESSERT

1. a **N3**
2. c **N2**
3. b **N1**
4. b **N3**
5. a **N4**
6. a **N2**
7. c **N1**
8. c **N3**
9. d **N1**

4 | EDITING: AFTER DINNER

DUSTIN: Oh, Carla, ~~you can~~ *can you* do me a favor?
CARLA: Sure, what is it? **N1**
DUSTIN: Could you ~~the~~ lend me some money? Since we're on this side of town, I'd like to stop by the pharmacy. I want to get a few things, but I don't have enough money. **N1**
CARLA: Of ~~the~~ course.
DUSTIN: Would you like ^*to* **N3** come in with me?
CARLA: Sure.

Unit 38 Achievement Test

1 | LISTENING: CAREER ADVICE

A.
1. ought to try **N3**
2. should I follow **N1**
3. shouldn't stay **N1**
4. you'd better not make **N4**

B.
<u>Question about advice</u>
1. Should I keep my present job? **N1**

<u>Statements of advice</u>
1. I think I ought to become a teacher. **N3**
2. But you shouldn't be irresponsible, either. **N1**
3. And you shouldn't talk to just one or two. **N1**
4. And you'd better make sure your wife supports you. **N4**
5. But you'd better not quit your job yet. **N4**

2 | PET ADVICE

1. a **N4**   3. c **N1**
2. c **N1**   4. b **N4**

3 | RON'S CAREER

1. b **N1**   4. c **N3**
2. c **N4**   5. a **N1**
3. a **N1**

4 | BASIC TIPS FOR DOG OWNERS

Note: Both contracted and noncontracted forms are acceptable.

1. ought to play **N3**
2. should put **N1**
3. shouldn't leave **N1**
4. 'd better not let **N4**
5. 'd better take **N4**
6. shouldn't give **N1**

5 | EDITING: BACK IN SCHOOL

TANYA: What do you want to do tonight?

RON: I ought ^to^ finish some homework. Then I ~~better had~~ **'d better / had better** **N1** study for a test.

TANYA: You're so busy with work and school. I want to help you. Should I ~~X~~ do something? **N1**

RON: I don't think you can really do anything. I should just organize my schedule better.

TANYA: Well, you shouldn't ~~X~~ work so much now **N1** that you're back in school. You ought to ~~working~~ **work** **N3** only in the mornings. That way, you can study more.

RON: You're right. Besides, ~~I've~~ **I'd / I had** **N4** better not complain. Going back to school was my idea!

Unit 39 Achievement Test

1 | LISTENING: PLANS FOR THE DAY

A.
1. Do you have to study **N1**
2. have to turn **N1**
3. have to go **N1**

B.
1. T **N1**
2. F **N1**
3. T **N1**
4. T **N1**
5. T **N2**
6. T **N2**

2 | FACTS AND CONCLUSIONS

1. j **N2**
2. e **N1**
3. i **N1, N3**
4. a **N1**
5. d **N1**
6. k **N3**
7. b **N3**
8. h **N2**

3 | AT DINNER

1. She has to lose **N1**
2. you don't / do not have to eat **N2**
3. Do you have to work **N1**
4. I don't / do not have to be **N1**
5. I had to go **N1**
6. your mom has to do **N1**
7. I have to unpack **N1**
8. I have to finish **N1**
9. Do you have to leave **N1**

4 | EDITING: AT THE HOTEL

DEBRA: That was a nice dinner. But Keith looks too thin! We have to ~~buying~~ **buy** him some food!

COLLIN: Well, you mustn't ~~X~~ forget that he is an **N3** adult. He can take care of himself. And he has plenty of food at his apartment.

DEBRA: Well, I want to take him some food, even if you think it's not necessary.

COLLIN: OK, but you ~~not~~ **don't / do not** **N2** have to go to the store right now. Why don't you wait until tomorrow morning? Let's go to bed. I'm so tired!

DEBRA: OK, but I ~~X~~ must brush my teeth, and I **N1** have ^to^ take a shower first. But you don't have **N1** to wait for me. You can go to bed now if you're tired.

PART XI Achievement Test

1 | LISTENING: SHOPPING FOR A PET

A.
1. Can you show **U37**
2. Would you like **U37**
3. Can I give **U36**

B.

Can or *may* for permission
1. You can pick the one you like. **U36**
2. But you can't keep it in there too long. **U36**
3. You may not write a check without a photo ID. **U36**

Offers
1. Would you like to take one of these? **U37**
2. Would you like to see some of our fishbowls? **U37**

2 | PET INFORMATION

A.
1. d **U38**
2. j **U38**
3. h **U39**
4. i **U39**
5. b **U38**
6. c **U39**

B.
1. f **U39**
2. i **U39**
3. e **U38**
4. a **U38**
5. h **U39**
6. g **U38**

3 | CONVERSATIONS IN THE STORE

1. I'd like **U37**
2. Could you **U37**
3. Could you trade **U37**
4. Would you like **U37**

5. I'd like U37
6. Should I U38
7. I'd like U37
8. Where can I U36
9. I'd like U37
10. May I feed U36
11. Could you feed U37
12. Should I clean U38
13. don't have to U39

4 | ANOTHER CUSTOMER

1. b U36
2. d U37
3. d U37
4. d U36
5. d U36
6. b U37
7. a U38
8. a U36
9. a U38
10. c U36
11. b U36
12. a U37
13. a U37

5 | PARROTS

1. should U38
2. have to / had better U39, U38
3. better not U38
4. ought to U38
5. don't / do not have to U39

6 | EDITING: TITO'S WEBSITE

Note: Both contracted and noncontracted forms are acceptable.

If you have a child, you should ~~X~~ think carefully before adding a dog to your family. Some dogs are great with children, but you have to *be* U39 ~~being~~ careful with others. You always have *to* U39 watch your child when he or she is with a dog. A dog can be a wonderful addition to a family, but you *'d better* U38 ~~better had~~ understand that it is a big responsibility as well.

Before you buy any dog, you'd better ~~X~~ see U38 how it acts with the child. Don't take the dog home if the dog and your child do not get along. You *don't have* U39 ~~have not~~ to take the dog home to know that you're choosing the right dog.

to buy U39 You don't have ~~buying~~ a specific kind of dog to be sure that it is good with children. Training your dog is more important than the kind of dog that it is.

Your dog shouldn't ~~X~~ conflict with your U38 *to* U39 lifestyle. You have be sure you have the time and energy to care for your child *and* a dog. Would *you like* U37 ~~like you~~ to see tips on dog training? Click here.

PART XII Diagnostic Test

1 | LISTENING: STOCKMANS

A.
1. sweeter U40
2. Which store U40
3. the freshest U43
4. the same as U42
5. in town U43
6. different from U42
7. rarely U41

B.
1. S U43
2. ADJ U42
3. ADJ U42
4. ADV U41
5. C U40
6. C U40

2 | MAKING A RADIO AD

1. different from U42
2. as exciting as U42
3. fast enough U42
4. too boring U42
5. very nice U42
6. loud enough U42
7. too loud U42
8. the same volume as U42
9. too soft U42
10. too quiet U42
11. loud enough U42
12. as loud as U42

3 | AD FOR COMPUTER ONE

<u>Comparative adjectives</u>
1. larger U40
2. more knowledgeable U40
3. flatter U40

<u>Superlative adjectives</u>
1. the most helpful U43
2. the most popular U43
3. the cheapest U43

<u>Adverbs</u>
1. slowly U41
2. fast U41
3. badly U41
4. easily U41

4 | ADVERTISER OF THE YEAR

A.
1. Which advertiser is more creative? U40
2. Which advertiser is more successful at increasing sales? U40
3. Which advertiser's ads are funnier? U40
4. Which advertiser is friendlier to clients? U40
5. Which advertiser is more hardworking? U40

ANSWER KEY | 295

B.
1. most excellent U43
2. most creative U43
3. quickly U41
4. most colorful U43
5. most popular U43
6. the smallest U43
7. definitely U41
8. hard U41
9. patiently U41
10. the greatest U43
11. sincerely U41

5 | EDITING: THE CAR COMMERCIAL

Meet the world's most ~~perfectest~~ *perfect* car. Forget about driving ~~noisy~~ *noisily* U41 along the road. We made *the* U43 quietest car possible. It has the most ~~powerfulest~~ *powerful* U43 engine. It's more ~~comfortabler~~ *comfortable* U40 than any car ever made. We believe that your safety is more important *than* U40 your image. But you'll look good in our car, and you'll be in the ~~most safe~~ *safest* U43 car ever built. Live ~~good~~ *well* U41, and drive this car. Go the ~~farest~~ *farthest* U43 that you can go. The Millennium Fantasy. It's one step ~~more close~~ *closer* U40 to perfection.

Unit 40 Achievement Test

1 | LISTENING: COMPARING SCHOOLS

A.
1. Which is N9
2. more expensive N4
3. stronger N2
4. smaller N2
5. much bigger N7
6. which are N9

B.

Comparative adjectives ending in *-er*
1. lower N2
2. closer N2

Comparative adjectives ending in *-ier*
1. friendlier N3

2 | COMPARING WEATHER

1. windier N3, N9
2. warmer N2
3. more humid N4, N9
4. higher N2
5. greener N2

3 | COMPARING CITIES

1. quieter / less noisy N4, N5
2. higher / bigger / larger N2
3. farther from N6
4. much worse N7, N6
5. harder / more difficult N2, N4
6. less interesting / more boring N5, N4
7. more expensive N4
8. better N6
9. cleaner N2
10. more beautiful / prettier N4, N3
11. less busy / quieter / more boring N5
12. lower / better N2

4 | EDITING: THE DECISION

Hi Marta,

I finally decided which school to go to. I'm going to go to Cornwell University in Greenwood—not Grant Medical College in Carberry. The main reason is that Cornwell University is ~~more cheap~~ *cheaper* than ~~Carberry~~ *Grant Medical College* N8. I also like that Greenwood's neighborhoods are quieter than ~~Carberry~~ *Carberry's neighborhoods / neighborhoods in Carberry* N8. Plus, Greenwood is less dangerous. Greenwood may be more boring than Carberry, but I'm sure I won't be ~~boreder~~ *more bored* N2 than I was growing up in Gronlid. I'll be too busy studying. Also, I think the Cornwell campus is nicer. But the best news is that I'll be closer to home, so it will be easier for you to visit me. By the way, which highway is ~~more fast~~ *faster* N2, N9 for driving to Greenwood, Route 10 or the Interstate?

See you soon,

Andrea

Unit 41 Achievement Test

1 | LISTENING: *STORY OF LOVE*: ACT 1

A.
1. slowly N2
2. expensive N5
3. well N4

B.

Adverbs: adjective + *-ly*
1. quietly N2
2. quickly N2
3. clearly N2

Adverbs: same form as adjectives
1. early N3
2. late N3
3. long N3

2 | STORY OF LOVE: ACT 2

1. nervously [N2]
2. shyly [N2]
3. slowly [N2]
4. comfortable [N5]
5. really [N2]
6. well [N4]
7. carefully [N2]
8. gladly [N2]
9. quietly [N2]
10. patiently [N2]
11. properly [N2]
12. happy [N5]
13. impossible [N5]

3 | STORY OF LOVE: ACT 3

1. hard [N3]
2. serious [N2]
3. angry [N2]
4. calm [N2]

4 | EDITING: STORY OF LOVE: ACT 4

Danielle runs to Mario's home and ~~happy~~ *happily* tells him that she wants to marry him. The day of the wedding, Danielle's father suddenly arrives at the chapel. He looks ~~sadly~~ *sad* [N5]. He does not usually apologize ~~good~~ *well* [N4], but he decides to try. He says to Danielle softly, "I thought ~~hardly~~ *hard* [N3] about you and Mario, and I decided that you have my blessing to get married." Danielle smiles ~~warm~~ *warmly* [N2] and says, "Thank you!" Mario and Danielle get married, and they live happily ever after.

Unit 42 Achievement Test

1 | LISTENING: PHOENIX, ARIZONA

A.
1. cool enough [N1]
2. to survive [N3]
3. very concerned [N4]

B.

<u>Too + adjective</u>
1. too hot [N2]
2. too miserable [N2]
3. too warm [N2]

<u>As + adjective + as</u>
1. as hot as [N5]
2. as strong as [N5]

2 | ANTARCTICA

1. light enough [N1]
2. too cold [N2]
3. warm enough [N1]
4. very dry [N4]
5. as dry as [N5]
6. the same amount of rainfall as [N6]
7. too expensive [N2]

3 | ACROSS THE UNITED STATES

1. a [N2]
2. c [N1]
3. b [N2]
4. c [N5]
5. b [N2]
6. a [N2]
7. c [N6]
8. b [N4]
9. a [N1]

4 | EDITING: TOO MUCH RAIN

In my opinion, Swansea is ~~too way~~ *way too* rainy. I like the sun, and it's too cloudy here for me. I enjoy being outside, but sometimes I get wet *as* [N5] a mop! Also, my clothes always get dirty from the muddy streets, and I'm ~~to~~ *too* [N2] poor to spend all my money cleaning them. Sometimes the streets are wet enough ^*to* [N3] ride a boat in. Unfortunately, the weatherpeople don't know ~~enough soon~~ *soon enough* [N1] if it's going to rain. Sometimes the day starts out beautiful and sunny, but then it gets ~~wet very~~ *very wet* [N4] by lunchtime. The weather in Anglesey isn't the same ~~from~~ *as* [N6] the weather here in Swansea. So I think I'll move to Anglesey, where it's much drier!

Unit 43 Achievement Test

1 | LISTENING: OMAR

A.
1. on the team [N6]
2. the biggest [N2]
3. the most handsome [N4]
4. at this school [N6]

B.

<u>Superlatives ending in -est</u>
1. the smartest [N2]
2. the coolest [N2]
3. the nicest [N2]

<u>Superlative ending in -iest</u>
1. the friendliest [N3]

<u>Irregular Superlative</u>
1. the best [N5]

2 | JESSICA

1. prettiest [N3]
2. most interesting [N4]
3. worst [N5]
4. most wonderful [N4]
5. most expensive [N4]

3 | THE DANCE

A.
1. the tallest
2. the oldest
3. the largest
4. the greenest
5. the most beautiful
6. the sweetest
7. the rarest
8. the finest
9. newest

B.
1. One of the richest businessmen
2. One of the best chefs
3. one of the most famous bands
4. one of the greatest parties

4 | EDITING: JESSICA'S DIARY

I had the ^most^ incredible evening last night. Omar took me to the most ~~wonderfulest~~ ^wonderful^ dance in the world. They had the nicest of everything. Omar is the ~~most great~~ ^greatest^ guy I know. He's also the most popular guy on campus. It was the ~~bestest~~ ^best^ date of my life.

PART XII Achievement Test

1 | LISTENING: JED'S WEBSITE

A.
1. Which color
2. the simplest
3. which picture
4. the nicest
5. the same size as
6. the same color as
7. clearly

B.
1. C
2. C
3. S
4. ADJ
5. ADJ
6. ADV

2 | DEVELOPING JED'S WEBSITE

1. dark enough
2. too difficult
3. different from
4. good enough
5. too low
6. the same level as
7. very easy
8. too large
9. too busy
10. plain enough
11. as simple as
12. different from

3 | JED'S RADIO ADVERTISEMENT

Comparative adjectives
1. more experienced
2. larger
3. friendlier

Superlative adjectives
1. the most knowledgeable
2. the cheapest
3. the most popular

Adverbs
1. badly
2. hard
3. perfectly
4. late

4 | TOP WEB DESIGNER

A.
1. Which web designer is more modern?
2. Which web designer is more creative?
3. Which web designer is more helpful to other designers?
4. Which web designer is nicer to customers?
5. Which web designer is more artistic?

B.
1. most interesting
2. most famous
3. quickly
4. definitely
5. most exciting
6. easiest
7. highest
8. hard
9. carefully
10. technologically
11. greatest

5 | EDITING: THE HOTEL WEBSITE

Stay in the world's ~~luxuriest~~ ^most luxurious^ hotel. Stay in ^the^ nicest hotel possible. You're guaranteed to ~~real~~ ^really^ enjoy your stay with us. We have the most ~~deliciousest~~ ^delicious^ meals. Our beds are more comfortable ^than^ any others. Our prices are lower than our ~~competitor~~ ^competitor's prices^. When you stay with us, you'll relax ~~good~~ ^well^. You'll feel ~~gooder~~ ^better^ here than at home. Our hotel is the ~~goodest~~ ^best^ that you can find. The Charles Hotel Suites. It's ~~wonderfullest~~ ^the most wonderful^ place on earth.

Test Generating CD-ROM

General Information

The test generating CD-ROM (TestGen®) that accompanies the *Focus on Grammar Assessment Pack* provides you with the TestGen software program and a testbank of hundreds of items per level. You can use the software program to create and customize tests. With TestGen, you can:

- create tests quickly using the TestGen Wizard
- select questions by part, unit, or grammar topic
- edit questions
- add your own questions
- create multiple versions of a test

Because the items in the TestGen testbank are different from those in the printed tests, you can use TestGen to create additional tests, review quizzes, or practice exercises.

Organization of Items in the *Focus on Grammar* TestGen CD-ROM

The *Focus on Grammar* TestGen CD-ROM includes five testbanks, one for each level of *Focus on Grammar*. Within each testbank, the items are divided by part of the Student Book.

Each *Focus on Grammar* test item is labeled for easy sorting. You can sort by grammar point or unit. See "How to Create a Test" for an example of a test with items sorted by grammar point.

How to Create a Test

There are two ways to create a test using the TestGen software. You can create a test manually, or you can use the TestGen Wizard.

Using the TestGen Wizard to Create a Test The TestGen Wizard is the easiest, fastest way to create a customized test. Follow these easy steps to create a test.

STEP 1
Select a **Testbank** from the **Testbank Library** window.

STEP 2
Click on **Use the TestGen Wizard to create a new paper test** icon.

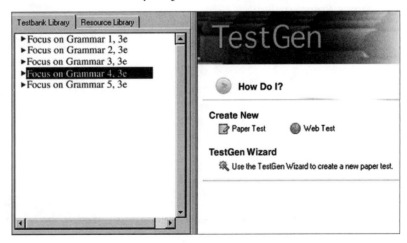

STEP 3
When the **TestGen Wizard** launches, you will be prompted to enter a name for your test. After assigning a name to your test, click the **Next** button to proceed.

STEP 4
Select the part or parts you want to include in your test.

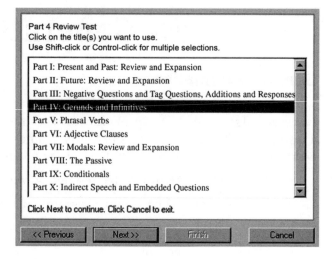

STEP 5
On the next screen, you will choose "Select questions randomly" or "Select specific questions from a list." Choose **Select questions randomly** and click the **Next** button.

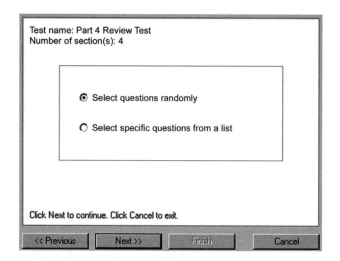

STEP 6
Use the drop-down list to choose questions randomly by Question Type, Section,* Grammar Point, or Unit.

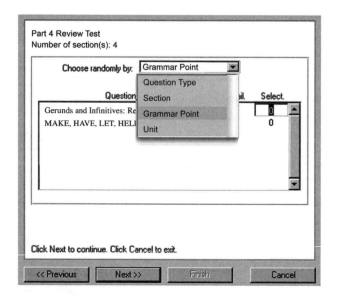

* "Section" refers to *Focus on Grammar* parts. Each level has 8 to 10 parts.

STEP 7
Under the "Select" column, choose the number of items you want in the test. Click the **Next** button to continue to the **Test Summary**.

STEP 8
The **Test Summary** window will display the name of your test, the number of sections (parts) you selected, the selection method, and the total number of questions on the test. Click **Finish** to build the test.

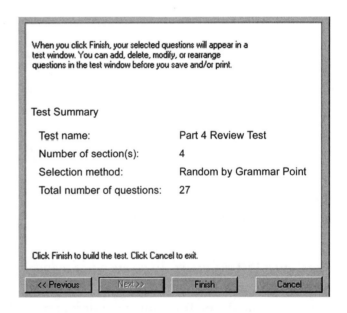

STEP 9
The **TestGen Wizard** will close, and a **Test Window** will open with your selected questions.

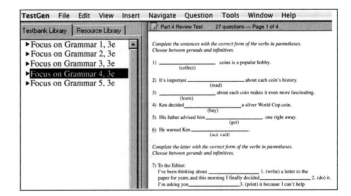

STEP 10
To put your questions in the correct order, click on the **Question** menu at the top of the screen and select **Sort**.

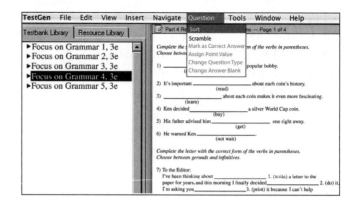

STEP 11
Next, click **Keep questions in the same order as they are in the testbank** under **SmartSort by test bank order** and click **OK**.

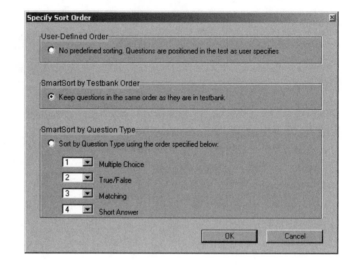

STEP 12
Finish by saving and/or printing the test.

Creating a Test Manually To create a test manually:

1. Open the TestGen software and select a **Testbank** from the **Testbank Library** window.
2. Click on the **Paper Test** icon in the startup pane. A new blank test appears.
3. Click on the arrows in the **Testbank Library** window to expand the outline and see the testbank questions.
4. Drag and drop each question you want to include into the **Test** window.

For more information, see the User's Guide located on the TestGen CD-ROM in the "Resources" folder.

How to Create New Questions

To add a new question to your test:

1. Click the place in the **Test window** where you want to add a new question.
2. In the menu bar, click **Insert > Question**.
3. Choose a **Question Type** from the drop down menu.
4. Double-click on the new question in the **Test** window.
5. Type the question and answer into the appropriate fields.

How to Edit Questions

To edit a question in your test:

1. Click on the **Tools** menu at the top of the screen and select **Preferences > Test Options.**
2. Click on the **Descriptors** tab.
3. Check **Correct Answer** to display the answers in the Test window.
4. Return to the test window and double-click on the question you want to edit.
5. Make any changes you want to both the question and answer.

How to Change the Order of Questions

If you want to move a question to a specific location in the test:

1. Click on the **Tools** menu and select **Sort.**
2. Click **User-defined order.**
3. Click **OK.**
4. Now you can drag the question to any location you want in the test.

Other TestGen Features

You can modify your TestGen test in many ways. You can change the display, create questions with graphics, edit direction lines, and much, much more. To learn more about the features that the TestGen software offers, go to the *Focus on Grammar* Companion Website (www.longman.com/focusongrammar) and click on the **TestGen** link.

TestGen 7.2 System Requirements

Windows®

Operating System:	Microsoft® Windows NT®, Windows 2000 or Windows XP	
Processor	233MHz or faster Pentium-compatible processor	
Random access memory (RAM)	128 MB	
Available hard disk space	20 MB (varies depending on testbank size)	
Web browser*	Windows NT®	Internet Explorer 5.5 or Netscape® Navigator 6.2.3
	Windows 2000	Internet Explorer 5.5, 6.0 or Netscape Navigator 6.2.3
	Windows XP	Internet Explorer 6.0 or Netscape Navigator 7.0

Macintosh®

Operating System:	Mac OS X v 10.2, 10.3, 10.4**
Processor	PowerPC G3, G4, or G5 processor
Random access memory (RAM)	128 MB
Available hard disk space	20 MB (varies depending on testbank size)
Web browser*	Internet Explorer 5.2 or Netscape Navigator 7.0

*Required only for viewing TestGen tests on the Web with TestGen Plug-in and for viewing TestGen Help.

**The TestGen application is supported on Mac OS X v 10.3 and 10.4. The TestGen Plug-in is not currently supported on this platform.

Installing TestGen

Windows Computers

- Insert the TestGen CD into your computer's CD drive.
- Open **My Computer**. Then double click on the CD drive icon.
- Double-click on "tgesetup.exe."
- Follow the directions on the screen to complete the installation. Once the installation is complete the program will begin automatically.

Macintosh Computers

- Insert the TestGen CD into your computer's CD drive.
- Double-click on "TestGen 7 Setup."
- Follow the directions on the screen to complete the installation. Once the installation is complete the program will begin automatically.

Note:

If you have existing versions of TestGen on your computer, you will receive a message providing you with the option to remove earlier versions of the program. Click *Yes* to remove the older TestGen versions and continue (recommended).

Removing older versions of the TestGen program does not delete or otherwise compromise tests and testbanks created with earlier versions of the program located on your computer. You can convert older tests and testbanks simply by opening them in the TestGen 7.2 program.

Product Support

The *User's Guide* can be found on the TestGen CD in the "Resources" folder (see TG7UserGuide.pdf). It provides detailed instructions about how to use all of TestGen's tools and features. Once TestGen has been installed, the *User's Guide* is also available by clicking "Help" in the TestGen menu at the top of the screen. To view the *User's Guide*, Adobe® Acrobat® Reader® is required. This free software can be installed from the Internet at the following address: www.adobe.com/acrobat.

For further technical assistance:

- Call Pearson's toll-free product support line: 1-800-677-6337
- Send an email to media.support@pearsoned.com
- Fill out a web form at: http://247.pearsoned.com/mediaform

Our technical staff will need to know certain things about your system in order to help us solve your problems more quickly and efficiently. If possible, please be at your computer when you call for support. You should have the following information ready:

- Product title and product ISBN
- Computer make and model
- RAM available
- Hard disk space available
- Graphics card type
- Printer make and model (if applicable)
- Detailed description of the problem, including the exact wording of any error messages.